Entrepreneurship in Latin America

Entrepreneurship in Latin America

Perspectives on Education and Innovation

Edited by Scott Tiffin

Foreword by Iván Sanabria Piretti

 PRAEGER

Westport, Connecticut
London

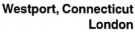

Library of Congress Cataloging-in-Publication Data

Entrepreneurship in Latin America : perspectives on education and innovation / edited by Scott Tiffin; foreword by Iván Sanabria Piretti.
    p. cm.
   Includes bibliographical references and index.
   ISBN 0-275-98040-5 (alk. paper)
   1. New business enterprises—Latin America. 2. Entrepreneurship—Latin America. 3. Small business—Latin America. 4. Latin America—Economic conditions—1982–. I. Tiffin, Scott.
  HD62.5.E583 2004
  338'.04'098—dc22   2004017677

British Library Cataloguing in Publication Data is available.

Library of Congress Catalog Card Number: 2004017677
ISBN: 0-275-98040-5

First published in 2004

Praeger Publishers, 88 Post Road West, Westport, CT 06881
An imprint of Greenwood Publishing Group, Inc.
www.praeger.com

Printed in the United States of America

The paper used in this book complies with the Permanent Paper Standard issued by the National Information Standards Organization (Z39.48–1984).

10 9 8 7 6 5 4 3 2 1

Contents

Foreword

Dr. Iván Sanabria Piretti

Entrepreneurship is about combining people with good ideas, vision, and courage, who risk their own capital–and their investors'–in new products and services. I also associate entrepreneurship with innovation, technology, and, ultimately, a motor that stimulates economic growth, progress, and well-being. Entrepreneurship is an economic and social phenomenon arising from the wide range of opportunities globalization offers and the enormous speed with which knowledge can be communicated nowadays. Latin American economies have started perceiving the benefits of entrepreneurial start-ups and their role in the success of free trade agreements during the last decade. As a Latin American entrepreneur, however, I believe our governments and business leaders can do more to promote this interesting phenomenon, especially now that the feasibility and value of entrepreneurship has been proven in our own particular context. We simply cannot overlook its importance!

Entrepreneurship in Latin American has recently become an appealing research topic for academics, a must-know area for our policy makers, and a common subject in the syllabus of students involved in business issues. I was unaware even of the term *entrepreneurship*, while actually being a young entrepreneur. However, after having been there, my partners and I actively promote public awareness on the need to create and maintain the appropriate conditions for many other start-ups to be born and nourished, and motivate others to pursue their entrepreneurial dreams by sharing our good and bad hands-on experiences when establishing our company, Artinsoft.

Let me tell you, briefly, the story of the start-up of Artinsoft, which is now one of the world's leading providers of innovative migration and upgrade technologies. The company's main product, Freedom®, is a set of programming tools that, using artificial intelligence technologies, enable companies to migrate their existing software systems into newer and more flexible computing languages (e.g., Java™, the Internet language, and .Net, Microsoft's newest development platform). Migrated systems are cheaper to maintain, can be easily evolved to support new business models, and allow companies to reach more clients. In only 10 years, our firm evolved from being the resourceless project of three recently graduated engineers and their university professor, to a 230-employee company, which has attracted the attention of global players such as Oracle, Borland, Microsoft, and Intel. What is behind this fascinating story?

As a co-founder, I can assure you that an idea, vision, research skill, enthusiasm and self-confidence are the main assets to succeed in such a knowledge-intensive business. To start with, Artinsoft had plenty of these capabilities. The company was a university spin-off from the Institute of Technology located in the city of Cartago, Costa Rica. A professor with a PhD in artificial intelligence encouraged three of his best master of science students in computer science to pursue his vision–the development of a rapid, secure, and cost-effective migration technology. The company was founded in 1993 and situated in a small rented farmhouse of a dog obedience training school in the hills of Ujarras de Cartago, where we started doing research to develop our own migration technology. We started programming with only two computers due to lack of capital.

In order to support the required research effort, we developed an Enterprise Resource Planning and Scheduling (ERP) software to support Costa Rican medium- and large-size businesses, and later we brought angel investors on board who provided the business-oriented vision needed. Together with the software, Artinsoft also provided consulting services on industrial organization to take full advantage of the package. Close proximity to the clients, the fact that the software was relatively cheap with respect to large international software houses, and that is was written in Spanish constituted the main ingredients for success. In a few years the company's reputation spread rapidly and big companies from Central and Latin America approached Artinsoft to buy the ERP software. With this product, we learned and acquired the necessary experience and capital to later manage the development of Freedom®, our flagship product.

The major breakthrough was still to come. In 1998, after 5 years of research, Oracle suggested that one of its main clients approach Artinsoft to implement Freedom® for an important software evolution process. We were hired by one of the major European software companies, and the project was successfully completed at a very low cost. This allowed us to finally validate our initial idea and technology. Furthermore, this gave us the opportunity to interact with other global players and be known worldwide.

Artinsoft's solid technical expertise and international reputation attracted the attention of Intel Communications Fund, which invests in companies that help decrease the barriers associated with porting communication applications. In February 2001, the fund invested in Artinsoft to upgrade and develop new migration software systems to bring applications closer to Intel's technologies. Later that same year, Microsoft Corporation also invested in Artinsoft to provide upgrade technology and consulting services to millions of developers targeting Microsoft .NET platform using Artinsoft's industry-leading technology. Clearly, this gave us the final boost to become a leading firm in the field. Interestingly, none of these technology giants had ever invested in a Latin American technology company before.

The success of Artinsoft underlines the importance of capability building and learning in the development process of entrepreneurial start-ups in Latin America. Of course, we also benefited from a highly qualified workforce in the IT area within Central and Latin America. For instance, the Costa Rican government's *informática educativa* plan implemented in the late 1980s, which promotes the idea that each school must have at least one computer, has proved to be very successful in helping many youngsters develop skills in the new information technologies.

Nevertheless, we believe that the appropriate conditions for many more start-ups to succeed depend on the subtle combination of several critical factors. After almost a decade of hard and tenacious work, we classify the critical factors in the success of knowledge-intensive start-ups into two groups: *internal factors*, those inherent to the company culture and the decision-making process; and *external factors*, those related to the environment where the company exists. Among the critical internal factors we identify are (a) the clear definition of the company vision and mission, together with the continuous review of the strategy to accomplish the mission, and the way each of the members in the organization helps in the implementation of the strategy through teamwork; (b) a continuously evolving, client-oriented organizational culture, working methodology and values; (c) the careful match between people, profiles, and job descriptions; (d) the investment in serious research and the use of technology (for instance, Artinsoft staff includes an outstanding group of six PhDs in computer science from schools such as Oxford University); (e) continuous personnel technical training; and, last but not least, (f) an outstanding marketing and sales team. As all the founding partners of Artinsoft agree, plenty of time and effort would have been saved by understanding each of these factors if we had had some basic guidance like the information start-ups can easily obtain today from universities and their business incubators in Costa Rica.

We also think that, although start-ups may see internal factors achievable simply based on their individual commitment to success, external factors are real development barriers that cannot be overcome without well-coordinated joint efforts between government and industry associations. Among these critical external factors we identify (a) high quality education and qualified professionals; (b) competitive infrastructure such as telecommunications, ports, and customs services; (c) training and support from universities to promote entrepreneurial capacity for their students; (d) coordinated effort between universities and industries to produce professionals with appropriate skill-sets; (e) access to and attraction of investment capital; and (f) a fresh international projection versus the traditional perceptions of our countries. To illustrate this last factor, I sometimes had to face customers who asked questions like "What does a *banana republic company* know about software?" which unfairly labeled the quality of our products and services in the past.

This book, *Entrepreneurship in Latin America*, carefully reflects on these and other critical factors of entrepreneurial success from the academic and industrial perspectives. Among other fascinating topics for people in industry, university, and government, the authors analyze mechanisms to support and promote entrepreneurial start-ups, like incubators and venture capital issues. Also, they consider university experiences in transforming curriculum design to promote innovative thinking. As a whole, this book gives us plenty of evidence to realize how important it is for further research to be done in this field in Latin America.

CHAPTER 1

Introduction

Scott Tiffin

Enterprise creation in Latin America has long been a preoccupation of economic policy, development studies, and actions to promote small and medium firms throughout the region. Rodrigo Varela seems to have been the first to use the explicit concepts of entrepreneurship, working in Columbia in the mid-1980s, following closely on the emergence of this literature in North America. However, it was not until a decade later that research began to appear in more countries of the region and in a more sustained manner. I began surveying aspects of entrepreneurship in Latin America (venture capital and local innovation clusters) in the late 1990s (Tiffin and Bortagaray 2002; Tiffin and Couto 1999). Finding little available literature, I initiated a first series of research projects in the Southern Cone to build teams and generate analyses, with the support of the International Development Research Centre. A few years later, I was able to expand on this at Babson College. The results of the Babson-sponsored research were presented in a symposium held on campus involving some four dozen academics from across the region and the United States–the first major international research event on this topic. After the symposium, I decided to diffuse the chapters more widely and began this book, which the Business School of the Universidad Adolfo Ibáñez in Chile subsequently supported.[1]

Now research in entrepreneurship has taken root across the region. PhD graduates in this field have begun to appear. More regional and local conferences have been held.[2] Courses and university incubators to support new student ventures are growing rapidly across the region, with

Brazil in the lead and Argentina, Chile, Columbia, Costa Rica, and Mexico following close behind.

This book represents the first overview of entrepreneurship in Latin America. It highlights the work of researchers from many countries. Most contributors are university professors entering a field that is still very new for Latin America and who are working individually with few resources. Some have contributed research papers, others have written practitioner reviews. In a variety of styles, they portray the central concerns and the current capabilities for research and teaching. Their contributions will, I hope, encourage further research.

The Importance of Entrepreneurship

All Latin American countries are euphemistically characterized as "developing." There is a highly polarized debate over the role that business plays in development. The current dominant view is that market-oriented globalization serves development. The minority view points to the steadily worsening economic situation of most people in the world and inculpates market-oriented globalization (Aga Khan 2003). What most authors in both camps agree on is that self-reliance and sustainability are fundamental to economic and social development. My own view, shared by many of the authors in this book, is that entrepreneurship presents great potential to promote development because it harnesses the latent drive of individuals and social groups for self-reliance by giving them the tools to create wealth within an ordered framework of industrial capitalism.

In the past few years, entrepreneurship in Organization for Economic Cooperation and Development (OECD) countries has attracted great attention as a key source of industrial wealth and power (OECD 2001; GEM 2002; Porter 2002). Successful entrepreneurs have become gurus of the business world and mythical heroes of the popular imagination. Individuals like the founders of Apple Computer incarnate the popular image of the entrepreneur—penniless, maverick students tinkering in their parents' garages, then swiftly rising to transform their humble start-up businesses into colossal multinational enterprises that push ahead the boundaries of knowledge and culture with a relentless cascade of innovative products. Although only a small fraction of entrepreneurs reach such heights, countless individuals are nevertheless inspired by these modern fairy tales to start up and grow their own firms.

As the authors contributing to this book point out, it was the great Austrian economist Josef Schumpeter who came up with the concept of entrepreneurship as the basis for economic evolution in the form of "creative destruction." Although his work lay dormant for several decades, in the last 20 years a great volume of research has arisen around some of his key ideas. It shows that entrepreneurship, linked to technological innovation, is indeed a major factor in creating new firms and new employment. As well, entrepreneurship helps the economy to evolve and to bring scientific knowledge into production. Many academics are now busy devising and testing theories of how entrepreneurship works and what it does. The authors contributing to this book indicate which ones they find important to their situations. Particularly intriguing to me is the recent work of Hausmann and Rodrik (2002), which conceptualizes economic development almost as a process of random "self-discovery." They argue that economic/industrial/political systems are immensely complex and that what really happens is that a swarm of entrepreneurs just keeps testing all the opportunities. Most die off, unsuccessful, but some succeed in a process of trial and error! In the path of the successful entrepreneur, imitators rush in, extending the basic concept and building up the niche. This is interesting as an evolutionary theory, or perhaps a theory that abandons theory as too complicated; whatever your view, it aptly describes the essence and importance of entrepreneurship.

Defining Entrepreneurship

Entrepreneurship is still a young, rapidly expanding field. Not surprisingly, the word *entrepreneurship* has different meanings to different people—it defies precise definition. To help develop the field in Latin America, it is important to suggest a definition and to describe the main aspects of entrepreneurship that take the region's unique characteristics into consideration. A good starting point for a definition might be something like "a process of identifying a business opportunity, planning to exploit it by creating a new company or corporate division, gathering resources to set it up, and evolving management styles and structures to achieve rapid growth and profitability."

Many words and concepts are involved even in this bare-bones definition. Let us put some flesh on it by describing what entrepreneurs do and what they are like. Because the authors in this book go into some detail with the literature on this topic, I will not repeat their work but rather give my own overview of factors I see as most relevant to Latin America. First, entrepreneurs are people who are skilled at spotting opportunities and methodically planning to turn these opportunities into practice through hard work over a number of years. The second factor is risk management. Entrepreneurs take risks, but the key is in taking finely calculated risks and in carefully managing those risks so that the chances of failure are minimized. Entrepreneurs are not gunslingers. Third is innovation. Entrepreneurs are innovators; they do something that is new. *New* of course varies from slightly different to completely unheard of, but entrepreneurs are always agents of change to some extent. Fourth, entrepreneurship is about wealth creation. Successful entrepreneurs are people who often start with very little but who, step-by-step, accrete resources of capital and knowledge to build products, jobs, organizations, and profits. Finally, entrepreneurship is about getting something done on one's own steam–self-reliance. Entrepreneurs are quintessentially self-motivated. But entrepreneurship is not really about individual action; far from it–it is the work of teams that work well together. In other words, entrepreneurship is a collective, as well as individual, social action. Teams can also be cooperative enterprises, or nongovernmental organizations (NGOs), or nonprofit social groups. Ultimately, entrepreneurship is an engine for sustainable development in any community in the world.

We also have to be very clear about what entrepreneurship is not. In Latin America, there is often a misconception that entrepreneurship is about small enterprise. The region has a long tradition of creating public support mechanisms for small and medium enterprises (SMEs). There is a tendency for many business schools, banks, and public agencies to claim they have been supporting entrepreneurship for years, because they have been involved with SMEs. It is true that there is some overlap when start-up entrepreneurial ventures remain small. They may remain small because of the wishes of their founders, and the literature calls these *lifestyle ventures.* Otherwise, they are small because they failed to grow. Start-up entrepreneurship is not about staying small but about starting with very little and then achieving rapid and sustained growth to be able to compete in national, regional, and global markets. Corporate entrepreneurship is the same: starting with few resources on the margins of an established enterprise but striving to achieve rapid and sustained growth. The motivations, skills, financing, and structures in a real entrepreneurial venture, whether startup or corporate, are all oriented to attaining much larger scale, structure, and products than SMEs.

In Latin America there is often confusion about venture capital, which is the emblematic financing mechanism for entrepreneurship. Most countries claim to have venture capital industries, but people are usually referring to private equity and public loan schemes. Private equity placements are investments that go to mature enterprises for such things as acquisitions, expansions, and new product development. They are not investments in the early stage of an unproven company where the bet is on high growth and a potential for a quick initial public offering (IPO–listing on the stock market). Many credit and loan facilities exist to support business start-up or project development, but these are very different in style and skill set than the risk-equity investing that is essential for entrepreneurial ventures. Venture capital is equity investment—where investors take shares in the enterprise.

With this description and definition of entrepreneurship in mind, we can now ask what entrepreneurship should include as an academic field in Latin America at this time. My own view is that the following topics are the most relevant, and they have been used in selecting the chapters in this book:

- Enterprise start-up and growth
- Corporate entrepreneurship and entrepreneurial family business
- Technical entrepreneurship and local innovation systems
- New venture financing
- Entrepreneurship for NGOs, cooperatives, and marginalized social sectors
- Public policy, incubators, and clusters
- Entrepreneurship education for business, science, and engineering students

Enterprise Start-up and Growth

This is the core of entrepreneurship: taking a raw idea, starting with few resources, putting a business plan together, assembling a team, getting investment, and starting up the firm. A long period then ensues until the process "ends," by taking the company public in an IPO on the stock market or, more commonly (but less desirable to investors), by selling ownership to another firm. Some firms really do follow the pattern up to the IPO, at least in Canada and the United States. And if the great majority do not, then at least this is the benchmark process most entrepreneurs strive to emulate or dream about in their few hours of daily sleep. Start-ups are the focus for nearly all the entrepreneurship research in Latin America at the present.

Corporate Entrepreneurship and Entrepreneurial Family Business

A great deal of entrepreneurship is carried out by visionaries, mavericks, or calculating bureaucrats within large, mature firms. These individuals are seeking ways to revitalize their companies (or public organizations) so that they act in a more nimble and innovative manner. Often, they are science-research driven, and they use corporate entrepreneurship as a tool to innovate the new products. That is, they create a corporate structure that can gather the teams, intellectual property, and risk finance to exploit the latent market potential of the raw technological knowledge. This is known as corporate entrepreneurship, as alluded to earlier, or intrapreneurship. It is, needless to say, a hot area for business schools, as start-up entrepreneurship becomes a mature intellectual field, with the added incentive that Fortune 500 firms pay professors much higher consulting fees than debt-ridden start-ups founded by impoverished students. In Latin America much of the mature business sector is structured around family lines, a unique and important feature to take into consideration. Because so much of Latin American business operates within a family ownership and management context, it is important to look at corporate entrepreneurship within a family context. Family business is a reasonably well-researched field in Latin America, but corporate entrepreneurship is entirely new.

Technical Entrepreneurship and Local Innovation Systems

Entrepreneurial firms gain a greater competitive advantage by basing their business plans on products or services involved with innovation of technology. Naturally, there is more risk, more time to bring to market, more skills required, a need for more support from the surrounding innovation system, and much more capital needed to pay for the research and design. For this reason, technical entrepreneurship is likely to be significantly harder to realize in Latin America than in developed countries. However, this type of entrepreneurship is still an important topic to consider in Latin America for two reasons: first because it is needed so badly to help transform dependent resource-based economies into knowledge-based economies,[3] and second because there is already a relatively strong science and technology establishment in place in some countries, and public policies are promoting commercialization, innovation, transfer, and entrepreneurship from their end. In countries like Brazil, we currently see almost no involvement of business schools in entrepreneurship but a very strong involvement of many engineering schools, who bring the perspectives of industrial engineering and product design and development. Technical entrepreneurship in Latin America needs to be studied within local innovation systems–to consider how to build and manage these local innovation systems. Even though a firm in Latin America may start out with the same quality of staff, ideas, and funding, the fact that it works in a weak or incomplete innovation system means it faces severe additional hurdles. In developed economies with a strong market and technological infrastructure, the systems are much stronger and can be taken for granted by those involved with technical entrepreneurship at the firm level. This is not so in Latin America.

New Venture Financing

The goal of most entrepreneurs in developed economies is to get equity investment, even though only a tiny fraction of start-ups receive any formal venture capital. Nevertheless, the presence of venture capital is critical in any entrepreneurial culture because it sets the tone of best practice and the goals to attain. In Latin America, there is less awareness and interest in venture capital; a generalized culture of personal relationships, with weak legal structures for protecting minority shareholder rights, make venture capital somewhat problematic. Indeed, there is little venture capital available, overall, for entrepreneurs in Latin America. It is not that there is a shortage of money or concentrations of funds; the problem is that too much flows straight out to Miami or Geneva or is directed to unproductive local investments, such as overly conspicuous consumption. Research on venture capital in Latin America needs to include the whole spectrum of funding: informal Angel financing; formal, professional venture capital funds; knowledge-based banking; and stock market operations. In addition, there needs to be an understanding of the knowledge that is brought by venture capitalists in helping build the companies, because this is equally as important as their cash. Research should also show how entrepreneurship can create high-quality local investment opportunities and, with time, help put some of the flight capital to work locally. There is a great deal of informal venture capital invested within closed family groups; it is important to investigate this and to point out ways of professionalizing these funds to get higher results.

Entrepreneurship for NGOs, Cooperatives, and Marginalized Social Sectors

Nearly all the literature on entrepreneurship relates to firms in a capitalistic economic system. However, entrepreneurship applies to many other sectors where the objective may be to create a not-for-profit firm, an NGO, or a cooperative. Cooperatives are ideal candidates for learning how to be more entrepreneurial and, at the same time, how to extend their social mandates. Entrepreneurship can also be a collective social phenomenon, practiced by social groups and villages. These are unexplored topics but obviously are of great importance to all of Latin America. The challenge is to bring together a market-driven and competitive, professional paradigm into settings that may have a very different ideological structure and much lower levels of education. The great attraction of entrepreneurship is that it is something that all social levels and types of organizations and individuals can engage in to realize strategic objectives and create wealth. It is both technique for success and an attitude that success is possible.

Public Policy, Incubators, and Clusters

Popularly, the notion of entrepreneurship epitomizes the heroic role of the individual working in a minimalized market system. The reality is that the successful entrepreneur works as a member of a team and that the company works within a complex, sophisticated support system, which the public sector painstakingly creates and manages. Appropriate public policy is critical to entrepreneurship. One of the most obvious instruments of public policy is the incubator. An incubator is an organization that usually has a physical presence but whose main strength is offering relationship services, promotion, and training to start-ups. Brazil is very advanced in the creation of incubators, although we may question how well staff is trained for these sophisticated tasks in a period of such rapid expansion. Most other countries of the region are beginning to follow in Brazil's pioneering track. Incubators are not the whole answer; they are only key nodes in what was referred to above as local innovation systems or, more popularly, clusters. Clusters are the networks of organizations and relationships that support innovation and entrepreneurship. Public policy to build innovation clusters is just starting in Latin America and is a key area to consider.

Entrepreneurship Education for Business, Science, and Engineering Students

The models for entrepreneurship education come mostly from the United States. How well they apply to different social and cultural settings in Latin America is open for discussion. There are some interesting experiments now going on (described in this book) in which universities are imitating, adapting, and extending the benchmark teaching technologies developed in places such as Babson College. However, there are deeper questions than just how to write business cases and teach them that relate more to the underlying social values of students in Latin America. In Brazil, for instance, entrepreneurship is centered in engineering schools—not business schools. In most countries of the region, there are strong repercussions from a business failure, which rightly inhibit many young people from following their entrepreneurial instincts. Education in many Latin American countries tends to emphasize rote learning and the acceptance of hierarchical authority and established knowledge—inimical to building an entrepreneurial spirit. As well, there is a long tradition (now diminishing, thankfully) of educated people not "rolling up their sleeves and getting their hands dirty," also inimical to entrepreneurship. Lastly, entrepreneurship education needs to be considered as a part of science and engineering curricula. This is a very new topic that few universities have begun to tackle but that should also be considered central to what entrepreneurship means for Latin America.

Entrepreneurship in Latin America

What is the extent of entrepreneurship in Latin America? What characteristics does it have? What is its impact? How does the situation differ from country to country? We have very few answers as yet to these questions. The Global Entrepreneurship Monitor (GEM) studies done by Babson College and the London Business School (GEM 2000; 2001; 2002) are one of the major sources of comparative data. They portray a startling picture of Latin American countries consistently among world leaders in terms of start-ups. Table 1.1 shows the ranking of the countries that GEM has studied in Latin America. In 2002, 37 countries were studied. The rankings are based on what GEM calls the Total Entrepreneurial Activity Prevalence Rates, which is the number of people per 100 adults (18–64 years old) in the labor force who have started up a business in the last 42 months. It measures both opportunity-based entrepreneurship (i.e., formal enterprises created by people who have other employment options but prefer to set up a company) and necessity-based entrepreneurship (i.e., informal, smaller companies created by people who perceive that they do not have any other option to secure employment).[4]

The other major source of comparative studies comes from the Inter-American Development Bank (Kantis, Ishida, and Komori 2002; and being extended in 2003), which compared several Latin American countries with several Asian countries. The main findings were there was indeed significant entrepreneurship in Latin America but significantly less sales, profitability, employment, and access to financing than the Asians.

There are currently no registries of entrepreneurship courses in universities, comparative information on venture capital, or databases on incubators across Latin America or in regional organizations such as Mercosur, Caricom, or the Andean zone. Probably only Brazil has national data for incubators (kept by Anprotec) and venture capital (maintained by the Asoçiação Brasilera de Capital de Risco). To give an overview of entrepreneurship across the whole region, we are reduced to offering a few opportunistic and anecdotal pieces of evidence. For example,

Table 1.1
World Entrepreneurship Ranking

	2000	2001	2002
Argentina	7	7	5
Brazil	3	1	7
Chile	–	–	3
Mexico	–	–	8

Figure 1.1
Number of Incubators in Brazil

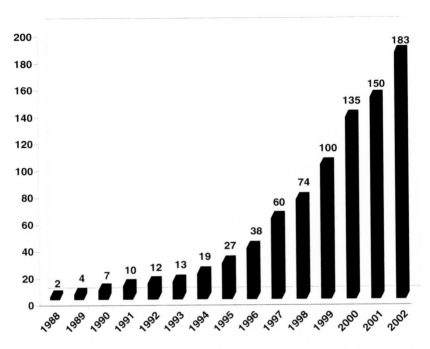

Anprotec (2002) data show an exponential rise in recent years in the number of incubators, given in Figure 1.1.

The business magazine, *AmericaEconomia*, was planning to attract younger readers with a new section for their magazine that centered around entrepreneurship and technology-based start-ups (that is, before the economic slumps of 2002). The Brazilian business weekly *Exame* has major features on this topic (e.g., "Novos Negocios," 6 Março 2002). BALAS (the Business Association for Latin American Studies) is planning to hold its 2004 conference at Babson on entrepreneurship. In addition, the 2002 Academy of Management conference in Denver had a workshop on this topic. The Universidad Adolfo Ibáñez Conference on Entrepreneurship in Latin America, following up in 2003 the Babson symposium of 2002, is the only regional research conference.[5] Various instructional and promotional events have been held in Colombia and Argentina in the past few years.

In terms of investment in education, Brazil is clearly the major player. Nearly all the Brazilian teaching and research in entrepreneurship is being carried out by industrial engineering schools; business schools are still oriented more to large (and multinational) enterprise. In 2001, the Universidad de São Paolo at São Carlos graduated what may be Latin

America's first PhD in entrepreneurship. In Spanish-speaking countries, the University ICESI in Colombia was an early entrant into the field, but Argentina is the leader in terms of scale and diversity, with major involvement in the field by the Universidad de San Andres, Universidad Nacional de General de Sarmiento, and the Universidad Austral. The Instituto Tecnológico Autonomo de Mexico is beginning work on entrepreneurship with a focus on family business; Instituto Tecnólogico y de Estudios Superiores de Monterrey is grafting entrepreneurial approaches onto its existing business curriculum. Instituto Tecnológico de Costa Rica has a growing program, focused on an engineering base. In Chile, the Universidad del Desarrollo has begun an ambitious program to focus its business school curriculum completely around entrepreneurship, in an alliance with Babson College. The Universidad Adolfo Ibáñez and the Universidad de los Andes, along with the Universidad de Chile, now also undertake teaching and limited research in this field. In Cuba in the late 1990s, the Instituto Superior Politécnico José Antonio Echeverria was attempting to reconcile entrepreneurship with Marxist theory and commercialize the huge technological base built up in fields such as medical biotechnology.

To try to overcome the limitations of existing data, I undertook a small comparative study of critical variables in startup entrepreneurship, technical entrepreneurship, venture capital, and entrepreneurship education.[6] The data gathering was done by telephone, using the opinion of key informants, and was also taken from published sources where possible. Expert informants were exceptionally knowledgeable people, such as the prospective founder of a venture capital firm in a country where there were none, or a senior government bureaucrat involved with promoting incubators, or an academic who had just completed a study on the topic. Countries surveyed were Argentina, Brazil, Chile, Costa Rica, Ecuador, Mexico, Uruguay, and Venezuela–a sample that covers most of the Latin American range of characteristics. Presenting these data in tabular form would be concise, but readers might be tempted to ascribe more accuracy to the numbers than warranted. Therefore, I summarize the highlights in more qualitative manner as follows.

Start-up Entrepreneurship

The percentage of people who started a business in the last 3 years was highest in Brazil, Mexico, and Venezuela, at 10%. The other countries were portrayed as much lower, averaging around the 3% mark. Brazil, Chile, Mexico, and Uruguay led the group in terms of percentage of these businesses founded by women, around 35%. The participation of women in start-ups in Ecuador and Argentina was perceived as much lower. In terms of "necessity-based entrepreneurship" (i.e., people starting firms because they had no other employment opportunities), Ecuador, Uruguay, and Venezuela topped the list with nearly all new firms falling into this category. Comparatively, Mexico, Costa Rica, and Argentina were less than half, and Chile was a very small figure. This perhaps reflects Chile's relatively strong economy and social value structures, which are the closest in the region to a developed country.

In terms of class breakdown, the middle class was seen to represent about half of the sources of new ventures. In Argentina, Costa Rica, and Venezuela, this percentage was significantly higher. Mexico and Brazil were seen as having the greatest participation by the lower class, and for Ecuador it was the opposite. The overwhelming majority (around 90%) of businesses was described as family-focused, with little interest in sellout as they grew, with the exception of Argentina, where this number was less than a third.

Entrepreneurship is perceived as a very risky activity, where the social implications of failure are seen in most countries as "serious." In Venezuela, interestingly, our respondent saw the possibility of failure as "minor." Perhaps this reflects the intense swings of a petroleum economy that create boom and bust cycles, seen as normal.

It has been stated that the red tape associated with setting up a new enterprise can be stifling. The World Economic Forum's Global Competitiveness Report data for 2002 seem to confirm a problem here because most countries require the passage of about 60 days to complete the formalities. In Mexico 90 days are required; in Argentina, 45; and in Uruguay, 30.

Technical Entrepreneurship

Given the importance of creating knowledge-based economies, I also gathered some data on technology-based entrepreneurship–which are even sketchier because this is a completely new concern and hard to get at directly. Informants estimated that in Chile and Ecuador, 0% of startups were based on technological innovations or doing meaningful research and development (R&D). Costa Rica was estimated at 10%, which could be reasonable, given the focus on engineering education and the huge impact of the Intel investments, which are well-integrated into the local economy. Uruguay and Brazil were extreme exceptions, with estimates of 50%. In the Uruguayan case, given the small numbers involved, there could be strong bias from a few firms.[7] The Brazilian estimate could well be true, considering that entrepreneurship is so strongly supported by universities and their incubators and is focused almost exclusively in engineering schools. This is very encouraging. The next step of course, would be to examine the depth of science and technology involved in the innovation. In a later chapter, Dornelas and Tiffin give some data on this topic and find some of the innovations focusing on relatively simple repackaging, although the managers labeled it R&D.

As for support to technical entrepreneurship, Brazil overwhelms the rest of Latin America in its investment in incubators. Anprotec (2002) data list well over 220, and key informants say the number is still climbing. Argentina comes next with about 20, which may have declined after the Internet bubble collapsed. Then come Mexico and Chile. The other countries have about one each. These numbers quickly become out of date as incubators catch on across the region and new projects quickly come on stream. In the cases of the countries with a number of incubators, it is estimated that about a third have a strong focus on technology-based firms, with the rest involving technology-based firms along with general business proposals.

The Global Competitiveness Report for 2002 presents World Bank data on the number of U.S. patents per million population, which are all extremely low, averaging less than 1. Costa Rica leads with 1.8, and Argentina follows with 1.5. All countries do have funds supporting R&D, and again Brazil leads the pack by a huge margin both in terms of number of funds and the size of these funds, far more than all of the rest of Latin America combined. It is guessed that about half of these funds are oriented to promoting commercialization or transfer of technology into innovations. Brazil makes the largest investment in R&D of any country as a percentage of GDP, around 0.81%. This is, of course, extremely low by OECD standards. Ecuador is lowest at 0.02%. These statistics give a good general impression, but drawing broader inferences is risky. For example, Chile comes out fairly close to Brazil in this index, but far less than Brazil, Argentina, and Mexico in another closely related one, which is production of PhDs per capita (Brunner 2001, 10). And Venezuela is a strong third in R&D as a percentage of GDP, but in terms of innovation and entrepreneurship is exceptionally weak. This large figure for Venezuela must refer to in-house work done by the state oil company and closely linked firms, which has little influence on the rest of the economy.

Venture Capital

The 2002 Global Competitiveness Report made estimates of availability of venture capital. These were based on key informants' perceptions. On a scale of 1 to 7, with 7 as the best, Brazil comes out first with 3.7 and Chile and Costa Rica next. These seem reasonable in terms of what we know in general about the state of venture capital. Surprising, however, are their estimates for Venezuela and Ecuador, both at 2. Low, to be sure, but my expert informants (both of whom were engaged in exploring the set up of venture capital firms, and both linked to Babson College) claimed there were no formal venture capital funds and virtually none available informally. Suffice to say that any of these qualitative measures based on relative impressions needs to be used with great caution.

Informants estimated that in most countries, these funds were informal; that is, they were not professionally managed in companies set up for this purpose but delivered by family, friends, and acquaintances. In Ecuador and Venezuela, they estimated 100%, and all the rest of the countries, slightly less. Brazil was the major exception to this, where the situation was inverted and nearly all venture capital is formally managed. This is not surprising, given the relatively advanced state of the industry in this country. Brazil leads in terms of the number of funds, the size of these funds, and the amounts invested–by huge margins. In terms of focus on technology investments, however, Costa Rica leads; it was estimated that all of the investments have been made in technology firms. Brazil follows closely behind, with Argentina and Mexico next at around half or less. Chile confirms the low level of technology innovation, with about 20%, and Ecuador and Venezuela share the last spot at 0%. IPOs are rare events, and reliable data on them seem to have been compiled across the region. Some informants claimed that no meaningful IPOs have taken place in Latin America for entrepreneurial firms, but our data portrayed Argentina as the leader with a "handful" and Brazil and Chile following with 2 events each.

Entrepreneurship Education

Brazil, once again, leads overwhelmingly in terms of the number of universities with courses on entrepreneurship: over 200. Mexico is next with about 40, then Chile at 10, and Argentina just behind, followed by Costa Rica. We may be underestimating Argentina here, as we redid the survey for Chile 8 months later than the Argentinean one. However, in Chile there is one university that is trying to create a specialization in entrepreneurship–the Universidad del Desarrollo, which is closely linked to Babson. Costa Rica and Argentina also have universities with a very strong focus on entrepreneurship. Interestingly, Brazil shows none. In all countries, a significant number of entrepreneurship training programs operate outside of the university environment (except that, in this case, the number of such courses in Brazil is hardly larger than those in other countries of the region).

The style of education in the business schools varies greatly. The leaders in the United States tend to have a system based on the case method, which, as Ed Cale explains in this volume, is highly conducive to imparting the values and techniques needed to train entrepreneurship. Our informants state that all business education in Ecuador, Uruguay, and Venezuela follows the case method. About half in Argentina and Chile does as well. But in Mexico and Brazil, it is a very small percentage—almost none in Brazil. This seems to make sense, because until very recently no business school in Brazil had any involvement with entrepreneurship. The business schools left it exclusively to the engineering schools, so they could concentrate on large business.

Based on remarks made to me in a student forum at Babson, I also decided to gather some impressions on the qualifications of business school students focusing on entrepreneurship in these countries. At Babson, which has a worldwide reputation for this specialty and very high admission standards, all the students of entrepreneurship are highly qualified in academic terms. However, the current reputation of entrepreneurship in Latin America shows a different reality: In Brazil, Ecuador, and Mexico, students going into this area were seen as average, and in Chile, lower than average. In Argentina, Costa Rica, Venezuela, and Uruguay, however, they were seen as above average. These are highly subjective ratings, to be sure, but they give some pause for further thinking and obviously, more analysis.

Summary

In summary, my investigation found lots of variability with a few major patterns consistent with general knowledge. Brazil is the giant, going beyond all the other countries of the region combined in terms of its commitment to this field. Brazil sets the tone for an overwhelming focus on technology-driven entrepreneurship and an emphasis on incubators as the prime motor of public policy intervention. However, it is interesting to note that although Brazil leads in terms of the total number of technical degrees granted per year, it is only by a small margin over Argentina. This investment in entrepreneurship is clearly anomalous in Brazil. Argentina has the university, industry, and research infrastructure in place to advance rapidly once it is able to refocus its attention, but it is currently making investments much lower than its innate capability. Mexico seems to be seriously underinvesting relative to its technological, financial, and industrial capacity, perhaps as a result of a *maquiladora* or branch-plant assembly mindset. Chile is starting to awaken from its single-minded focus on export of high-quality natural resource products; in some areas it is advancing quickly but in others very seriously underinvesting in intellectual capital. Costa Rica is a small star, carefully marshalling its tiny resources to focus on a few areas and harvesting impressive results. Uruguay remains a mystery: a country with high education and social levels, no major structural problems, but unable to mobilize. Ecuador is consistently at the bottom, but although down, it is not out. At least two major business schools are vigorously beginning to create major entrepreneurship centers.[8] In Venezuela, under the current situation, it remains impossible to predict what the future may hold relative to entrepreneurship.

The Portrait of Entrepreneurship in This Book

This book began as a collection of academic research papers. Over the months of its development, it changed shape, conforming to the reality of entrepreneurship in Latin America. As soon as the initial research funding from Babson ended (paying for expenses and bringing people to the conference in Boston), so did the participation of some of the authors; they simply had no means to continue with research. More descriptive chapters, produced by practitioners, were offered. Then, new topics focusing on incubation and teaching came in, which reflected significant investments being made throughout the region. Country participation shifted radically; all the Argentinean authors pulled out, faced with more pressing issues during the chaos and collapse of their country in 2002. An Ecuadorian chapter on social entrepreneurship in an indigenous community was turned down at the last minute, after two drafts, unable to reach the formalization necessary for a book of this type. Persistent digging brought to light long-standing involvement by universities in Peru and Columbia, and replacement chapters came in unexpectedly. But just days before submitting the book manuscript, a Brazilian chapter was unable to secure funding for translation and had to be dropped.

Here is a summary of what this book contains. First, a statement from Iván Sanabria Piretti, a senior executive in a very successful high-tech start-up now operating globally out of San Jose, Costa Rica. Dr. Sanabria Piretta and the other entrepreneurs in his company are perfect exemplars of what is needed, desired, and possible throughout Latin America!

The chapter by Juan José Llisterri and Pablo Javier Angelelli of the Inter-American Development Bank (IDB) is a strong overview of the regional situation, resulting from recent and ongoing research the IDB has been supporting in various countries of Latin America and some comparisons with Asia.

Next, a chapter by Dr. Jeannine Horowitz Gassol discusses entrepreneurship curriculum in Venezuela at the Universidad Simón Bolívar. Her chapter shows that positive entrepreneurship activities can be carried out even in the face of the most hostile of situations—a generalized social, political and economic collapse in Venezuela. It is important to read her portrayal of a country suffering extreme distortions caused by an economy based exclusively on resources (petroleum). Her chapter describes the difficulties faced by all countries in the region, and the hope that entrepreneurship will help get out of the dead end trap of resource-based dependency.

Dennis Ray's chapter is a good one to follow the Venezuelan case, because he treats Latin American entrepreneurship in a global context of center-periphery relations. His view is not only more macro (where most entrepreneurship literature is resolutely micro) but is also a good critique of common assumptions about the triumph of global capitalism and the inevitable spread of its benefits. Dr. Ray concludes with ideas about how entrepreneurship can seize upon opportunities presented by globalization.

Then comes a series of chapters on incubators, business plan competitions, and entrepreneurship courses. This is clearly where the bulk of attention and experience lie at present in Latin America:

- Dr. Rodrigo Varela and Jorge Jimenez Prieto, from ICESI, Columbia presents the results of a significant research project on the impact of entrepreneurship programs in three universities.
- Dr. Germán Echecopar from Universidad Adolfo Ibáñez reports on research done in Chile to understand how incubators can improve their output of successful startups.
- Juan Carlos Leiva looks at business plan competitions in Costa Rica at the ITEC.
- Dr. Pedro Arriagada Stuven focuses on curriculum development in Chile at the Universidad del Desarrollo.
- Dr. Edward Cale discusses the implications of transferring Babson's entrepreneurship curriculum to a Latin American context.
- Alexandra Solano, Angélica Mora, and Pedro Marquez describe curriculum design at ITESM in Monterrey, Mexico, and reflect the expertise in this area that keeps this university the leader in business and engineering in Latin America, as well as a strong player internationally.
- Sergey Udolkin Dakova addresses the promotion of entrepreneurship in Peru at the Universidad del Pacífico.

Dr. John Bourne, from the United States, puts an interesting and important twist on the education theme when he describes how distance education based on Internet technologies could be usefully applied to rapidly diffusing entrepreneurship education in the region.

Several research papers are related to local innovation clusters, technical entrepreneurship, and family business:

- Gonzalo Jimenez and I have created an index to measure the capability of cities to promote knowledge-based start-ups.

- Dr. José Dornelas and I studied technology-based start-ups coming out of Brazilian incubators.
- Dr. Imanol Belausteguigoitia compares family-based entrepreneurship in Chile and Mexico.

Venture capital is treated by Alicia Castillo Holley, who runs a technology-oriented seed fund in Chile, and by Gustavo Harckbart and Dr. Antonio Botelho, who describe the situation in Brazil.

Dr. Judy "J J" Jackson and Olga Pizarro present the results of a survey of female entrepreneurs in Chile, coming up with some important findings about the primacy of social concerns that women have in entrepreneurship, for themselves, their family, and their children. Eva Jonathan also tackles the issue of gender in high-tech entrepreneurship in Brazil. In my statement about critical issues for entrepreneurship to consider in Latin America, I left out gender issues; I prefer to treat this important topic within any of the other ones, to avoid ghettoizing it, but a good case could be made for making this a separate area of study.

Developing the Field and its Application

The chapters in this book touch on all of the categories suggested previously as the important issues of entrepreneurship in Latin America, with the exception of social entrepreneurship. They also suggest the possibility of adding an eighth category: gender. Now the work really begins, as these chapters show how little we know about any of these areas, even in the countries of Latin America with the strongest investigative capabilities.

What suggestions can we make about further developing this field and getting the knowledge into curriculum, executive training, and public policy? First, the obvious—we need more research! More exactly, we need research carried out in conjunction with stakeholders. In other words, the research should not just be for the sake of academic publications but to take input from users who define what the critical issues are, and who must be involved in applying the knowledge as well as funding its generation. Gibbons (2003) describes this "Mode 2" research as being increasingly important and widespread in advanced economies. However, there are costs of emphasizing Mode 2 research, because rankings for business schools consider publication in journals that are more academic than practical. Perhaps the ranking gurus for Latin America, such as *AmericaEconomia*, can be persuaded to modify their methods to take consideration of this stakeholder-oriented research.

Other closely related elements in the research equation are the production of PhDs in Latin America. Where are the PhD programs in business administration in this region? Are there any? There is a continual flow of bright students who go primarily to the United States to get PhDs and then come back to teach at an undergraduate or MBA level. Time is long overdue for business schools to invest in creating PhD programs, so the region does not remain intellectually dependent in this area.

To create PhD programs is costly. But it is possible to set up consortia, as is done in developed countries, to develop specialized management PhDs.[9] The problem with consortia in Latin America is that there is little precedence to date of universities cooperating to generate critical mass. There is a great deal of competition, exacerbated by the fact that many universities see themselves primarily as businesses, competing for money by teaching undergraduates. This must change in order for universities to compete on a global level. Latin American universities can help accomplish this by pushing for more careful national accreditation of universities, accompanied by rigorous pruning of those that do not measure up and providing a portion of research and enrollment subsidies to private universities.

Overall, there is a desperate lack of research funding. What is available comes almost exclusively from the public sector. There is little culture of industry-sponsored research, and there are very few tax incentives for this.[10] No significant foundations seem to be operating at national or regional levels to emulate the wonderful work the Kauffman Foundation has done in the United States for many years to build up the field of entrepreneurship and American universities as leading producers. Even if Latin American professors do manage to obtain small grants and publish a paper, this is only the first step. Their average international colleagues enjoy far more funding for learning, researching, and publishing, and therefore have a much higher level of output of higher-quality works with greater impact. And this average level of productivity is also far lower than for the leaders who enjoy privileged links to wealthy sponsors with cutting-edge problems. Thus, there are two large gaps that only money can close.

Finally, the picture is complicated by several counterproductive academic value systems. There are few Latin American scientific journals and conferences of importance. I have on several occasions heard Latin American colleagues express little interest in attending Latin American entrepreneurship conferences when they could go to a European or North American conference—where the real action is. The situation is worse for publications. It is difficult for Latin American management academics to publish in international journals on topics that are relevant to their situations; one avenue for top journal publication is to entice a foreign colleague with an international project to work with them. In the United States, some academics have told me they would like to do Latin American work but that they were reluctant because they felt the outputs would be difficult to publish in top journals; a few actually kept their Latin American activities hidden from their department chairs, for fear of negative repercussions. A recent report on international education by the International Development Research Centre (Smart 2003) alludes to the same widespread situation in Canada. We could start to go deeper into social value structures and development dependency theory,[11] but maybe it is best just to cut the Gordian knot here, accept that these are classic chicken and egg situations, and begin to accept responsibility for changing this situation.

So we have a need for research to be done in cooperation with stakeholders; more research funding, especially from industry; local production of PhDs; cooperation of research units to create critical mass; and support for Latin American scholarly initiatives by Latin American intellectuals and professionals. These are all issues in which individuals involved in entrepreneurship research, teaching, and management can take positive action.

References

Aga Khan, S. 2003. "Desarrollo sustentable, una idea desvirtuada." *Le Monde Diplomatique*, May: 6–7.

Anprotec. 2002. *Panorama*. Associação Nacional de Entidades Promotoras de Empreendimentos de Tecnologias Avançadas.
http://www.anprotec.org.br/arquivo-pdf/panorama2002.pdf.

Brunner, J. J. 2001. *Chile: Informe sobre Capacidad Tecnológica*. Santiago: United Nations Development Program (UNDP).

Gibbons, M. 2003. "Globalization and the Future of Higher Education." In *Globalisation of Universities: Private Linkages and Public Trust*, edited by G. Breton and M. Lambert. Paris: UNESCO/IAU/PUL.

Global Entrepreneurship Monitor (GEM). 2000. "GEM Global 2000 [executive or summary] Report."
http://www.gemconsortium.org/category_list.asp?cid=113.

Global Entrepreneurship Monitor (GEM). 2001. "GEM Global 2001 [executive or summary] Report."
http://www.gemconsortium.org/category_list.asp?cid=113.

Global Entrepreneurship Monitor (GEM). 2002. "GEM Global 2002 [executive or summary] Report."
http://www.gemconsortium.org/category_list.asp?cid=113.

Harrison, L., and S. Huntington. 2000. *Culture Matters: How Values Shape Human Progress*. Boston: Basic Books.

Hausmann, R., and D. Rodrik. 2002. "Economic Development as Self-Discovery." *US National Bureau of Economic Research Working Paper*, no. 8952, (November). http://ksghome.harvard.edu/-.drodrik.academic.ksg/SelfDiscRev2.pdf.

Kantis, H., M. Ishida, and M. Komori. 2002. *Empresarialidad en economias emergentes: Creacion y desarrollo de nuevas empresas en America Latina y el Este de Asia*. Washington, DC: Banco Interamericano de Desarrollo.

Organization for Economic Cooperation and Development (OECD). 2001. *Entrepreneurship, Growth, and Policy*. Paris: OECD.

Porter, M. 2002. *Research Triangle: Clusters of Innovation Initiative*. Cambridge, MA: Harvard University Press.

Smart, C. 2003. *The Campus Roundtables on the Internationalization of Canadian Research*. Draft, Ottawa: International Development Research Centre.

Thurow, L. 2000. *Building Wealth: The New Rules for Individuals, Companies, and Nations in a Knowledge-Based Economy*. New York: Harper-Business.

Tiffin, S., and G. Couto. 1999. "A Survey of Venture Capital in Latin America." Presented at Third International Conference on Technology Policy and Innovation, Austin, TX.

Tiffin, S., and I. Bortagaray. 2002. "Local Innovation Clusters in Latin America." In *Technology Policy and Innovation*, vol. 5, edited by M. Heitor, D. Gibson, and M. Ibarra. Westport, CT: Quorum Books.

World Economic Forum (WEF). 1996–2002. *Global Competitiveness Report*. Geneva: World Economic Forum. http://www.weforum.org/site/homepublic.nsf/Content/Global+Competitiveness+Programme%5CReports%5CGlobal+Competitiveness+Report+2001–2002.

Notes

1. Thanks are due to the anonymous Babson Alumni from Latin America who generously donated funds that were applied to the original research projects; to Enrique Ostalé, Dean of the Business School at the University of Adolfo Ibañez, who supported the book project as part of his vision of transforming the school into a major research producer; to Dr. German Echecopar, Director of the Entrepreneurship Center, who provided funding; and to Marina Schorr, whose energetic assistance kept the authors on track.

2. The Babson symposium has evolved into an annual research conference for the region. The second conference was held at the Business School of the Universidad Adolfo Ibáñez in October 2003 and is planned to rotate among the main research centers in Latin America.

3. Lester Thurow (2000) makes a good all-round case for this topic.

4. The GEM data are used in public with great enthusiasm by proponents of entrepreneurship in Latin America, but in private moments the data are treated with equal degree of skepticism. There are vast differences between

a necessity-based, subsistence, family company in a poor district of a Latin American city and a robotics firm spun out of MIT with half a dozen PhDs backed by millions in professional venture capital and research contracts from DARPA.

5. Especially noteworthy is a set of conferences on entrepreneurship development held by the Universidad ICESI in Columbia, at a national and subregional level.

6. There are some sources of good original data the GEM studies by Babson College and London Business School), and some good compilations (Brunner 2001), but they are highly focused on specific topics, and there is virtually no systematic overview in the entrepreneurship field at this time for the region.

7. For example, there is a strong and profitable firm doing advanced biotech paternity testing, which I visited in Montevideo, but not many other start-ups.

8. Personal communication from John Newman, recently an entrepreneurship professor at Babson College, engaged in a design project for one of these schools in Ecuador.

9. As an example, in Montreal, four major universities got together a decade ago to create a specialized PhD in Technology Management: UQAM, McGill, Universite de Montreal, and Concordia.

10. Chile is a major exception, where the corporate donations for university research allow for 50% of the gift to be applied to reduce tax payable, and the remaining 50% generates a second credit calculated as a business expense worth 15%, the standard corporate tax rate. Thus the total credit can be worth a maximum $0.5 + 0.5 \times 0.15 = 0.575$ of the original gift, or the gift can cost a firm as little as 42.5% of its cash value to the university. However, there is to date limited awareness in industry of these incentives and very little flow to university-level education, partly because of a current preference for primary and secondary education projects. In addition, there are no incentives for such donations from individuals.

11. For those who do not mind being politically incorrect, take a look at the recent book by Lawrence Harrison and Samuel Huntington, *Culture Matters: How Values Shape Human Progress.*

CHAPTER 2

The Inter-American Development Bank and the Promotion of Entrepreneurship: Lessons Learned and Recommendations for New Programs[*]

Pablo Javier Angelelli

Juan José Llisterri

There is evidence to indicate that entrepreneurship[1] contributes to economic growth, to an increase in productivity, to the rejuvenation of the social-productive fabric, to innovation, and to the generation of new jobs. A recent study shows that company creation rates (1988–96) are associated in a positive way to economic growth (1989–99) in the countries of the Organization for Economic Cooperation and Development (OECD) (2001). The behavior pattern is similar when considering the proportion of adults involved in the creation of new companies as an indicator of entrepreneurship (Reynolds et al. 2000). Audretsch and

[*] The views and opinions expressed in the paper are those of the authors and do not necessarily represent the official position of the Inter-American Development Bank.

Thurik (2001) also found empirical evidence that suggests that an increase in entrepreneurship leads to higher rates of economic growth and lower unemployment rates.

The role of the new companies is also significant with regards to the creation of job opportunities, particularly for young people, who constitute a group with a higher unemployment rate than the average for the economically active population in many developed and developing economies (OECD 2001). It is at a local or a regional level that the impact of entrepreneurship is often most clearly seen. In geographical areas with higher company creation rates and greater entrepreneurship, the use of economic resources is more efficient, and economic growth and the population's living conditions are usually superior to those in areas where entrepreneurship is weaker.

In the countries of Latin America, diverse evidence indicates that the rates for company creation and growth of the created companies is lower than those for industrialized countries. For example, the statistics in the economic censuses in the region show that the average age of Latin firms is much higher than in developed countries, which reflects a scarce entry of new companies into the market. A study that compares the performance of new companies in Latin America and in East Asia found that the Asian firms grow 2.5 times faster than the Latin Americans ones (Kantis, Ishida, and Komori 2002). Another recent study indicates that big Latin American companies, in both the real and the financial sector, are small not only in absolute terms, but also in relation to the size of their home-country economies (IDB 2001).

Policies aimed at promoting entrepreneurship are acquiring increasing importance in many countries around the world. The trend is also present in Latin America, although it is more recent. This is due to three different reasons. First, there are few initiatives and little time has elapsed since they began to be implemented. Second, it is difficult to gain access to the information about the characteristics and results of these programs. Third, because the existing programs concentrate on different factors that affect the process of creation of companies—such as the availability of production factors and specialized services, the value that society attaches to companies and to business persons, the degree to which the educational system generates the entrepreneurial motivation, the simplicity and efficacy of the regulatory framework for economic activity, the individuals' entrepreneurial potential, and the individuals' capacity to relate and to cooperate with other economic agents—their design and their results are not comparable.

The objective of this chapter is to study the experience of the Inter-American Development Bank (IDB) in the promotion of entrepreneurship in Latin America, in order to extract lessons and policy recommendations. Between 1995 and 2002, the IDB[2] invested 177 million dollars in

42 programs intended to promote the creation of companies. Nine initiatives concentrated on the introduction of innovations in the educational system, the development of sustainable training and incubation services, and the strengthening of managerial contact networks. The characteristics and results of these nine programs are discussed in the first section of this chapter. The remainder of the projects, which are analyzed in the second section, seek to develop risk-capital markets for new and small companies. The last section of the chapter compares the central aspects of the explored programs and evaluates under what conditions it may be more convenient to broach comprehensive strategies for the promotion of entrepreneurship.

Culture, Education, and Entrepreneurial Spirit

Education, the values transmitted by the family, social context, and entrepreneur role models are important aspects in the generation of the motivation and the abilities for individuals to consider the option of launching a company. In Latin America, however, the educational system and the family are not the most effective environment to motivate and train entrepreneurs. The university only has a relatively significant role in the creation of technical knowledge. The influence of the family does not appear to be too significant either, although it is recognized that relatives contribute to the shaping of important values, for example, the capacity to work hard (see Table 2.1). In addition, role models provided by exemplary entrepreneurs do not seem to play the motivational role they have in other regions of the world. Asian entrepreneurs, for example, grant greater recognition to the motivational influence of other business persons whom they admired and whom they wanted to imitate.

Job experience, more than education, the family, or exemplary entrepreneurs, is the factor that has the biggest impact in the generation of motivation and abilities for undertakings (see Table 2.1). This situation is worrisome considering that urban juvenile unemployment is rising in many countries of the region and that it almost duplicates or is near to doubling the unemployment averages (International Labor Organization 2002). Considering that job experience is an essential factor in the motivation and training of future entrepreneurs, as long as the number of youths who do not gain access to the labor market increases, a decrease is to be expected in the total number of individuals with the desire and capabilities to be entrepreneurs.

The introduction of reforms in the educational system and in the social, cultural, and business environment, as well as the reduction of juvenile unemployment, could contribute to increases in the number of people who are motivated and capableof creating companies. However, policies to promote entrepreneurship that pursue these objectives are

Table 2.1

Importance of Different Contexts for the Creation of the Motivation and Abilities to Launch a Business in Latin America (Percentages of Entrepreneurs) (IDB 2002)

Competencies	High School	Technical Institutes	Universities	Job Experience	Training Courses	Family
Solving problems	8.0	8.7	33.9	77.4	18.3	30
Business motivation	3.6	3.1	15.1	53.5	7.2	35.7
Risk taking	2.0	1.1	13.7	66.8	7.2	29.5
Negotiation	2.5	1.7	11.4	76.3	11.9	20.3
Teamwork	8.4	5.0	28.5	68.6	12.8	14.8
Creativity	8.4	5.9	28.1	49.0	11.5	24.6
Technical knowledge	4.2	12.8	45.6	52.3	25.3	5.5
Marketing	0.6	3.7	24.6	55.5	27.8	5.6
Management	2.3	3.6	28.4	62.7	21.4	12.6
Capacity for work	2.0	1.7	13.1	62.9	3.0	42.9
Communication	6.7	3.7	20.1	61.6	15.9	25.9
Motivating others	3.7	2.0	13.3	65.7	17.9	22.9

not very numerous. A successful example from outside the region is the strategy to increase the rate of creation of companies implemented between 1993 and 2000 by the Scottish Enterprise (Scotland's economic development agency). This case provides some ideas about how the culture and attitudes toward entrepreneurship can be changed. The main challenge faced by this policy was to persuade more people to become business persons. To this end, between 1998 and 2001 the Scottish Enterprise implemented the Personal Enterprise Campaign program, an initiative that included TV advertisements, an interactive road show, instructional materials, and a follow-up through local offices. This program has been one of the most expensive and innovative initiatives to spread the entrepreneurial culture. It is estimated that more than 40,000 people participated in the initiative and 15,000 were present at specific events. An evaluation carried out by the University of Glasgow suggests that as a consequence of the program 2,870 new businesses and 6,600 jobs were created. However, the Scottish Enterprise experience indicates that is difficult to generate cultural changes over the short term. For example, between 1992 and 1999 the percentage of Scottish adults not interested in starting a new business decreased from 37% to 32%, and the increase in the number of adults committed to the development of a new business rose marginally, from 1.2% to 2.4%. The influence of this change in the culture of Scotland did not manifest itself directly, either, in the creation of new companies (Scottish Enterprise 2000).

Reform policies in formal education, at the primary, secondary, tertiary, and university levels, are more frequent than programs to spread the entrepreneurial culture. Education, as a mass mechanism for the transmission of knowledge, models, and motivation, has the potential to facilitate the development of a more entrepreneurial society. An extra-regional policy example in the education area is that of the CEED[3] (Center for Entrepreneurship Education and Development) in Nova Scotia, Canada. This public-private institution was created in 1995 within the Department of Education of Nova Scotia. The role of the CEED is mainly concentrated in drawing up curriculums and methodologies for entrepreneurship education, training teachers, and introducing courses on entrepreneurship in high school and university education.

An example of the activities of the CEED is the development of the Entrepreneurship: A Way of Life course, the methodology of which concentrates on learning through experiment and the development of attitudes, abilities, and knowledge necessary to be an entrepreneur. It seeks to have the students apply knowledge acquired in different activities: at school, in the community, in tutorships, and in the creation of new businesses. The course includes 110 hours of classroom activities developed as a complement to Nova Scotia high school syllabi to introduce entrepreneurship at this educational level. Since the 1997–98 school year, Entrepreneurship: A Way of Life has been the most popular elective course in the high schools of Nova Scotia.

The experience of the IDB in programs for spreading entrepreneurial education and culture is very restricted. Only two initiatives exist that have as an objective the introduction of entrepreneurial education in the formal educational system. The first is being implemented in Chile, Ecuador, Paraguay, and Peru. Its goal is to develop capabilities and skills among impoverished young people who are getting a high school education.[4] The main activities of the program are developing educational materials appropriate to each country's realities, implementing courses in the schools, making the project known in the business community to motivate and commit business persons' participation in the educational programs, and establishing coordination among the participating institutions in each country. As a result of the program, it is hoped that 395 high school teachers and 32,000 students between the ages of 14 and 19 will receive an entrepreneurial education.

The second program is in the province of Río Negro, Argentina. Its objective is to introduce innovative methods and contents to train youths who attend the formal public school system. The activities include the development of a syllabus and a handbook for the training of young entrepreneurs, the training of 5 facilitators and 20 teachers in entrepreneurial education, and the introduction of courses at schools to train 750 youths between 16 and 24 years old. One aspect that sets this initiative apart is that it includes a system of scholarships and technical assistance to underwrite the first phase of the creation of 100 new undertakings proposed by the students trained. This aspect gives the program a more comprehensive character and increases its potential impact on the creation of companies. The program is carried out by an alliance between the Fundación Gente Nueva and the Fundación Jorge Kitll. Both institutions have experience in educational matters and entrepreneurial development.

When comparing the problems mentioned at the beginning with the supply of programs, it seems evident that opportunities exist in the region for introducing reforms in the educational systems so that they contribute more effectively to creating entrepreneurial motivation and capabilities. These reforms should consider the importance of exposing students to the job market to shape them as future entrepreneurs. The results of programs such as those in Chile, Ecuador, Paraguay, Peru, and Argentina must be carefully analyzed in order to ascertain what obstacles exist to the introduction of new content to promote entrepreneurship in the schools. Another area for opportunity is the increase in the esteem in which the society holds entrepreneurs, where the experience of Scotland could be significant. Lastly, it should be considered that although this type of policy has the potential to reach large groups of people, mainly teenagers and youths, its impact on the number of people interested in creating companies and on the rate of creation of companies can, as the case of Scotland shows, be small or even nil over the short term. The focus of these programs should be of medium and long-term duration.

Networks, Business Services, and Creation of Companies

This section analyzes how business services and networks influence the creation of companies and what is the role of support policies in these fields. Entrepreneurs can use the services of consultancy companies, universities, chambers of commerce and unions, nongovernmental organizations (NGOs), and technological institutes to launch their business. They can also use their networks of formal and informal relationships to gain access to resources that are out of their reach. The networks can facilitate access to business opportunities, information, technology, and also solutions to the problems faced in the initial development of the companies. Some authors point out that informal networks (friends, family, other business persons) are more effective than formal ones (banks, institutions, lawyers) for business development. In Latin America, however, the importance of formal and informal contacts evolves over time. As progress is made in defining and implementing the entrepreneurial project, the contacts that are more formal and linked to the business world acquire greater significance.

Table 2.2 presents some data on the use and impact of business services and networks for the entrepreneurs of the region. In the creation of the project, business services contribute to shaping the entrepreneur's skills, whereas the networks are important in identifying the business opportunity. At the launching stage, the networks are more important than the services of universities and union organizations in obtaining information and technology. The same situation is repeated in the first years of development of the companies, when contact with customers and suppliers is valued more highly than the services of business associations, public institutions, and consultancy firms to solve the problems of the company's growth. In sum, the services incorporated in the interactions of entrepreneurs with their networks of contacts are more useful and valued than those offered by companies and training or consultancy institutions.

This can be due to three reasons. First, the design and methodologies of the services for entrepreneurs that are offered by the training and consultancy firms and institutions are not suited to their needs. Second, the supply of these services is insufficient. Third, the entrepreneurs may not have the capacity to meet the total cost of the services. The policies and programs for training courses, incubation and the development of networks that are discussed below broach these problems.

The IDB has financed three programs to promote training and technical assistance services for entrepreneurs. Through the first one, the execution of which concluded in the year 2001, the Advisory Center for New Companies (ACNC)[5] was created in Argentina. This center was created with the objective of providing sustainable orientation services, training, and technical advice for people who wanted to set up or readapt a new company in the city of Buenos Aires and its surroundings. The pattern of services that ACNC introduced in the market was based on three successive stages: sensitization workshops to attract customers, evaluation of companies or business ideas, and training and technical assistance. More than 1,000 companies received assistance under the program. In the beginning, the beneficiaries were mainly

Table 2.2
Importance of Business Services and Networks in the Process of Creation of Companies in Latin America (IDB 2002)

	Creation of the Project	Launching	Initial Development
Business services	Training courses make a small contribution to creating business skills (see Table 2.1)	4 out of 10 entrepreneurs use the services of universities and business associations to obtain information and technology	Between 15 and 20% of entrepreneurs use the services of business associations, public institutions, and consultancy firms
Use of networks	7 out of 10 entrepreneurs identify the business opportunity in discussions with other people, who generally are friends, co-workers, or other business persons from their own city	6 out of 10 entrepreneurs rely on their contacts to obtain information and technology. Commercial and institutional networks are more important than personal ones	Half of entrepreneurs recognize that interaction with customers and suppliers helps them to solve the problems of initial growth

people who wanted to start a new business. However, as the implementation advanced, the group of beneficiaries tended to concentrate more and more on the owners and managers of small and medium-sized companies. This change in ACNC's strategy was due to the need to achieve greater financial sustainability, because the experience of the first months of operation indicated that the probability of recovering costs was higher among the more established managers than among the individuals who wanted to undertake a new business. Only 3% of the potential business persons participating in the sensitization workshops were willing to pay for the evaluation and the technical assistance.

The second training initiative has as its goal support for the transfer of the Empretec methodology (see Box 2.1) to institutions, teachers, and business persons in El Salvador, Guatemala, and Panama. An interesting characteristic of the design of this program is that the definition of the group of beneficiaries emphasized the presence of women and employees from big companies. The inclusion of these segments makes it possible to have a bigger customer base, and in the case of the employees, helps to strengthen the role of big companies as incubators of new businesses. The program was executed at the end of 1999 and by now has

Box 2.1
The Empretec Program[6]

Empretec is an UNCTAD program created in 1988 with the objective of building up institutional capacity to support the development of entrepreneurs with a high potential for growth. The program has 50 national Empretec centers set up in 24 countries, and 280 instructors and interviewers trained and certified in accordance with international standards. To gain access to an Empretec course, individuals are strictly selected through a system of personal interviews. Only a quarter of those who register enter the program to participate in a two-week workshop (25 participants, a third of them female) that encourages the individuals to center on their roles as business persons. The program challenges them to critically examine their personal strengths and weaknesses. The method of training is highly interactive and experimental. It includes structured exercises, working in groups, evaluation tools, and other vehicles to challenge the participants to focus on such aspects as their capacity and willingness to seek and achieve quality, productivity, and growth, and to be aware of the necessity for continuous improvement as a competitive strategy in each aspect of their own and their business attitudes. The evaluations indicate that more than 85% of participants in the workshop noticed a change in their personal and business attitudes. The workshop not only has an impact on each individual's motivation and skills, but also generates self-confidence and promotes strong links among participating business persons, who later organize themselves for mutual help and the exchange of information and experiences.

achieved some results. In the three countries, private and public-sector leaders became involved in launching the Empretec offices. In El Salvador, FUNDEMAS, an institution led by a highly regarded local businessman, was set up. In Panama, the Fundación Empretec Panamá was created, also with the backing of large corporations and public institutions. The Managers' Association leads the program in Guatemala. As for the training of teachers, approximately 20 people were trained in the three countries. In terms of people trained, the results through the end of 2002 were 196 in El Salvador, 257 in Panama, and 164 in Guatemala. The participation of women in the courses ranged between 40 and 50%. As in the case of ACNC, this experience indicates that to achieve sustainability in the training services it is necessary to diversify the kinds of customers it benefits, including people who want to be business persons, but mainly established business persons and employees of big companies or those from the public sector.

The New Youthful Companies program in Peru[7] is the third initiative in the training area, and its objective is to promote a business culture and to foster private investment in innovative initiatives by university youths of up to 30 years of age. The focus is much more comprehensive than in the two previous cases. Its activities include training teachers and advisors to provide courses on drawing up business plans, offering these courses to university students, implementing a nationwide business plan competition, and furnishing of guarantees and technical assistance in support of the projects selected in the competition. Carrying out this program is the Asociación Pro Bienestar y Desarrollo (PROBIDE) of Peru, an organization with experience in the area of education and strong links to the local business community. The bonds between PROBIDE and the Peruvian business community are one of their critical assets for the benefit of the program's services. The youths who are selected through the business plans competition not only receive guaranteed access to a bank credit, but can also be part of the PROBIDE network of contacts, which increases their business opportunity possibilities and their access to other strategic resources, such as information, technology, partners, and suppliers. In Box 2.2, some results of the program are presented. In this respect, it is worthwhile to note that in this case it was indeed possible to concentrate on the training of potential entrepreneurs, although this training was free of charge.

Company incubators are, along with training programs, among the most common forms of service to promote entrepreneurship. The incubators are organizations that provide physical space and technical support (product development, laboratory tests, administrative and legal support, marketing, etc.), for a limited time, for the setting up of technology-based or traditional companies. The incubators are generally located in areas close to universities and research centers, and they can be spots for the transfer of scientific knowledge to industry. For example, many businesses that are created by teachers or researchers undergo their first development stages in organizations of this type.

Box 2.2
Some Results of the New Youthful Companies of Peru Program

Between mid-2001 and the end of 2002, the program trained 50 regional coordinators and 500 teachers in techniques for drawing up business plans. These teachers and coordinators, in turn, trained more than 4,000 youths, who, working in teams, presented almost 800 business plans in the Believe in Order to Create competition. Two committees of professional people and business persons selected 112 of the 800 business plans that were presented in the competition. The finalist projects were submitted to the credit committees of diverse financial institutions for them to give their opinion regarding their financing. In the cases in which the answer is positive, the Private Guarantees Fund set up by the program will guarantee the credits granted. These projects will also receive technical support from PROBIDE during the first years of operation.

Regarding training programs and programs for the spread of entrepreneurial culture, company incubators aim for a more restricted public, and their impact on the creation of companies may take place over shorter periods. The beneficiaries of the incubation services are generally individuals who already have a business plan. Another aspect that characterizes the incubators is their concentration in high-technology sectors. The experience of Brazil illustrates the aspects discussed. In that country, the number of company incubators rose from 68 in 1997 to 135 in the year 2000. A recent study indicates that through the year 2001 the number of graduating companies was about 315, approximately 50% of which are in the sector of information and communications technology. A survey of 103 companies that had graduated shows that in 64% of the cases the performance of the firms would have been worse without incubators and that the service most valued by managers is the facilitation of market access (Ministry of Science and Technology 2001).

The IDB has backed three company incubation programs. The first one is in Santa Catarina, Brazil, and its objective is to increase the productivity of small, state companies through support for the creation of new technology-intensive companies. The activities of the project are to put into operation three company incubators, train managers and employees in companies in the region, and disseminate the experience into the rest of the country. To obtain access to the incubation services, entrepreneurs have to demonstrate that the product to be developed is technology-intensive, that the project is technically viable and profitable, that they have financial resources, and that the environmental legislation is complied with. The incubation services are provided for periods of 2 to 3 years and seek to create companies with a lower mortality rate, greater capacity for technological innovation, and larger growth than companies that are not incubated. Carrying out the project is the National Industrial Learning Service of Santa Catarina.[8]

The other two incubator programs operate in Uruguay and Panama. Both have as an objective the creation of information technology (IT) companies. The goals are 50 new companies in the case of Uruguay and 19 in Panama. Access to the incubators takes place through competitive processes in which the entrepreneurs must demonstrate that the product or service is innovative and based on IT, that theirs are emerging companies, and that the product or service is marketable. The business persons who fulfill these requirements receive training to draw up the business plan, which must be submitted to a committee that decides who is finally admitted to the incubator. The incubation may be in the facility or off-site. In the first case, the entrepreneurs develop their business project at the physical location of the incubator, making use of its infrastructure services. Remote (virtual or off-site) incubation does not require physical infrastructure services because the entrepreneurs are located at their own offices, although it offers the benefit of all the other services. The project in Uruguay is carried out jointly by the Technological Laboratory of Uruguay (LATU) and ORT University, and in Panama the operator is the Fundación Ciudad del Saber.[9]

The importance the entrepreneurs allocate to networks has slowly been brought into the design of policies for the promotion of entrepreneurship. Several of the programs that are already in execution, such as the new youthful companies of Peru and the incubators, also contribute, in spite of it not being among their main objectives, to strengthening and diversifying entrepreneurial networks. The mechanisms to promote networks include stimulating teamwork; the creation of entrepreneur clubs, forums and associations; and different forms of transfer of knowledge from established business persons to those who want to or are already in the process of starting their business, among other possibilities. The promotion of networks, however, is one of the most complex and less-experienced areas in the promotion of entrepreneurship, and one in which only now good practices are beginning to be identified. (See Box 2.3.)

Among the programs backed by the IDB, Business Capacity Development in Latin America is the one that incorporates the objective of strengthening networks in the most explicit way. The objective is to extend the methodology of Endeavor[10] first to Uruguay and Chile, and then to a third country. The Endeavor methodology is based on a rigorous process of identification and selection of entrepreneurs, who then are backed in the drawing up of a strategic and financial plan and in the development of bonds with local and international investors and with local universities. The program, besides including the start-up of the Endeavor offices and methodology in three countries, also incorporates carrying out 20 case studies of successful entrepreneurs and writing 40 articles to be disseminated through the Web site of Endeavor.

A review of the programs financed by the IDB in the areas of training and incubation of new companies shows that priorities have been to facilitate the development or the transfer of support methodologies to entrepreneurs and to create institutional capacity in the region. The cases of ACNC and Empretec show that, when sustainability is sought, the possibility is lower of reaching those who should be the beneficiaries of these programs. It is also clear that, unlike the policies discussed in the previous section, the training and incubation programs reach fewer people, although their impact in the creation of companies could be more direct and over shorter terms. One can also think that if these initiatives are combined with strategies for the dissemination of suc-

Box 2.3
Good Practices for the Promotion of Networks

A recent study, based on the analysis of five successful programs in the United States, points out the following recommendations for the development of networks.

- Leadership with high visibility: One should not underestimate the power of a leader with a vision that can mobilize people around an idea or a project. Many activities need a "champion" with the passion and intellectual credibility to carry them forward in a successful way.

- Relationships, not contacts: The development of networks means establishing not only contacts among people but also relationships–that is to say, the creation of spaces of trust for the exchange of information and the development of leadership capabilities.

- Small groups: Networks with many participants are easier to create than those with fewer people. However, the latter are more effective in generating exchanges of information and collective learning. At the beginning, the effort should be to identify the right people rather than to generate large groups.

- Commitment over the long term: The programs for network development should be over the medium and long term. In general, the achievement of results in this type of initiative requires a minimum of 3 or 4 years.

- Facilitation, not intervention: The role of a program's officials is to develop networks, "to be there but not to be stand out," to provide administrative support to the network, but to avoid intervening in guiding the activities.

- To link people, not companies: People can relate to one another, companies cannot. In consequence, the network development programs should not build alliances among companies, but instead bonds among people who want to share ideas and learn from one each other.

---

cessful cases, they could contribute to spreading entrepreneurship in society. The development of networks does not appear to be a high priority, and this aspect should be reconsidered. As was shown at the beginning of this section, entrepreneurs prefer the use of the services incorporated by the networks. Training and incubation services can be more effective in facilitating the creation of new business if they help entrepreneurs to establish relationships with other people who provide them with resources for the undertaking. A last point to highlight is the participation of highly regarded business persons in the leadership of the programs, an aspect that appears to be a basic condition to give credibility and summoning-power to the operating institution.

The Financing of the New Companies

It is common for entrepreneurs to base the launching of their business on the use of their own funds and loans from family and friends, and, to a lesser extent, on external sources of financing. In Latin America, however, access to external sources is more difficult than in other regions of the world. The contrast is evident when it is compared with Asian entrepreneurs who have easier access to private bank loans, to the guarantees and subsidies of national public institutions, as well as to a nonformalized risk capital, the so-called business angels (see Table 2.3). Because of the insufficient access to external financing, a little over two-thirds of Latin American entrepreneurs are negatively affected by the conditions under which they launch their business activities. Their scale of operation or technological level is inferior to the one desirable in order to be competitive, or they must begin to operate later than planned.

The problem of access to financing is still more marked in the first years of company life. Personal savings and the support of family and friends tend to become less frequent as the business grows and there is a bigger demand for capital. Although, in this phase, Latin American entrepreneurs tend to use more bank credit, the number of Asian entrepreneurs who use financing continues to be greater. In East Asia, the proportion of firms that use external sources of financing during their first years of life doubles the one seen in the launching phase, whereas in Latin America only a barely positive evolution is observed. This statistic is completed with a certain increase in access to corporate risk capital in Asia that contrasts with its marginal presence in Latin American countries (see Table 2.3).

The IDB has broached the small company's problem of access to capital and financing through different programs and instruments, ranging from initiatives to improve the regulation and supervision of financial systems to risk-capital funds.[11] Although all these programs seek to improve efficiency in financial markets, risk-capital funds appear as the best option for meeting the needs of companies that are beginning to operate. Between 1995 and 2002, the IDB, through the Multilateral Investments Fund (MIF), invested $163 million in 33 capital funds for small companies. For their part, local partners, including both private investors and development organizations, have invested $273 million.

The typical MIF operation limits its participation to a maximum of 50% of total capital; it includes private-sector partners to contribute the remaining part of the capital and works through an administrator with outstanding experience in the matter. These programs seek to begin the creation of a local investment-fund market that contributes an effective financing for the launching and development of companies through the

Table 2.3
Where Do Latin American and East Asian Entrepreneurs Obtain
Financing? (Percentages of Companies) (IDB 2002)

Financing Sources		Launching		First Three Years	
		East Asia	Latin America	East Asia	Latin America
Internal	Personal savings	66.7	87.2	54.3	63.7
	Relatives/friends	33.7	24.1	23.6	21.0
	Credit cards	10.6	10.2	10.0	9.1
External	Private investors	17.4	9.2	14.8	6.5
	Venture capitals	5.9	3.5	10.6	1.3
	Banks: loans	24.8	18.7	39.9	23.8
	Banks: overdrafts	6.1	13.0	9.7	18.1
	Public institutions: loans, guarantees	12.1	2.1	23.5	4.1
	Public institutions: concessions	5.3	0.9	8.3	1.3
	Local governments: loans, guarantees	5.8	0.9	12.8	1.0
	Local governments: concessions	3.1	1.4	5.0	1.3
Others	Customers (advances)	10.2	19.6	10.4	19.7
	Suppliers (commercial credits)	15.6	39.2	19.5	43.5
	Factoring	2.9	5.4	5.7	9.1
	Tax payment postponements	2.9	11.1	4.3	13.2
	Service payment postponements	1.8	3.3	3.2	4.7
	Wage payment postponements	1.4	3.3	2.7	4.4
	Purchasing secondhand equipment	23.2	33.6	17.2	27.5
	Others	2.3	3.8	2.8	7.3

demonstration effect and the introduction of new investment technologies. They also seek to contribute to training experts in the management of investment funds for small companies.

The investment funds in which the MIF participates are characterized by the following aspects: (1) investments of between $50,000 and $1,500,000, while the large private capital groups generally invest amounts above $5,000,000; (2) the annual sales of beneficiary companies do not surpass $3 to 5 million and they have fewer than 100 employees at the time of investment; (3) the co-investors are organizations oriented toward development, such as development institutions, NGOs, or private strategic investors; and (4) they finance the creation of companies and other investments in the initial phase, an approach with high risk but possibilities for high yields.

Nine of the 33 investment funds supported by the MIF are still in the initial structuring and start-up phase. The other 24 are already structured and most of them have already made investments. In total, 105 small companies have already received support from the investment funds, with an average amount of $500,000. It is too early to evaluate the financial results of the investments of the MIF in terms of capital earnings or losses racked up when withdrawing the investments. It is expected that the investment fund yields will behave according to a J curve, with a decrease in the net value of goods at the beginning, because in the first years the small size of the fund's management costs reduce the capital. Afterwards, within 5 to 10 years of the fund's existence, a growth in yield is expected.

The impact of the investment funds on entrepreneurship in Latin America is restricted if the number of companies that benefit is considered. For each million dollars invested, two new companies are backed. However, the impact will be substantially bigger if these interventions are able, via the demonstration effect, to stimulate other investors into entering the industry. For this to happen, it is necessary to advance in the solution of the legal and regulatory problems that limit the possible investment structures; generate contingent liabilities (due to tax debts, social dues, and lack of compliance with environmental standards); hinder optional share purchasing plans, which forces the establishment of offshore companies and significantly increases transaction costs, and affect the rights of minority partners (Morrison and Forrester LLP 2001).

Policy Discussion and Recommendations

The experiences analyzed in this chapter allow for the observation that there exists a wide range of possibilities to promote the creation of companies. The programs of educational reform and spread of the entrepreneurial culture concentrate especially on the young population and seek to change the attitude of individuals and endow them with entrepreneurial capabilities. The training, incubation, and development of networks programs support groups of people who already have motivation and ideas to begin a business. Lastly, risk-capital funds facilitate the development of companies that were recently constituted and have high growth potential. Table 2.4 summarizes the entrepreneurial process stages, the type of beneficiaries, and the prospective results of the different types of programs discussed in this chapter.

Table 2.4 shows that certain complementarities exist among the analyzed programs. It also allows the thought that it may be convenient to design more comprehensive initiatives for the promotion of entrepreneurship. For example, the successful cases of a risk-capital program can positively influence the culture and reinforce the results of educational reforms that seek to increase the number of people with entrepreneurial motivation. At the same time, insofar as there are more well-trained people motivated to launch a business, risk-capital funds will have more and better options to choose their ultimate customers. At least three factors should be kept in mind to decide the degree of comprehensiveness of a promotion program for entrepreneurship: the starting point situation, the degree of substitution among different types of areas or programs, and the type of companies that they seek to promote.

When a weak entrepreneurial and institutional background characterizes the starting point, there will be a greater need to operate in a comprehensive manner. In the Scottish case, briefly remarked on earlier in the chapter, due to the fragility of the entrepreneurial context at the beginning of the 1990s, the strategy that Scottish Enterprise designed was of a comprehensive and articulated kind, with the purpose of reversing the negative or neutral incidence, according to the case, of the different factors that limited the creation of firms: culture and education, networks, support spaces for the identification of opportunities and the drawing up of the project, access to financing, and technical assistance. In the United States, on the contrary, where the culture, education, regulatory environment, and central role of civil society institutions are very favorable to entrepreneurial development, the public role is focused on such topics as financing, the development of networks, or access to information.

The need for comprehensiveness may also be smaller in a case in which a type of program can affect several factors that determine the entry of firms into the economy. For example, a program aimed at improving the supply of risk capital, which in its initial development only affects companies, could, if it enjoyed very sizable resources and all its investments were successful, generate demonstration effects with

Table 2.4
Typology of Programs to Promote Entrepreneurship

Program Type	Stage of the Entrepreneurial Process and Beneficiary Type	Expected Results and Time Frames
Education and spread of the entrepreneurial culture	They facilitate the creation of new companies. The beneficiaries are mainly adolescents and the young, but the whole population can be reached by these initiatives.	Over the medium term, an increase takes place in the number of people who want to be entrepreneurs and there are more individuals with business skills.
Training, incubation, and development of networks	They facilitate the start-up and the initial development of new companies. The beneficiaries are people with entrepreneurial potential and a business idea/plan, sometimes in technology-intensive sectors.	Over the short term, better-qualified business persons. Over the medium term, few new companies in the economy.
Risk capital	They facilitate the initial development of new companies with high potential for growth.	Over the medium term, a few successful new companies in the economy and more developed risk-capital markets.

regard to other people, and stimulate them to undertake new projects. Nevertheless, if the context does not systematically operate in favor of entrepreneurial development, a strategy focused on one or a few factors will present limitations over the a medium and long term. Soft-pedaling activity in certain areas that operate over the medium term (for instance culture and education), concentrating, for example, on financing, may cause effects on the rate of creation of undertakings over the shorter term, but it will surely require having ample budgetary resources that are capable of generating very powerful incentives making entrepreneurial initiatives a very attractive option, beyond the possible existence of other factors which operate in the opposite direction.

The company profile that it is sought to promote is the final element to consider in determining the degree of comprehensiveness. If the objective is the increase of the entrepreneurial base in a wide sense, there should be comprehensive and articulated efforts. If, on the contrary, the objective is to develop companies with a quick growth or with a certain sectorial profile, policy instruments could be concentrated, for example, on incubator programs or the development of risk-capital funds.

The last observation is about the institutions that carry out the programs. Several factors appear to be critical for carrying out programs promoting entrepreneurship. The first is specialized knowledge in the program area, be it education, training, incubation services, or risk-capital management. The second is entrepreneurial leadership and knowledge of the business world. The third is the working approach, which should be based on the shaping of networks and on the design and furnishing of sustainable services. The existence of institutions with such characteristics should also be an element of analysis in the decision on the scope of entrepreneurship promotion programs.

References

Acs, Z., and D. Audretsch. 1998. "Innovation, Market Structures and Company Size." In *SME Development and Management: Contribution to a Necessary Debate*. Universidad Nacional de General Sarmiento.

Anprotec. 1999. Annual IX Seminar of Technological Parks and Incubators, Brazil.

Audretsch, D., and R. Thurik. 2001. "Linking Entrepreneurship to Growth." OECD Directorate for Science, Technology, and Industry. Cited in *Entrepreneurship, Growth and Policy*. Paris: OECD.

Center for Entrepreneurship Education and Development. 2000. *The First Four Years*. Halifax, Nova Scotia, Canada.

Entrepreneurship in Emerging Economies: Creation and Development of New Companies in Latin America and East Asia. 2002. Database for the study. IDB, 2002.

Gartner, W. 1988. "Who Is an Entrepreneur? It Is the Wrong Question." *American Journal of Small Business* 12: 11–32.

Gibb, A. and J. Ritchie. 1982. "Understanding the Process of Starting a Small Business." *European Small Business Journal, DFC*.

Inter-American Development Bank (IDB). 2001. *The Business of Growth: Economic and Social Progress in Latin America*. Washington, DC.

Inter-American Development Bank (IDB). 2003. *Support from the BID Group to the Micro Company Sector*. Washington, DC.

Inter-American Development Bank (IDB). 2003. *Support from the BID Group to the Small and Medium Company Sector*. Washington, DC.

International Labor Organization. 2002. *Labor Panorama 2002*. www.oit.org.pe/spanish/260ameri/publ/panorama/2002/index.html.

Johannisson, B. 1993. "Designing Supportive Contexts for Emerging Enterprises." In: *Small Business Dynamics: International, National and Regional Perspectives,* C. Karlsson, B. Johannisson, and D. Storey (eds). Routledge: London.

Kantis, H., M. Ishida, and M. Komori. 2002. *Entrepreneurship in Emergent Economies: Creation and Development of New Companies in Latin America and East Asia.* Inter-American Development Bank, Washington, DC.

Kayne, J. 1999. "State Entrepreneurship Policies and Programs." Kauffman Center for Entrepreneurial Leadership, www.entreworld.org.

Morrison and Forrester LLP. 2001. *The Need for Legal and Regulatory Reforms in Argentina, Brazil, Chile, El Salvador and Mexico to Promote Risk Capital Investments in Small and Medium Size Enterprises.* Unpublished report. Washington DC.

Ministry of Science and Technology. 2001. "Companies Graduated from Brazilian Business Incubators," Brazil.

Organization for Economic Cooperation and Development (OECD). 1997. *Small Businesses, Job Creation and Growth: Facts, Obstacles and Best Practices.* Paris.

Organization for Economic Cooperation and Development (OECD). 1999. *To Stimulate the Managerial Spirit.* Paris.

Organization for Economic Cooperation and Development (OECD). 2000. *Outlook of Small and Medium Enterprises.* Paris.

Organization for Economic Cooperation and Development (OECD). 2001a. *Entrepreneurship, Growth and Policy,* Paris.

Organization for Economic Cooperation and Development (OECD). 2001b. *Putting the Young in Business.* Paris.

Reynolds, P., W. Bygrave, E. Autio, L. Cox, and M. Hay. 1999–2002. *Global Entrepreneurship Monitor.* Executive reports, www.entreworld.org.

Science and Technology Ministry. 2001. "Graduated Companies in Brazilian Incubators." Brazil.

Scottish Enterprise. 2000. "The Scottish Business Birth Rate Inquiry 2000." Discussion paper, www.scottish-enterprise.com.

Notes

1. Entrepreneurship is defined in this work as the capacity of individuals to create companies.

2. The programs financed by the IDB in the 1995–2002 period that were included in this study are those whose beneficiaries are young people or business persons who are going through the first stages of the creation process of their companies, including the gestation, launching, and initial development (first three years of operation). All of the projects included in the present work were financed by the Multilateral Investments Fund (MIF), one of the three institutions that are part of the IDB Group. For further information, see www.iadb.org/mif.

3. For further information, see http://www.ceed.ednet.ns.ca.

4. This program seeks to extend the services of Junior Achievement International (JAI) to geographical environments not yet reached by this organization. JAI is an institution affiliated with Junior Achievement, Inc., which was founded in 1919 in Springfield, Massachusetts. JAI was established in 1994 to develop entrepreneurship programs outside the United States and has operations in 112 countries. For further information, see www.jaintl.org/about/history.asp.

5. For further information, see www.fundacioncane.org.ar.

6. For further information about the Empretec program, see www.empretec.net.

7. For further information, see www.creerparacrear.org.pe.

8. For further information, see www.sc.senai.br/incubadoras.jsp.

9. For further information, see www.latu.org.uy and www.ciudaddelsaber.org.pa.

10. For further information, see www.endeavor.org.

11. For a detailed analysis of these investments see the following reports: *Support from the IDB Group to the Small and Medium-Sized Company Sector* (March 2003); and *Support from the IDB Group to the Micro-Companies Sector* (March 2003.)

CHAPTER 3

Entrepreneurship and Development: Venezuela Case Study

Jeannine Horowitz Gassol

Even though the existence of entrepreneurship has been known for a long time now, its relevance and importance in economic and social development is still a matter of debate and study. Entrepreneurship cannot be viewed as a recipe that simply can be followed to form successful enterprises, because in reality it involves a very complex and not completely understood process. As entrepreneurship is strongly linked to innovation, the concerted promotion of the latter becomes extremely important, particularly in nations with poorly developed innovative capabilities.

Venezuela represents an example of a country with tremendous resource potential but with an oil-based rental economy that has generated little innovative and productive capabilities. The rental mentality and the "top-down," all-encompassing policies implemented in the past have failed to promote economic diversification, innovation, and competitiveness adapted to global markets, and have generated a paternalistic culture contrary to entrepreneurship. The results have been a poorly developed infrastructure, a very high poverty ratio, high unemployment, and a general feeling of stagnation and failure that in turn has created an extremely explosive political and social situation.

Having spent most of my career and thinking process on different aspects of innovation and economic development in both developed and underdeveloped countries has convinced me that change for successful development cannot be accomplished through the ambitious and general programs designed in the past, but rather through the implementation of specific, targeted, "bottom-up" and systemic projects, which are tailored to their surroundings and are, from the very onset, evaluated and continuously improved. These projects can create cascade effects, pull rather than push the necessary policies, and establish effective coordination of resources in the networking fashion needed today.

This chapter looks at entrepreneurship in a broader developmental context using Venezuela as a case study. An incipient entrepreneurship program being developed at the University Simón Bolívar under the very adverse conditions existing in the country at the time this chapter was written is also presented. The program has been designed in a bottom-up fashion, considering at all times the environment where it is inserted. Its major objectives are changing the mentality of university students from employees to entrepreneurs, promoting feasible university technological enterprises that can in turn boost national innovative capabilities, and creating a network of stakeholders represented by research centers, universities, businesses, industries, governmental and nongovernmental agencies, and financial institutions, to name a few. In this active manner and through real case action, it is hoped that a realistic innovation system can be generated that can pull effective reform policies toward a real, sustainable development.

An Entrepreneurship Overview

The Living Webster dictionary defines *entrepreneur* as "the person who organizes, manages and assumes the risks of a business." The word is also used to describe "a successful businessman." In Spanish, the word used is *emprendedor,* which in the *Diccionario Ideologico* is defined as "the person who gives rise to things difficult or risky." As one searches throughout the literature, one finds different definitions of the term *entrepreneur*, which are applied to define different things, but two things are always present: entrepreneurship involves taking advantage of opportunities, and putting ideas into practice.

Economists, in general, still consider entrepreneurship a metaeconomic event (as well as technology) and cannot yet explain its influence in the economy (Drucker 1986). Not surprisingly, the conclusions drawn from an entrepreneurship study performed by the Business Council for the United Nations (Reynolds et al. 2001) were that entrepreneurial development is a complex phenomenon and that its causes and impact need further study. Investment in research and technology development appears to not only create new wealth, but also creates new high-quality jobs that tend to lower the level of necessity entrepreneurship in the more technologically sophisticated countries studied. The study encouraged research and technology development as a means to increasing economic growth and well-being, while at the same time, stating that universal one-size-fits-all or best-practice solutions may not be an optimum strategy for policy development.

Latin American countries (generally viewed as developing nations) are not technologically sophisticated countries and do not contribute significantly to world innovation (Institute for Scientific Information 1994). In addition, the Latin American business environment is in general less friendly to new ventures than other countries (Kantis, Ishida, and Komori 2002). This, of course, raises the question of to what degree entrepreneurship and development are linked, because policies in Latin American countries have not been able to promote the entrepreneurial spirit among their population except for necessity entrepreneurship, and worse so, have curtailed the possibility of entrepreneurial success.

Venezuela: An Example

Venezuela is a striking example of underdevelopment and lack of innovation and technological entrepreneurship, and because of its unique characteristics merits an in-depth study. It is a country blessed with a significant amount of natural resources, among which petroleum clearly stands out. In addition, it has plentiful water, good land for agriculture, immense biological biodiversity, an advantageous global position, a mild climate, tremendous mining potential, beautiful natural scenery, and few natural threats (no volcanoes, tornadoes, or hurricanes, apart from the odd earthquake occurring every 40 years of so). It is a relatively large country (approximately 1 million kilometers square) with a relatively small population (around 25 million). Despite all of these comparative advantages, Venezuela is definitely an underdeveloped country and, at the time this chapter was written, undergoing a critical political, social, and economical situation with no short-term solution at hand. These factors place it among one of the less-desired countries for foreign investment and entrepreneurship.

What has happened here? Well, a critical analysis of Venezuela's history would reveal many interesting aspects of how culture and attitude can shape a country's future, which is not our purpose here. To make a long story short, let us say that Venezuela's history began at the end of the fifteenth century, being as it was the first continental place where Columbus set foot in 1498. It then became part of the Spaniard colonization enterprise, established as a simple *Capitania* because it lacked the rich indigenous culture of Peru and Mexico and did not have many riches to offer in the way of gold. It gained independence as a country in 1830, but until the beginning of the 1900s, Venezuela suffered a never-ending list of *caudillos* that kept the country in constant civil unrest. It was not until the discovery of oil at the beginning of the twentieth century that Venezuela became more than a "banana republic," switching from an agricultural-based economy to a petroleum one, particularly under the strict dictatorship of Jose Vicente Gomez that lasted 27 years, until 1935. In 1935, Venezuela began its democratic history, with a 10-year interruption that occurred from 1948 to 1958 during the dictatorship of Marcos Perez Jimenez. After Perez Jimenez, Venezuelans experienced a long period of democracy under a primarily bipartisan government system with free elections. During the petroleum boom of the 1970s, Venezuelan rulers created the illusion of leading the country toward a fast development. In reality, however, the line followed encouraged widespread inequality and poverty, generating a social crisis that ended in 1991 with two coup d'état attempts by Hugo Chavez Frias that ended the traditional bipartisan system. Chavez was elected president in 1998, promising a revolution that would end corruption and inequality and establish the changes that the country required. After 4 years of Chavez's government, with little change being perceived by the majority that elected him, the country entered another phase of social and political unrest marked by a frontal confrontation between government supporters and an opposition coalition that has basically shut down the country and brought it very close to a civil war.

With regards to economic development, for most of the twentieth century until today Venezuela's economy has been heavily based on an oil industry that created a rental-based economy with little diversification. In 2001, oil accounted for 80% of exports and over 25% of the National Gross Product.[1] During the 1970s and most of the 1980s, Venezuela implemented a deficient policy of import substitution with the intent to diversify its economy, which resulted in overprotected enterprises with poor competitive abilities in a global market. At the end of the 1980s and during the 1990s, it became generally recognized that Venezuela needed to increase its competitiveness through the development of endogenous technology. Therefore, an attempt was made to develop university-level human resources (engineers and scientists) and to promote research through an ambitious scholarship and grant program. However, the human resources produced were not put to use effectively, resulting in a tremendous brain drain for the country,[2] and the contribution that Venezuela made in the scientific area was not generally translated into marketable products nor inserted into an economic or social context. Badly designed economic and social policies–very top-heavy with theoretical dogmas that made their implementation close to impossible–ended up benefiting few and promoted dependency. In addition, generalized corruption and lack of an efficient and transparent judicial system curtailed entrepreneurship and investment. The results, therefore, have been a poorly developed industrial and technological infrastructure, a deficient financial system, a very high poverty ratio, high unemployment, and, thus, an explosive social and political situation.

The Entrepreneur in Venezuela

Recently, entrepreneurship has become a fashionable concept in Venezuela. The belief is that it will help solve the country's present maladies, specifically underemployment and low productive capabilities, but there is not a real understanding of what entrepreneurship implies and how it is tied up with innovation and development. The general perception is that a large proportion of the Venezuelan population is highly uneducated and unprepared to perform complex technical and technological work (some place the proportion as high as 80% but under the present situation any figure presented constitutes guesswork). The number of companies (particularly small and medium sized) that are going bankrupt due to the current conditions is undetermined, although the sum given by several business organizations is greater than 50%.[3] Most of the innovation is done in universities and research centers that are, for the most part, government financed, but the knowledge remains primarily in academic papers and theses and is not readily transferred to the productive sector.[4]

In an effort to help generate businesses, and thus employment, in a highly recessive economic situation, the present government has been designing several financing projects such as the Pam Pyme and the Promotion of Microenterprise Programs through the Ministry of Production and Commerce. Some of these are intended to be linked to entrepreneurship programs coordinated through universities, private consulting firms, and nongovernmental organizations, emphasizing the design of business plans with a future hope of establishing diverse self-sustained (meaning not free) managerial and business services for the potential entrepreneur. I believe that these programs, unfortunately, will have the same results as other policies implemented in the past, and that is that they will remain mainly ineffective as long as they continue to be designed without taking into consideration how they can be implemented, continuously evaluated, and improved through the analysis of real cases. In a country that has no registered organizational history, where policies are changed without having first performed the necessary analysis of their applicability or done a success or failure study, the tendency is to repeat the same errors over and over again, therefore demonstrating a lack of social innovation.[5]

We must remember that becoming an entrepreneur can be a difficult and almost impossible endeavor if all the factors that influence its viability are not present (culture, infrastructure, and information, to name a few). The questions that remain are the following: Are we aware of what these factors are? Do we manage them adequately in our present system? And above all, do we know what kind of entrepreneurship we should be promoting and to what purpose? In my opinion, none of these questions have been answered in Venezuela.

One of the most obvious steps to take toward developing entrepreneurship is to change the attitude of the average Venezuelan. It is almost a consensus that the Venezuelan population is, in general, highly adverse to risk and wants a very quick reward for effort. This is not surprising considering that the country's economy is a rental one, that the population is used to paternalistic policies, and that ever-changing government policies and the lack of a transparent and consistent judicial system promote a "grab what you can, when you can" type of culture. Personal motivation toward entrepreneurship can be perceived as a fundamental precondition, but I am convinced that motivating toward obtaining an entrepreneurship mentality will be useless and even counterproductive, if the motivated entrepreneur is not presented with feasible ideas on what to entrepreneur into and, if afterwards, finds so many insurmountable obstacles as to make the task impossible. Where will these feasible ideas come from? How can we help these ideas become real entrepreneurial endeavors? These questions also remain to be answered.

Universities and Entrepreneurship in Venezuela

A nation that, on the one hand, is very rich in natural resources, but, on the other hand, lacks the basic infrastructure (legal security, social services, financial stability, etc.) necessary to promote a sustained development, can represent another example of what has been termed "the curse of resource wealth." The resource wealth, however, can also represent a wealth of opportunities, which are the basis of entrepreneurship. The trick then becomes finding ways to promote the widespread exploitation of these opportunities by "pulling" forward developmental policies that increase innovation capabilities in products and services and help Venezuela compete in a global economy.

Undoubtedly, Venezuelan universities represent a very important developmental factor. Although they are primarily viewed as the centers for high-level human resource development in all areas of knowledge, they are also one of the few places where innovation is perceived as a necessary and required product, even though the transfer process of this innovation remains very incipient. The University Simón Bolívar, in particular, is a good example of an innovative university. It is considered a technological university with a social conscience. It was founded in the early 1970s as an experimental public university devoted to scientific and technological education but providing, in addition, a strong humanistic background to scientists and engineers. During its more than 30 years of existence, it has achieved a national reputation as being one of the best universities in the country. Unlike other public universities, its organizational structure is based on a matrix structure, having no faculties but rather academic departments that house the professors under an interdisciplinary structure, and academic coordinations that coordinate the academic curricula. National comparisons place the University Simón Bolívar as the university with the highest numbers of doctorate-level faculty, and national and international companies consider it a producer of high-quality professionals at the undergraduate level. Even though a very strong part of the academic requirements for faculty is research and development, it is primarily measured by the ability to publish in academic journals. The research carried out helps ensure to a certain degree that faculty keeps up-to-date and furthers the indirect transfer of new knowledge via education, but it lacks the culture and effective mechanisms for the transfer of this knowledge into more practical applications necessary for development. In addition, resources for research are scarce, and obtaining them involves a difficult, tiring, and often despairing process that causes faculty to search for research projects that will ensure publications in order to comply with university regulations, leaving little time to promote transfer activities and original innovation. Undergraduate students are not, in general, very inclined to work on university research projects, because it demands more time and effort, and prefer the alternative of *pasantías*,[6] hoping to establish future contacts and employment. The lack of doctoral programs also hampers the involvement of students in research. Around 10% of faculty are involved in industrial-related projects, but more as a means of augmenting their decaying salaries than as a form of promoting academia.[7] In many cases, these efforts are not considered valid activities by academic standards and very little student involvement is seen in them.

I have observed over the years that even though the quality of technical teaching is high, students are taught inside an environment that emphasizes an employee mentality more than an entrepreneurial one, and are expected to find "good" jobs in "good" companies. Nowadays, in the poor economic situation the country is facing, jobs, good or bad, have become rare commodities that are very difficult to obtain.

Faced with the bleak situation in which the country is placed, many will adhere to the notion that Venezuela must change 180 degrees in its policy and strategy if any successful development is to be accomplished. The very explosive social situation that Venezuela faces today implies that many things are going very wrong and that relatively fast solutions are needed. The country, however, cannot afford to continue to implement large encompassing programs that arise as palliatives of the situation but do not create enduring bases for insertion into the twenty-first century. Trying to alleviate the overspread poverty without creating stable job opportunities based on innovative production will result in more paternalistic behavior and continued dependence on the government's exploitation of natural resources. In addition, everlasting, successful changes will not take root if real necessities and feasible projects do not pull them, in a bottom-up fashion. Governments must take advantage of what the nation has already achieved over the years and improve upon what has been developed (regardless of who developed it), instead of trying to effect change by destroying what is there, convinced that a new conceptual proposal (which in truth tends to be an old one resuscitated) will become a saving formula. There is an old Spanish saying that fits Venezuela historical policy very well: "When a new Saint comes, the old one stops performing miracles." This has been made evident by changing governments that implement "new" policies without first having analyzed the real effects of former ones.

The universities can be crucial in creating the driving forces of effective change because they are respected and admired. The University Simón Bolívar, therefore, must find ways to help graduating students find means of sustenance and, preferably, sustenance that arises from applying the knowledge acquired during their stay in the university, as well as making a more concerted effort toward developing innovation at a national level.

An Entrepreneurship Program for the University Simón Bolívar

I believe that by taking advantage of the university's two major activities, higher education and research, an entrepreneurship program targeted to the realistic creation of university-founded enterprises that are also linked to research centers and industry can help change the mentality of university students from that of simple employees to innovative entrepreneurs and provide them also with high-value added ideas and opportunities for the generation of a technology-based economy in Venezuela. Many of these ideas and opportunities can arise from the university's research efforts and university-business links and thus drive the creation of innovative small and medium-sized businesses and business intrapreneurship projects that maintain research ties with the university, and, in turn, boost the university's innovative capabilities. The different projects resulting from the entrepreneurship program can assist in diversifying Venezuela's markets, increase its competitiveness, and trickle innovative thinking downwards into the work force. The needs of these projects will help push, in an organized manner, the long-awaited economic, political, and social changes.

Because the university's budget had been deficient for a number of years and very few funds were available for investment in new programs, the entrepreneurship program was designed in a bottom-up fashion that would focus on coordination of available resources to ensure their effective use. The primary aspects of the activities of the entrepreneurship program are summarized in Figure 3.1.

The starting point of the program would be developing academic courses directed toward undergraduate and graduate students. The undergraduate course would be an elective course that I called The Entrepreneur and the Development of Businesses, targeted to undergraduate students from scientific and engineering fields, and aimed at

Figure 3.1
Principal Activities of the Entrepreneurship Program

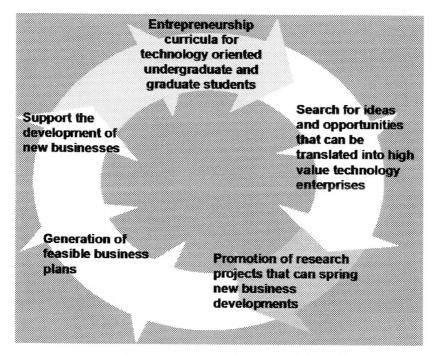

providing them with hands-on knowledge on how to establish a business in their fields of expertise. By using a feasible idea, the course was intended to instruct, in one academic trimester, about the different aspects involved in establishing a successful business. I believed that technology ideas for entrepreneurship projects for undergraduate students should ideally come from the faculty and that their involvement as technical advisers was critical. However, from previous experience I had become aware that involving the faculty in the program would be difficult, either because, in general, they did not understand the concepts presented to them, or were extremely jealous of their research and distrustful of external involvement. The reasons for this merit a whole chapter on university culture and, therefore, will not be addressed here. It is sufficient to say that in order to help change the culture, I would need to embark on a promotion scheme for which I did not have enough resources. I therefore decided to concentrate on the minority of professors who were willing to participate, hoping to create showcases that would pull in the rest.

The graduate course would be an elective course that I called The Entrepreneur: How to Become a Leader in Your Company, directed toward graduate students in the specialization of business management. Because most of the students pursuing this degree are working professionals from diverse companies, the course would focus on performing in-company projects that would improve the company's competitive ability and help the students become company leaders.

The search for ideas and opportunities for projects would promote ties with other universities, research centers, businesses, government institutions, and private institutions. Ties would also be generated with alumni associations and student associations with the objective of creating a network of stakeholders of the program. As projects would progress to the stages of implementation, more linkage ties would have to be developed with diverse institutions, generating a coordinated network of resources (Figure 3.2).

The objectives of the program would be the following.

- Strengthening of technological and managerial capabilities;
- Promotion of an entrepreneurship and innovation spirit and culture;
- Improvement of research and development capabilities as well as technology management in universities;
- Development of better products and processes in the productive sector;
- Generation of enterprises with a high technological content; and
- Promotion of financing mechanisms and policies better suited for entrepreneurship development.

Figure 3.2
Links with the Entrepreneurship Program

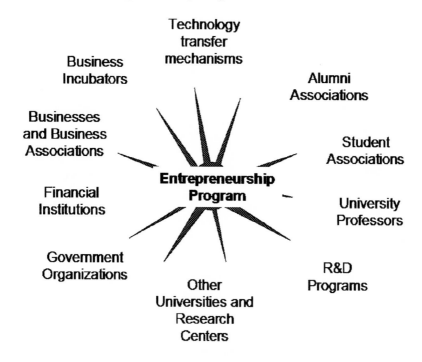

An Entrepreneurship Program for the University Simón Bolívar

The Undergraduate Course

To date, the course has been given 6 times, once each academic quarter (12 weeks), each course having on average 25 students. The students who took this course came from different fields in engineering (mechanical, electrical, material sciences, chemical, electronics, computer, and production) and from chemistry, architectural, and urban studies. Apart from the students in production engineering, the rest had very little knowledge of business. At the beginning of each course, I asked the students to answer a number of entrepreneurship-related questions. Data was obtained from a total of 152 students.

In general, students perceived technological entrepreneurship as being a difficult endeavor (see Figure 3.3). When asked to evaluate obstacles to entrepreneurship (Figure 3.4), students placed lack of financing as the most important factor, followed by excess red tape on registering a business and other business transactions. Although lack of

Figure 3.3
Perceived Level of Difficulty for Technological Entrepreneurship

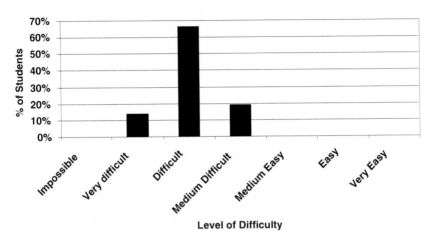

Figure 3.4
Level of Importance of Obstacles (7 Being the Highest and 1 the Lowest)

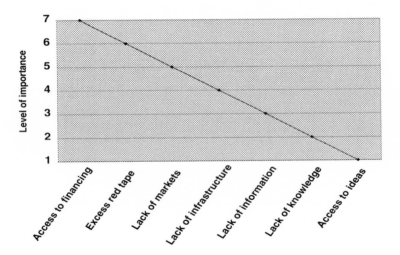

technological ideas was considered the a less-relevant obstacle, when faced with the task of having to generate an entrepreneurial idea, students invariably showed an inclination toward developing food franchises, becoming business consultants, or establishing any sort of business that would involve the commercialization of an imported good.

Access to financing is certainly a problem faced by small and medium-sized businesses in Latin America; however, many of these problems have their roots in the lack of confidence that financial institutions have on the projects proposed (Grupo DFC 2002).[8] Being able to develop solid business plans based on feasible ideas should improve the odds of obtaining financing.

Students really hoped to be able to obtain good jobs in solid companies and, if possible, abroad, and were, therefore, more inclined to do *pasantías* than research theses (Figure 3.5). In addition, they had little knowledge of the type of research being done at the university and obtained their technology information mostly from the required course reading (see Figure 3.6).

Figure 3.5
Student Preference of Work-Study in Industry or Research Theses

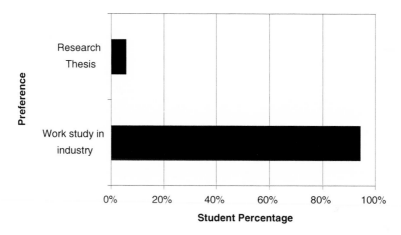

Figure 3.6
Technology Information: How Often Do You Read About Technology?

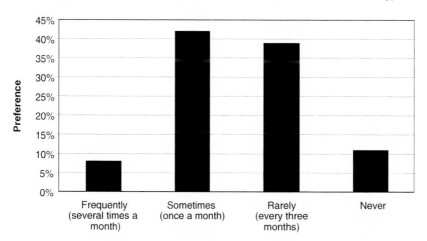

Students not only did not have much faith in the future of their country, but in addition, the training that they were receiving, while trying to absorb as much specific technical knowledge as was possible, did not steer them toward establishing effective uses for it. When I proposed that, as part of the course, we would search for ideas for establishing innovative businesses in their fields, I got back stares of bewilderment and skepticism. We began to discuss their particular fields of study, hoping to find ideas for projects that required a multidisciplinary group approach. While doing this, I would instruct them on the notions of creativity, motivation, innovation, and market orientation, keeping an eye, at the same time, on the country's political, social, and economical developments.

Once we hit what appeared to be feasible and interesting projects, I would then search through the university's faculty list to find amicable technical tutors for them. Needless to say, with the short time provided by one trimester and the time needed to find an idea, I had little time left but to concentrate on the aspects of the project that would relate to market studies and marketing plans.

As shown in Box 3.1, the projects undertaken throughout the courses have been varied. Some projects develop products or services that have resulted from the university's research efforts. Others deal with establishing new university services or bettering already existing ones. Some have been oriented toward the creation of production or service industries that can provide products or services that are already produced elsewhere, but have not reached the Venezuelan market.

The course has been able to get involved with ongoing university research projects such as the inter-university competition Formula SAE, where a specific formula car is designed and constructed. The competition requires the design of a business plan for its commercialization. The design and production of orthopedic equipment is also an ongoing university research project that has ties with the public orthopedic children's hospital. The project involving the design and production of oil drill heads is linked to a government-financed research institute, which has the capability of establishing a pilot production program that can be further expanded into a full production industry.

So far, the results obtained have been encouraging, although the political, economic, and social environment of the country has deteriorated, making the future even more uncertain than before and the process more difficult. For students, having the opportunity of working on innovative projects pertaining to their fields of study has provided them with a different perspective on possibilities. In addition, the knowledge acquired from each course has developed a pool of ideas from which to feed subsequent courses, as projects that were begun in one academic quarter can be

Box 3.1
Projects Undertaken

Technology-based projects:

- Production and commercialization of a new air filter (USB thesis)
- Polymeric Implants Biocorp: Production and commercialization of biodegradable bone implants (USB research)
- Production of dental prosthesis from innovative resins, porcelain, and metal alloys (USB research)
- Production of orthopedic prosthesis made from titanium alloys (USB research)
- Management of overnight deposits software
- Commercialization of molecular simulation software and services (USB research)
- Design and production of orthopedic equipment for cerebral palsy sufferers (USB research)
- Development of commercial uses of new alloys for engine coating (USB research)
- Development of a silver-coating industry for electronic components
- Production and commercialization of phosphate chemical compounds
- Commercialization of security systems
- Gelatin production from waste products
- Design and implementation of a health information system
- Production and commercialization of palm oil
- Design and commercialization of data interface transmission mechanisms
- Design and production of oil drill heads
- Business plan for the competition Formula SAE
- Production and commercialization of cashew nuts
- Production and commercialization of control systems for exercise machines (US Patent technology)
- Development of recycling businesses

Intra-university projects:

- Development of a Center of Students Affairs with online technology
- Improvement of management and business strategy of the student store
- Development of student residences
- Online services to promote cooperation courses for students in industry
- Student Center to provide Internet services and computer equipment
- Strategy to improve transportation to and from the university
- Development of university restaurants

picked up by other students in the next one, allowing the projects to be improved and therefore, increasing the chances of some of them actually being implemented in order to generate the desired showcases.

Because a course lasting one academic quarter does not give enough time to review the different aspects of developing an entrepreneurial idea, the initial course is being redesigned as two consecutive courses, each with the duration of an academic quarter. The first course will deal with aspects of creativity, motivation, and idea-forming, concentrating on later studies of the market and developing a marketing plan. In the second course, the initial project will be continued, focusing on production plans, financial aspects, and developing a more complete business plan. In addition, workshops and seminars are being designed that will address different and important aspects of the entrepreneurial processes such as negotiation, laws and bureaucracy, leadership, effective presentations, and more in-depth study of finance, technology management, and marketing.

Student interest and involvement is increasing, which has arisen from word-of-mouth publicity. Unfortunately, inserting the program formally into the university's system has turned out to be a difficult process because its implemented organizational structure has resulted in the absence of effective coordination mechanisms between the different academic departments and academic coordinations, and has generated the need for one-to-one promotion. In addition, the university has not been immune to the overall situation of the country, having received insufficient funds from the government, which has created a conflicted and paralyzed environment. In my view, students represent the most important resource available for development of the entrepreneurial program. They are an enthusiastic workforce that can help attract technical faculty, help insert the program into the university's system, obtain information, and promote interest in industry and government. Organization of this precious resource is one of the most relevant entrepreneurial projects that is being undertaken, as is the development of an information system that can help with the red tape, the search for financing, and the overcoming of other obstacles found in the path to becoming an entrepreneur.

The Graduate Course

As with the undergraduate course, the graduate course has also been given 6 times, each course having on average 9 students. Students participating in this course had a greater generalized knowledge of the different aspects of business. Because most of them already have jobs in varied companies, the objective of the course was oriented toward designing intrapreneurship projects that concentrate on innovation as a means of improving the competitive abilities of the companies they belong to. The type of companies represented include telecommunications, electrical distribution, oil, paint, ceramic, electrical equipment, banking, consulting firms, commercial stores, textile, and insurance, among others. Projects have involved evaluating the company's performance and designing strategic plans for improvement, as well as developing plans for incursion into new markets and designing new operating systems. It is hoped that the approach used in the course will in turn help pull these companies into becoming stakeholders and patrons of the entrepreneurship program. So far, the input that students have received from their companies has been highly favorable. Some students, however, use the course to further their personal ideas on establishing their own business. Of the personal projects, one of them is being further developed, getting it ready for the search for financing. The project involves the production and commercialization of California red worms for agricultural use.

What About the Future?

It is still too early to predict the outcome of the entrepreneurship program, and it is clear that many things remain to be done. By promoting the generation of innovative entrepreneurial ideas, we have but scratched the surface toward developing a competitive technology-based economy in Venezuela. It is now imperative that we begin to bring some of these projects to the market as showcases that will help insert the entrepreneurship program into the incipient national innovation system, creating links with varied organizations and programs, and, perhaps more importantly, helping pull this system toward a more realistic approach.

In order to achieve this, we must ensure the development of feasible business plans that will be channeled through the different government programs that are being created for this purpose, testing the real applicability of these programs and thus generating the necessary changes that will make these programs useful. In addition, we must stir the interest of potential private investors and promote industry involvement.

The present economic, political, and social situation is undoubtedly quite unstable, and the future uncertain, as government officials and opposition forces are in constant conflict. This makes our path a much more difficult one. However, when the program was designed, obstacles were expected and constant adjustments must be made. It would be naive to think that the entrepreneurship program could fix all of our present maladies and turn the country around in the short term and, therefore, patience is needed. However, success stories arising from the entrepreneurship program and, particularly, being able to present feasible enterprise plans can certainly help mitigate and begin to bring down the barriers that the present system and its subsequent culture have built against believing that Venezuela can overcome its shortcomings. Success stories can also help the country focus on tangible results rather than rhetorical theory. I am convinced that after so many years of trying to step out of underdevelopment, with supposedly everything in our favor but without succeeding, the desire for immediate and all-encompassing solutions compounded with a fear of failing has become engrained in the average Venezuelan mind, creating economic, political, and social paralysis. As Franklin D. Roosevelt once said, "The only thing we have to fear is fear itself," and as a country, we must overcome our fears.

References

Banco Central de Venezuela (BCV). 2001. *Informe Económico.*

Drucker, P. 1986. *Innovation and Entrepreneurship, Practices and Principles.* New York: Harper Collins Publishers.

Grupo DFC. 2002. *Acceso de las pequeñas y medianas empresas al financiamiento.* Informe de Trabajo. División de Micro, Pequeña y Mediana Empresa, Departamento de Desarrollo Sostenible, Banco Interamericano de Desarrollo.

Institute for Scientific Information (ISI). 1994. Observatoire des sciences et des techniques. *Science Citation Index of ISI Society,* December.

Kantis, H., M. Ishida, and M. Komori. 2002. *Entrepreneurship in Emerging Economies: The Creation and Development of New Firms in Latin American and East Asia.* Summary report. Inter-American Development Bank, Washington, DC.

Reynolds, P., M. Camp, W. Bygrave, E. Autio, and M. Hay. 2001. *Global Entrepreneurship Monitor.* Executive report. United Nations Association of the United States of America and the Business Council for the United Nations.

Notes

1. Banco Central de Venezuela (BCV). Informe Económico, 2001.

2. The Mariscal de Ayacucho Scholarship Program has no definite statistics on this.

3. The exposition of motives for the new law for the promotion and development of the small and medium-sized industry (still in discussion at the National Assembly), estimates that between 1989 and 1995 the sector suffered a 20% reduction. The economic situation has become much worse in the last 3 years.

4. As made evident by the Ministry of Science and Technology's efforts in trying to design and implement policies to increase the productivity and transfer capabilities of financed programs and institutions.

5. The Ministry of Production is at present establishing policies to promote the national industry based on the maxim *compre venezolano* (buy Venezuelan), which greatly resembles the failed import substitution policies implemented during the 1970s and 1980s.

6. A work-study program where students are expected to spend from 3 to 6 months working in companies doing a variety of projects.

7. Data to this effect was presented in the FUNINDES-USB Annual Report, where I was Director of Planning and Development. FUNINDES-USB (Foundation of Research and Development of the University Simón Bolívar) is the organization that coordinates university-industry relations.

8. Grupo DFC (2002) Acceso de las pequeñas y medianas empresas al financiamiento. Informe de Trabajo. División de Micro, Pequeña y Mediana Empresa, Departamento de Desarrollo Sostenible, Banco Interamericano de Desarrollo.

CHAPTER 4

Globalization, Entrepreneurship, and Entrepreneurial Support Systems in Latin America

Dennis M. Ray

The Multiple Faces of Globalization

Globalization has multiple identities. It represents a complex set of forces driving the global integration of industries and financial institutions, and the rapid diffusion of technologies, products, and cultural trends. This aspect of globalization is rooted in the economic competition among the major corporations in the rich countries.

In the early stages of industry globalization, intense competition creates many of the positive outcomes—lower prices, improved quality, greater choice—the advocates of globalization and liberalization applaud. But as national champions disappear, plants close, and unemployment in various industry-dependent communities grows, the earlier benefits of global competition diminish rapidly. The first global industry was petroleum, and by 1929 it had established mechanisms to fix prices, share markets, and avoid competition. A clear sign of industry oligopoly is when firms compete less with each other and more with suppliers, customers, and governmental regulatory agencies.

Globalization is also an ideological and political movement being promoted by strategic elites in the rich countries, led by the United States, and international institutions such as the IMF, World Bank, and World Trade Organization that largely represent the interests of these rich countries and their elites. The political and ideological doctrine of globalization with its emphasis on free trade, open markets, and economic liberalization has been a core component of U.S. foreign economic policy going back to the 1940s and 1950s.

It is important to distinguish between globalization as an inevitable force of industry consolidation and economic integration, and globalization as a political ideology of the strategic elites in the United States and elsewhere in the developed world. The former must be effectively addressed by elites in Latin America; the latter deserves the skepticism that has been articulated by the anti-globalization forces that operate on the fringe of the international system and articulate alternative visions.

The Economic Consequences of Globalization and Regional Dependency

The economic reality of globalization is represented not by the benign invisible hand of Adam Smith but by a clenched fist pointed upward celebrating the wealth and power of the rich against the poor and weak. The invisible fist should direct our attention to the fact that globalization redistributes income and wealth on a global scale. The United Nations Development Program's (UNDP) Human Development Report for 1997 offers a hint of this global redistribution process.

Globalization is proceeding apace, but largely for the benefit of the more dynamic and powerful countries of the North and the South. The loss to developing countries from unequal access to trade, labor, and finance is estimated at $500 billion a year, 10 times what they receive annually in foreign assistance (HDR 1997).

In Latin America, the forces of globalization are intertwined with a dependent regional economic system that has operated for the benefit of the United States for nearly all of the twentieth century.[1]

The dependent regional economic system has relied on three forms of international economic transactions–direct foreign investment, terms of trade, and foreign aid. Direct foreign investment (DFI) reinforces the power of rich countries and their leading corporations that control allocation decisions and, consequently, the distribution of wealth and income of an increasingly integrated global economy. This means control over a global value chain of natural resources from the ground in Latin America to final markets in the center, control over allocation of investment and job creation decisions, control over the economic bargain between labor and the corporation, and control over the allocation of revenue. Control is instrumental to allocation decisions and, ultimately, the distribution of wealth and income.

The loss of economic autonomy reinforces and exacerbates the distribution of wealth and power in the global system. An economic manifestation of this is that the repatriation of profits from foreign investment in poor countries has long exceeded the rate of new investment, and even the combined impact of new investment and local reinvestment. Still, DFI has great potential to stimulate economic development and is a reflection of a vibrant, growing economy.

Terms of-trade have favored industry over agriculture and technology over primary goods since the recognition of inter-sectoral relations in the U.S. economy in the 1930s. What *terms-of-trade* means is that it takes an increasing volume of primary goods to buy a tractor, a jet airliner, or outfit a modern hospital. The poor must run increasingly faster just to maintain their relative position. Industrial goods—at least those that remain distinctive—naturally inflate in price whereas commodities tend to deflate over time. Cumulative terms-of-trade losses by the developing countries amounted to $290 billion between 1980 and 1991 (HDR 1997).

There is a perverse new factor today and that is the $40 billion dollars in subsidies to U.S. farming corporations and an even higher level of subsidy by the European Union to its farms. Rather than promoting the values of economic liberalization and free trade, these subsidies reflect extreme protectionism.

The impact of adverse terms-of-trade is reinforced by the tendency of independent primary goods producers in Latin America to maximize their self-interest for themselves by maximizing production, which assures that market prices will drop for all. When primary goods are owned and/or controlled by foreign corporations, they develop Nth country sources of supply so as to minimize the power and leverage of any one source of supply. Corporations in rich economies have learned how to transform the commodities produced in poor countries—apparel (jeans), athletic shoes, music, and fast food—into symbolically differentiated products, thereby justifying high margins.

The regime of free trade creates another set of problems for Latin America. Developed countries impose the highest trade barriers on goods for which developing countries have the greatest competitive advantage: textiles, clothing, and footwear. The IMF estimates that these trade barriers have cost developing countries $50 billion per year (HDR 1994). Domestic agricultural subsidies and price supports by the industrial countries cost the developing and former centrally planned economies approximately $22 billion a year in foregone export revenues (HDR 1992; HDR 1994).

At the end of World War II, foreign aid was based on grants to reconstruct Europe and Japan. The United States invested in its own economic future by helping to reindustrialize its former enemies. Over the next decade, foreign aid progressively shifted from grants-in-aid to loans, and then in the 1960s from concessionary loans to commercial loans, and finally to commercial loans with risk premiums. The net effect has been that the repayment of past loans soon exceeded the flow of capital from new loans. Ideology had little to do with it; it was a reflection of the power of the lending countries.

With the emergence of the Cold War, aid lost nearly all pretense of being an instrument of economic development and became an instrument of national politics. During the last 50 years, the amount of aid from the rich has also declined steadily. The U.S. foreign aid budget has fallen from 0.24% of GDP in the mid-1980s to 0.1% in 2002, making the United States the least generous of 22 advanced economies (Chua 2004).

The three core mechanisms of the international economic system have progressively enriched the rich countries by decapitalizing the poor countries. This trend has been reinforced by flight capital—for example, rich individuals in Latin America who move their financial assets to the stock, bond, and property markets of rich countries—and by the flow of royalty income. The negative impact of global processes of decapitalization is magnified by national systems that take from the poor and give to the rich and privileged. The mechanisms for this national redistribution are often more exploitative, violent, and repressive in developing countries than in rich countries.

Center-Periphery Relations

The lens of center-periphery relations (Wallerstein 1979, 2004; Galtung 1971) is especially helpful to understanding the regional dependency system between the United States and Latin America in the twentieth century. If we think of the state system as a hierarchical system with an underlying institutional class structure, the world looks very different than for those who see it as a global market with increasingly uniform rules promoting free trade and investment.

The center is being pulled in opposite directions. The center is becoming narrower and more exclusive. At the same time, in some industry and technology niches, the center is being stretched and expanded to include places like Taiwan, Ireland, Brazil, Australia, or Finland. These complex forces of globalization are making the nation-state a less appropriate unit of analysis for describing much of the international system. Although nation-states remain the primary unit of economic analysis, globalization is driven by a few cities and economic regions—like Silicon Valley—that dominate an industry and drive its global integration. We must focus on cities and city-regions in order to understand what is happening with globalization and to formulate appropriate policies and strategies at the political and corporate level.

This is an opportunity for the most dynamic, entrepreneurial, and technology-based city-regions of Latin America. For the most part, the periphery operates outside the emerging global economy of high technology. But between the center and periphery, there is a large and diverse group of nation-states and city-regions, many in Latin America, that are linked to this global economy. They constitute, in a sense, the "middle class" of the international system. These globally linked city-regions constitute an important market for technology products. Companies from these city-regions, whether well-established or start-ups, have nearly the same potential to play in the global economy as their counterparts in the center *if* their founders and managers have the vision, competence, and strategic acuity to pursue an appropriate international strategy.

The Challenge

The challenge is to understand how the major city-regions of Latin America can become full participants in the evolving global economy. The challenge is also to develop policies that address the growing income gaps between globally linked cities and the surrounding countryside. This challenge may be more difficult because changing domestic distribution of wealth and income threatens a long-established social order.

Globalization is both a threat and an opportunity to the economies and peoples of Latin America. Optimists claim that the diverse competitive, economic, technological, and political forces that drive globalization will pull and push Latin American economies, industries, and firms into the global arena and bring prosperity. Critics of globalization should not be too quick to dismiss the possibility that a truly global system might, in fact, transform and transcend the regional economic dependency on the United States, especially as U.S. economic hegemony begins to weaken with the rise of a country like China. Pessimists would counter by arguing that Latin America already has a well-established role in the global economy as a supplier of primary goods, moderately low-cost goods, and evolving markets, and that further globalization will use Latin America for the benefit of corporations from the Northern Hemisphere, with a disproportionate distribution of costs and benefits. Cynics observe that the economic, political, and corporate institutions that drive globalization will ignore much of Latin America as not worth the effort, along the lines that Africa has become increasingly marginal-ized under globalization. To be used and exploited is bad; to become so marginalized as to barely exist on the radar screen of multinational cor-porations and international organizations is perhaps even worse. The choice of which scenario evolves does not entirely reside in the center. Therein lies the opportunity for Latin America.

Entrepreneurship

Much harm has been done to Latin America and the rest of the less-developed world since the collapse of the Berlin Wall in the name of free markets and economic liberalization. It has been a huge mistake to link entrepreneurship directly with the ideology of free markets and eco-nomic liberalization. The rationale for entrepreneurship is not laissez faire capitalism but self-reliance.

The contemporary world is largely dysfunctional in economic and political terms. For example, when a worker loses his or her job in the contemporary world, the social and economic safety net that once existed is today largely absent. Entrepreneurship taking the form of self-employment is the only viable strategy of personal economic survival in this situation. When a community loses a large foreign investor, there is no one outside that community who really cares. If a nation-state endures an economic or financial crisis, how will the rich countries of the world or the international governmental organizations (IGOs) respond? Argentina now understands the cold indifference of the advo-cates of economic liberalization and the international community. Self-reliance is the only solution that can be counted on. Community and national self-reliance demands that a country develop a strong, vibrant entrepreneurial community that can adapt to the challenges, threats, and opportunities of a chaotic global era. Self-reliance should not be equated with economic autarky; it must mean finding autonomy and economic self-determination in the context of full participation in the emerging global economy.

Entrepreneurship is the primary engine of job creation and wealth creation. Furthermore, the creation of new firms is not class-based. Although rich entrepreneurs may move to an upper class, anyone can become an entrepreneur. It is one of the few authentic and viable ave-nues of social mobility in any society. Cross-cultural sociological and his-torical research suggests that successful entrepreneurs come not from the rich but from either displaced elites or those who became marginalized by socio-economic or political change. Observation on the streets of just about any country in the world tells us that the most small business founders come from the underbelly of society. The wealth created by entrepreneurs is community-based, meaning that it originates locally, is embedded in community social networks, and is more likely to stay in the community than the wealth created by DFI. Entrepreneurship is the basis for building constructive international links based on reciprocal and interdependent commercial relationships, not hierarchical relationships based on exploitation and dependency.

None of these compelling advantages of entrepreneurship depends on laissez faire economics or a Washington version of economic liberalism. The old wealth of Latin America has been based on center-periphery relations. Those patterns are now reinforced by globalization and inhibit sustained economic development and prosperity to Latin America. New wealth is based on the willingness of individuals, communities, and nation-states to assume responsibility for their own well-being.

Entrepreneurial Support Systems

There is a methodology and science to be formulated for advancing community, national, and regional economic development through the encouragement and support of innovative entrepreneurship. Industrial relocation through DFI is a zero-sum process by which a new factory in country B means the closure of a factory in country A. For every country B, there are always countries C, D, and E willing to make greater concessions at some future date to attract DFI. In contrast, entrepreneurship is a positive-sum process.

Entrepreneurial support systems are the institutions, knowledge systems, and strategies that nurture and create entrepreneurs and new ventures. Entrepreneurial support systems are the foundation of applied economic development and, at their best, build powerful links between community-level initiatives and the global economy. Entrepreneurial support systems consist of business and technology incubators, private investor—sometimes called "angel investor"—networks, venture capital firms, university and national laboratory-based technology commercialization programs, an international technology licensing program, international business facilitation (especially entrance into the U.S. market), export promotion, guidance on global outsourcing, programs to attract expatriate and immigrant entrepreneurs with targeted skill sets and competencies, entrepreneurship and technology entrepreneurship education and training, entrepreneurial mentoring and skill development, and educational and skill development programs capable of filling the technology and knowledge-based jobs created by successful entrepreneurship.

To be effective, entrepreneurial support systems must adapt to distinctive local and national conditions. Their justification must rest on the value of job creation; wealth creation; creating and maintaining a civil society; and individual, community, and national self-reliance. An effective entrepreneurial support system is not about the exporting any one country's economic theories and ideology. Entrepreneurial support systems are about each community and each country finding its own voice and its own path in an increasingly interdependent world.

Entrepreneurial support systems should be viewed as scientific experiments in applied economic development. It is vital to distinguish between effective and ineffective approaches, and public policy must be capable of recognizing and building on best practices at home and abroad. This requires that a research base capable of developing the theory, metrics, data, and analysis so that the results of experiments and initiatives can be independently measured and evaluated. Much of what passes for measurement and evaluation today is designed to justify existing programs and existing budgets. When this happens, programs that begin with the intent of helping entrepreneurs become focused on helping themselves. The case for entrepreneurship and specific entrepreneurial support systems should be based on economic data, not ideology.

Equity Capital and Flight Capital

One of the major drivers of entrepreneurship in the United States, the UK, and Europe is the availability of early-stage equity capital in the form of angel investors and venture capital firms. Angel investors and venture capital not only bring critical financial resources to a new venture, but they bring entrepreneurial, managerial, industrial, and international experience. This capital and knowledge reduces the risk of new venture development. The reduction of risks is not a small matter because a culturally embedded attitude toward risk and failure is one of the major psychological barriers to entrepreneurship just about everywhere.

A benefit of the e-commerce revolution is that so much money poured into venture capital (VC) firms in the United States that they could not effectively invest all of it. Many VC firms sought to replicate their e-commerce investments in Europe, Asia, and Latin America. Firms that opened offices in Latin America considered a wider, more eclectic range of portfolio clients. Although fairly small and largely exploratory, these international initiatives are most positive and instructive of the latent potential of globalization. But much more needs to be done to create an adequate equity-capital base for Latin American entrepreneurship.

If we consider that there is a strong Latin population clustered in Miami, Los Angeles, and throughout the Southwest of the United

States—much of it affluent, some rich—these individuals are a potential source of early-stage equity capital for Latin American entrepreneurs. The development of the Internet, video conferencing, and low-cost air travel make it increasingly practical for high net worth individuals in the United States to consider investment in Latin America. The knowledge, industry savvy, and U.S. experience of individuals could be invaluable for Latin American entrepreneurs with a growth orientation and an opportunity with potential to succeed in South and/or North America.

Latin American flight capital is another source of capital that could be tapped for early-stage investment in Latin-based new ventures. The underlying rationale behind flight capital is the spreading of personal portfolios to minimize financial and political risk. The same goals can be achieved through angel investor networks that funnel some of that money back into Latin-based new ventures. Imagine a group of 20 high net worth Latin American businessmen in each major city of Latin America who each put $1 million into a fund and allocate another million to traditional portfolio investments in offshore stocks, bonds, and property. Half, or $10 million, would be invested in a portfolio of high-potential ventures. Each investor would share in responsibility for identifying and helping mentor high-quality entrepreneurs and their new ventures. They could create a rigorous and competitive process of screening and reviewing potential portfolio companies. The $10 million would coming from the United States and denominated in U.S. dollars and would be invested in new ventures still centered in the local market. The other half—$10 million—would be invested in helping these or other ventures enter the U.S. market. More or less aggressive versions of this model might be pursued, but the central point is that local money can and should be used to finance local ventures.

Attracting Entrepreneurs

A coherent public policy of entrepreneurial support would seek to attract expatriate entrepreneurs, immigrant entrepreneurs, and repatriated entrepreneurs. If none of these groups find the nation-state or city-region appealing, this is a clear signal that many things are fundamentally wrong.

Expatriate entrepreneurs are mostly small business founders but attracting them—whether to Costa Rica, Chile, or the Caribbean—is usually a positive sign for the potential of other kinds of entrepreneurship and the ability to find a niche in the global economy. Immigrant entrepreneurs, if they come at all, usually come in larger numbers than expatriate entrepreneurs. They bring with them an entrepreneurial spirit and skills that may be lacking domestically. Canada, Australia, and New Zealand have all sought to attract overseas Chinese entrepreneurs and have offered various political inducements–citizenship–for a certain level of investment. When the local entrepreneurial community is underdeveloped, an immigrant entrepreneur program can be a positive initiative.

Repatriated entrepreneurs are perhaps the most important. These are nationals who choose to come home to start a business after acquiring a university education and work experience abroad. Repatriated entrepreneurs have been a key to the economic development of Taiwan. In the mid-1980s, the Taiwanese government offered a variety of financial and other incentives to engineers and entrepreneurs from the United States to return home. Today the close economic ties between Taiwan and Silicon Valley are an important driver of globally linked high-tech entrepreneurship in both locales. The recent surge in the economy of the Republic of Ireland is now attracting Irish to return home, bringing with them capital and entrepreneurial and engineering skills. Vietnam and China are both seeking to induce overseas Vietnamese and Chinese to return home. Indian software entrepreneurs who have made their fortunes in the United States are increasingly going home to start new ventures or subsidiaries of their firms. The ability to induce foreign nationals to return home is probably a clear sign that a country has reached a critical milestone in its economic development.

Entrepreneurial Division of Labor

An effective entrepreneurial support strategy must nurture an appropriate entrepreneurial division of labor. The entrepreneurial division of labor reflects the relative contribution to employment, national income, and exports by multinational and large national enterprise, state-owned enterprise, and local small-medium and new enterprise. Most of what passed for national economic policy in the twentieth century offered a theoretical and ideological answer to the issue of an optimal entrepreneurial division of labor. Excessive reliance on multinational enterprise, state-owned enterprise, or local enterprise has liabilities and costs. Each type of enterprise has a capacity to make an economic, social, and technological contribution.

Center-Periphery Relations in an Age of Global Strategies

Between mid-1999 and early 2001, the author was founding director of a Global Business Accelerator (GBA) at the IC2 Institute of the University of Texas at Austin. During that time eight companies were recruited to GBA and another three were informally linked to GBA. Eight of the 11 companies were recruited from outside the United States. The experiment allowed the author to observe the challenges and opportunities presented to technology-oriented new ventures from the near periphery (two ventures from Mexico and one each from Slovakia, Finland, UAE, and New Zealand were included in the sample). In the analysis of the sample, an interesting pattern emerged.

For firms in globally linked city-regions, it was not enough to compete as exporters from their home base. They had to establish a direct presence in the center–the U.S. market–in order to realize the market potential of their innovation or product and have access to financial resources or a harvest event. Proximity to new technology was not a factor among this sample. When technology was acquired or sought, it was found in the periphery, India (software). What was especially interesting is that two of the three U.S.-based firms saw their market not at home in the center but offshore in the city-regions of Singapore and Malaysia. They did not have the resources or technology to compete in the center.

The implication is not that every technology venture must directly enter the U.S. market or that most U.S.-based technology ventures should seek out foreign markets in city-regions. To state our finding in the most generic terms, when there is often a discontinuity between the innovation/product and the home market, growth-oriented new ventures must think and act internationally in order to capture that full potential of their innovation. As it happened in this sample, the discontinuity for near-periphery ventures from various city-regions was in most cases tipped in favor of their opportunity having far more potential than their local market. For the center ventures, their opportunity did not measure up to the demands of the local market, and they needed to move offshore to the periphery to realize their potential.

A new model for technology-based firms from the periphery suggests that in order to realize the full potential of their innovation, these firms must become international at an early point. The key market for most is the United States because it offers potential access to private investors– for example, angel investors and venture capital–in addition to other benefits–the world's largest technological market, a wide range of corporate partners, customers, and access to "harvest events" (e.g., acquisition or an initial public offering). Israeli firms have been using this strategy for at least a decade, leveraging their ethnic contacts in the U.S. to seize opportunities and resources not available in a small, vulnerable home market in the periphery. Firms from Finland, Ireland, Australia, New Zealand, and Singapore have begun to consciously emulate this strategy with the support of local corporate sponsors, venture capital firms, incubators, and governments.

The basic premise of the strategy is that the research and development (R&D) and emotional heart of the firm can and should remain in the home country when a subsidiary or sister company is established in the United States. The U.S. arm of the firm then licenses technology and product rights from the parent in the home country and leverages this asset to raise venture capital and build an operating company. The relatively low cost of R&D in a periphery market creates a potentially powerful source of competitive advantage.

What does it take to succeed with this strategy? The prerequisites will be divided into three categories: firm-specific attributes, home country facilitators, and host (U.S.) country social capital requirements. Firm-specific attributes include:

- An innovative product, even if it is incomplete or not yet an internationally competitive product;
- A willingness to partner with other firms to develop an internationally competitive product;
- Experience living and working in the United States so as to minimize the time and cost of cultural learning;
- Sufficient resources to make frequent trips to the United States for at least 6–12 months until a U.S. affiliate is established, operating, and locally funded;
- The ability to prepare a business and marketing plan compelling to U.S. investors and communicate effectively with investors, suppliers, and customers; and
- A commitment to follow-up promptly and effectively on leads generated through international business trips to the United States and move quickly from strategic intent to operations.

Home country facilitators include:

- A local market sufficiently sophisticated to constitute a good beta test for the innovative product or service;
- A local market sufficiently attractive to financially support and sustain a full exploration of the U.S. market or, alternatively, sufficient local equity capital to finance entry into the U.S. market;
- A local market with a sufficient supply of scientists, engineers, designers, software engineers, and programmers with a practical and commercial orientation to sustain a steady, if small, flow of new products and technology-based new ventures;

- University or other business education that prepares local entrepreneurs and managers for the challenges and rigors of doing business in the United States, Europe, Japan, and/or China;
- Tax codes and regulations that facilitate the creation of sister enterprises or subsidiaries offshore;
- A telecommunication infrastructure to facilitate doing business via the Internet anywhere in the world, 24/7, at costs that are comparable to any OECD country; and
- A physical infrastructure that eliminates unwarranted hardship for either international travel or shipping.

Some might argue that home countries have a responsibility to create infrastructures and social capital offshore to help their national firms enter key markets. This is the implicit assumption around most commercial departments of national embassies and trade promotion departments. We take a contrary view on this point. Very few countries do this well and none do it better than a smart and hardworking corporate team. Empirical studies show that firms that rely on export promotion departments are more successful than those that do not demonstrate what statisticians call *autocorrelation*. By that we mean that firms that are meticulous and thorough enough to make full use of national export promotion programs will also be good at other forms of environmental scanning and social capital creation offshore. That does not prove that the former causes export or international business success. There are things, however, that national governments, local economic development agencies, incubators, and venture capitalists can do to facilitate the creation of social capital in center markets. They can cultivate relationships with incubators, investors, consultants, and industry specialists in the United States and other rich markets who can be called upon by local firms. They can maintain subscriptions to the databases of major market research firms so that local firms can do sound preliminary market research at little or no cost. Relationships and databases need to be very specific to a select number of industries because of limited resources. This is one of the virtues of industry and regional clustering.

Host countries also have a major obligation to help firms from the periphery successfully enter their markets. Perhaps only Japan with Japan External Trade Organization (JETRO) has taken this responsibility seriously. Although JETRO was intended to offset the bad publicity of Japan's aggressive export strategies and relatively closed domestic market, it is still a relatively good role model of what other rich countries should be doing. States and cities in the United States have active programs to attract foreign direct investment, but these are usually oriented toward large multinational corporations from Europe and Japan. There is relatively little interest in smaller or new ventures. In this context, the Economic Development Board (EDB) in Singapore provides a good example due to its openness to attract all types of foreign firms. Universities and incubators should also consider programs to facilitate entry into the U.S., European, and Japanese market. There ought to be more visibility in the technology and entrepreneurial community of the periphery about venture capital and angel investor networks in the United States.

Imagine a series of IGO (International Governmental Organization) and INGO (International Non-Governmental Organization) initiatives that could help not eight but a thousand emerging technology ventures from the periphery to successfully enter the U.S. market. Imagine, further, a thousand technology-based firms from the United States, the European Union, and Japan entering the markets of Latin America, bringing new technology, jobs, and a strong entrepreneurial orientation. The periphery firms could become viable players in the global economy, generating export revenue, remitting profits, upgrading their local technology and their competitive position, and serving as role models for other local firms. New ventures and small business firms from the center could bring technology and knowledge to the periphery's city-regions, addressing problems such as the digital divide, renewable energy, or productivity-enhancing innovations and software.

Conclusion

Given the reality of globalization, it is up to nation-states and city-regions to create developmental policies that capture as many of the benefits and minimize as many of the liabilities of globalization as possible. Make no mistake; this is a form of industrial policy. Although the United States has a hostile orientation to industrial policy, that is largely a combination of self-delusion and deceit. U.S. foreign economic policy, its defense budget, the U.S. tax code, and actions on behalf of large U.S. corporations with regard to expropriation in the 1960s and 1970s and intellectual property protection in the 1990s are all fundamental components of an industrial policy. If the United States can induce other countries to abstain from industrial policy, the resulting policy vacuum creates an environment where the United States can more readily exert its ideological will and impose its policy perspective on others. Articulating an industrial policy that has consistently combined both open markets and a strong commitment to state intervention and state-owned enterprises has not kept Singapore from maintaining close policy, economic, and corporate ties with the United States.

Putting emphasis on entrepreneurs and not large multinational corporations has many benefits. Governments typically seek foreign direct investment by large multinational corporations over multiple small investments because the investment is more visible, takes less political and administrative work, and promises to create a large number of jobs per investment. Most of this is based on the myth of "really big numbers." However, when governments make tax concessions, dilute labor protection, and waive environmental standards to attract foreign direct investment, the benefits of that investment are negated from the outset. This may either stem from distorted concepts of economic development or from the co-optation of local elites and decision makers. By *co-optation* we mean that the local elite makes decisions on behalf of foreign, not indigenous, interests and their position in society is tied to serving foreign interests.

Economic development is not about attracting foreign investment. It is about thousands and tens of thousands of entrepreneurs exploring opportunities and seeking to build companies, and private investors looking for and finding the best of these entrepreneurs and helping them with capital, knowledge, experience, and social networks. The genius of the entrepreneurial approach is that it is deeply embedded in local communities, and it has a potential to cut across class lines. When it develops an international orientation, it has the potential to incrementally redress the inequalities of wealth and income distribution in the global system. For entrepreneurship to redress the inequities of wealth and income in national systems, it must also find ways to share prosperity for it to fully realize it potential (Hall 2001).

Globalization will not and cannot accomplish this as an automatic and inevitable by-product of free markets. Left to its own devices, globalization will skew even more the distribution of wealth and income on a global basis and within countries, rich and poor alike. Given that the concentration of wealth and income in the United States has become even more skewed over the last generation, this should not surprise us. Latin America must find its own path between the old, failed policies of economic autarky and protectionism, on one hand, and the perverse consequences and failing policies of neo-liberalism and open markets, on the other hand.

References

Chua, A. 2004. *World on Fire: How Exporting Free Market Democracy Breeds Ethnic Hatred and Global Instability.* New York: Anchor Books.

Galtung, J. 1971. "A Structural Theory of Imperialism." *Journal of Peace Research,* 2.

Ger, G. 1999. "Localizing in the Global Village: Local Firms Competing in Global Markets." *California Management Review* 41, no. 4: 64–83.

Girvan, N. 1999. "Globalization and Counter-Globalization: The Caribbean in the Context of the South." Conference paper for International Seminar on Globalization: A Strategic Response from the South, University of the West Indies, Mona, February 1–2.

Hall, C. 2001. *The Responsible Entrepreneur: How to Make Money and Make a Difference.* Franklin Lakes, NJ: Career Press.

Human Development Reports (HDR), http://hdr.undp.org/reports/default.cfm.

Wallerstein, I. 1979. *The Capitalist World Economy.* Cambridge: Cambridge University Press.

Wallerstein, I. 2004. *World-Systems Analysis: An Introduction.* Durham, NC: Duke University Press.

Note

1. In Venezuela at the end of 2002, the clash was not between the proponents and critics of globalization but between those who had traditionally benefited from a particular pattern of globalization in the petroleum industry and those who wanted to use the local oil revenues for a different social agenda defined by an electoral process. See Chua (2004).

CHAPTER 5

The Effect of Entrepreneurship Education in the Universities of Cali

Dr. Rodrigo Varela

Jorge Enrique Jiménez Prieto

Entrepreneurship education started officially in Cali, Colombia, in 1976 when it was included in the industrial engineering program of the Universidad del Valle, first as a required course called Starting a New Business and later as a graduation project option. However it began to have a real impact when the main entrepreneurs of the region founded Universidad Icesi in 1979, because in their vision the idea was to educate new entrepreneurial leaders of the region to promote socio-economic development.

In order to do that, a specific academic unit was established January 1, 1985: the Center for Entrepreneurship Development (CDEE), with the mission of forging a new "entrepreneurial culture" with the permanent participation of the academic and entrepreneurial community, and the promotion of innovation and social responsibility.

The fundamental purpose of the CDEE is to motivate and to shape, through educational activities, the members of the community under its area of influence in the development of innovative and creative actions that will allow them to become, throughout their lives, creators of new and competitive organizations; leaders of the existing ones; and creators of wealth, productive employment, social well-being; and personal, professional and social satisfaction.

Under the heading of entrepreneurial education, the CDEE is committed to provide a learning, motivational, developmental, and supportive environment, which will significantly improve the disposition of the members of the community to act in creating new, competitive organizations and to preserve and grow existing ones, whether they are private or public, profit or nonprofit, and from any sectors of the economy.

The areas of creation, appropriation, and diffusion of knowledge in which the CDEE works are developing of the entrepreneurial spirit and culture; creating new enterprises; shaping of entrepreneurial leaders; furthering of entrepreneurial education; managing of family business; and managing of small and medium enterprises (SME).

The CDEE firmly believes that socio-economic development is basically a human process in which people find the appropriate ways to use production resources—natural, human, financial, technological, and informative. These creative and innovative human beings, capable of overcoming the limitations that the environment presents them with, skilled to take advantage of opportunities independent of the resources they may have, eager to transform their ideas into actions, capable of nurturing the economy, the business activity and the quality of life, are the business leaders that the CDEE seeks to shape. The culture and the vital energy that guides them and drives them is called *entrepreneurial spirit.*

The design of the center was a combination of the previous experiences that some academic members had had in the Industrial Development Program for Intermediate Cities and some international study trips to university centers that in the early 1980s were starting entrepreneurship programs.

In 1985 a curricular decision was made to allow every Icesi student to have academic training to become an entrepreneur. Through the years many educational, research, and extension programs had been carried out not only to develop the specific educational model that Icesi has been using, but also to produce academic materials in Spanish, based on the Latin American reality, to support the teaching activities. The Latin American Congress on Entrepreneurship (ten of which have been held in Colombia, two in Mexico, one in Chile, one in Costa Rica, one in Puerto Rico, and the next one in Panama) was the main procedure to expand the idea of entrepreneurship education to the broader Latin American academic community. *Innovando*, the information bulletin of the center that is published every semester, is also used for the expansion of the knowledge of the activities of the center.

At this time the CDEE has a total of 10 full-time faculty members and technical assistants to cover all the programs in entrepreneurship development and SME support. Many national and international projects have been done.

Through the years the center had been very interested in knowing its effect, and for that reason, in 1998, the CDEE approached Corona Foundation to finance a project that would allow a careful evaluation of the entrepreneurial activities of Icesi alumni. However, Corona Foundation asked that the evaluation cover the business administration, industrial engineering, and systems engineering programs in three universities in Cali (Universidad Icesi, Universidad Javeriana, and Universidad del Valle). Thus the alumni of six undergraduate programs [one business administration (day program), two business administration (evening program), two industrial engineering, and one systems engineering] who graduated in the 1984–1993 period were studied.

Research Goals

This empirical research was oriented to measure different aspects related to the effect that entrepreneurial education has had in the professional careers of the alumni of three different universities (two private and one public) and in six different undergraduate programs. The specific objectives were to:

- Measure the proportion of entrepreneur or intrapreneur alumni from each program;
- Characterize the business activities of the entrepreneurs;
- Evaluate personal characteristics of the group and check if they were able to differentiate between entrepreneurs and non-entrepreneurs;
- Identify the educational experiences that in their opinions were significant in their becoming entrepreneurs and establishing their own businesses;
- Receive feedback from alumni that would allow the university and the programs to improve their entrepreneurial education activities and provide better support, not only to current students but also to alumni; and
- Document the career path of some of our alumni and to write cases that could be used in academic courses.

Methodology

Basic Questions

Five basic questions were formulated to fulfill the research objectives:

1. What is the proportion of alumni who have started their own businesses? Under what conditions? What are their characteristics?
2. What other activities have they undertaken that could be considered entrepreneurial?
3. What are the entrepreneurial characteristics that differentiate entrepreneurs from non-entrepreneurs? What benefits do they consider were derived from their entrepreneurship-related courses and activities?
4. Which aspect of the university educational experience was basic for their entrepreneurial process? In what ways should the CDEE or related units keep working to help students and alumni become entrepreneurs?
5. What was lacking at the university level for the non-entrepreneur alumni? What should their university do in order to help them become entrepreneurs?

Sample Design

The population for the study was defined as all the alumni who had obtained their degrees in the period from January 1984 to December 1993. Once the population was defined, the first stage was to find out where each one of those alumni was, because it was necessary to contact them personally for the purposes of the research. This was one of the main difficulties of the research, because all the universities did not have updated databases for their alumni.

Through different mechanisms (professional directories, direct reference among alumni, old employers, parents' information, chain information development, etc.) new directories were developed covering statistically significant populations from each graduating class in every program.

A random stratified sample method was used to develop the sample for the first stage of the research. Table 5.1 shows the total population, the size of the sample, and the estimated error.

During the second stage of the research, an open invitation was given to all the participants interviewed in the first stage, but not all of them were willing to spend the time that the more detailed questionnaires required. Table 5.2 shows the sample for the second stage. The difficulty encountered in this stage was getting the students from the three universities to cooperate. This greatly affected the conclusion of the second stage.

Table 5.1
Sample for First Research Stage

Program	Total Alumni	Sample Size	Error (%)
Business administration–Universidad Icesi–Day program	429	185	5
Business administration–Universidad Icesi–Evening program	489	178	5
Systems engineering–Universidad Icesi	234	137	2
Industrial engineering–Universidad del Valle	316	140	5
Business administration–Universidad del Valle–Evening program	388	108	8
Industrial engineering–Universidad Javeriana	652	122	7
TOTAL	**2508**	**870**	

Table 5.2
Sample for Second Stage

Program	Total Alumni	Sample Size	Error (%)
Business administration–Universidad Icesi–Day program	429	84	20
Business administration–Universidad Icesi–Evening program	489	78	16
Systems engineering–Universidad Icesi	234	13	6
Industrial engineering–Universidad del Valle	316	50	16
Business Aadministration–Universidad del Valle–Evening program	388	48	12
Industrial engineering–Universidad Javeriana	652	49	6
TOTAL	**2508**	**322**	**13**

The third stage required in-depth interviews to cover all aspects of the development of the individual. Two limitations were encountered: one in terms of resources to cover the cost of the interviewers, and the other alumni willingness to spend 4 or 5 hours of their time. These facts forced the research team to concentrate their efforts on 49 alumni distributed as indicated in Table 5.3. This research stage does not support statistical based inference.

Table 5.3
Sample for Third Stage

University	Number of Alumni	Composition (%)
Universidad Icesi	39	80
Universidad Javeriana	6	12
Universidad del Valle	4	8
TOTAL	49	100

Information Gathering Techniques

For the first stage, which was oriented to questions 1 and 2 in the previous Basic Questions section, an independent telemarketing organization was hired to conduct a telephone survey of the 870 alumni from the three universities.

For the second stage, which was oriented to questions 3, 4, and 5, a research team was designed for each university, in which an alumnus was in charge of conducting the interviews and giving the three questionnaires used. This procedure was followed to avoid bias in the interview, to allow a greater level of reliability among the participants, and to avoid claims of intentional modification of results.

For the third stage, two psychologists were in charge of the process.

Processing Information

All the collected information was placed in magnetic media and processed with the help of SPSS when statistical information was required, or by Microsoft Word when transcription was required.

Results

First Stage

As shown in Table 5.4, there is significant difference among programs in terms of the percentage of alumni who at the time of the interview had their own business in operation and worked full-time in their business. The business administration (evening program) of Universidad Icesi presented the highest percentage with 23%, and the industrial engineering program of Universidad Javeriana presented the lowest one with 7%.

In Table 5.5 it is possible to see that there are also significant differences among the programs in the percentage of alumni who simultaneously had the roles of employee in an organization, and entrepreneur or investor in a business. The alumni of industrial engineering at Universidad Javeriana presented a very clear orientation to this two-track alternative.

Table 5.4
Currently Entrepreneurs

Program	Entrepreneurs (%)
Business administration–Universidad Icesi– Evening program	23
Industrial engineering–Universidad del Valle	19
Business administration–Universidad del Valle– Evening program	18
Business administration–Universidad Icesi– Day program	14
Systems engineering–Universidad Icesi	9
Industrial engineering–Universidad Javeriana	7

Table 5.5
Employee-Entrepreneur

Program	Employee-Entrepreneur (%)
Industrial engineering–Universidad Javeriana	19
Business administration–Universidad del Valle– Evening program	9
Business administration–Universidad Icesi–Evening program	7
Business administration–Universidad Icesi–Day program	6
Systems engineering–Universidad Icesi	3
Industrial engineering–Universidad del Valle	3

The unemployment situation of alumni is presented in Table 5.6. The business administration programs present the highest level of unemployment, whereas the engineering programs present very low unemployment. It is possible that the impact of a difficult labor market has obliged many students to create their own new companies.

It is very interesting to observe in Table 5.7 that a very high proportion of the alumni who were not entrepreneurs at the time of the research have had significant entrepreneurial experience in previous years. For the business administration alumni of Universidad Icesi that percentage is above 40%.

Table 5.6
Unemployment

Program	Unemployment (%)
Business administration–Universidad del Valle– Evening program	19
Business administration–Universidad Icesi–Day program	10
Business administration–Universidad Icesi– Evening program	10
Industrial engineering–Universidad del Valle	4
Systems engineering–Universidad Icesi	2
Industrial engineering– Universidad Javeriana	1

Table 5.7
Entrepreneurial Experiences by Non-Entrepreneurs

Program	Entrepreneurial Experiences (%)
Business administration–Universidad Icesi– Evening program	46
Business administration–Universidad Icesi–Day program	41
Systems engineering–Universidad Icesi	31
Industrial engineering–Universidad del Valle	29
Business administration–Universidad del Valle– Evening program	28
Industrial engineering–Universidad Javeriana	19

Given all the effort that the Colombian government and the trade agreements had placed in promoting export business, a research question was oriented to that area. As shown in Table 5.8 most of the entrepreneurs are oriented to local markets, some to national markets, and just a few to the international markets. Obviously more effort and more orientation to international business, markets, and trade are required to improve these results.

Table 5.9 shows the orientation of the businesses created by the alumni in terms of economic sector, and as expected the business administration students had a higher tendency toward service and commerce business. The industrial engineering alumni are more balanced in all sectors, but the Universidad Javeriana alumni are more involved in manufacturing. The systems engineering alumni are more service-oriented.

Table 5.8
Market Orientation

Program	Local (%)	National (%)	International (%)
Business administration–Universidad Icesi–Evening program	62	32	5
Business administration–Universidad Icesi–Day program	67	25	8
Systems engineering–Universidad Icesi	81	13	6
Industrial engineering–Universidad del Valle	70	23	7
Business administration–Universidad del Valle–Evening program	71	18	11
Industrial engineering–Universidad Javeriana	69	27	4

Table 5.9
Economic Sector

Program	Manufacturing (%)	Service (%)	Commerce (%)
Business administration–Universidad Icesi–Day program	17	34	49
Business administration–Universidad Icesi–Evening program	26	41	33
Systems engineering–Universidad Icesi	13	48	39
Industrial engineering–Universidad del Valle	26	36	38
Business administration–Universidad del Valle–Evening program	25	43	32
Industrial engineering–Universidad Javeriana	39	27	35

Table 5.10 shows how the alumni are establishing partnerships with their family members. The higher percentages are in the alumni of private universities, and the highest one is industrial engineering at Universidad Javeriana, in which 65% of the businesses had family partners.

Table 5.11 shows the distribution in terms of the level of ownership that the alumni entrepreneurs have in their businesses. It's interesting to observe that more than 50% of the entrepreneurs had majority in terms of ownership. It is interesting to note that the alumni of the public universities showed a higher concentration in ownership, with about 70% holding more than 50% of the ownership.

Second Stage

In the second stage, the sample was characterized according to the results of the first stage. Table 5.12 shows the composition of the sample and presents he main results derived from the second research stage.

Table 5.13 presents the main factors that were important in allowing the entrepreneurs of each university to start their businesses. Support of family and friends was accepted as a very important variable, especially for Icesi and Javeriana entrepreneurs, but project feasibility due to customer existence and resource availability, management formation at the university, and entrepreneurship orientation at the university also received high values.

Table 5.10
Family Partners

Program	Businesses with Family Partners (%)
Industrial engineering–Universidad Javeriana	65
Business administration–Universidad Icesi– Evening program	50
Business administration–Universidad Icesi– Day program	48
Systems engineering–Universidad Icesi	48
Industrial engineering–Universidad del Valle	41
Business administration–Universidad del Valle– Evening program	36

Table 5.11
Ownership Percentage by Alumni

Ownership Percentage by Alumni		Business Administration (Day) Icesi (%)	Business Administration (Evening) Icesi (%)	Systems Engineering Icesi (%)	Industrial Engineering Javeriana (%)	Industrial Engineering Valle (%)	Business Administration (Evening) Valle (%)
Less than 10%		6	5	13	4	7	0
Between 10%	and 29%	22	20	26	35	13	18
Between 30%	and 49%	16	23	6	14	10	14
Between 50%	and 99%	23	21	29	33	31	29
100%		31	30	26	14	39	39

Table 5.12
Sample Composition for Second Stage

Program	Entrepreneurs (%)	Intrapreneurs (%)	Employees (%)
Business administration– Universidad Icesi– Day program	57	7	36
Business administration– Universidad Icesi– Evening program	63	10	27
Systems engineering– Universidad Icesi	0	0	100
Industrial engineering– Universidad del Valle	52	4	44
Business administration– Universidad del Valle– Evening program	40	8	52
Industrial engineering– Universidad Javeriana	35	2	63

Table 5.13
Main Factors in Becoming Entrepreneurs

Main Factors in Becoming Entrepreneurs	Icesi (%)	Javeriana (%)	Valle (%)
Family and friends' support	68	67	41
Project feasibility due to customer and resource availability	65	73	61
Management formation at the university	63	33	37
Formation at the university	48	53	35
Entrepreneurship orientation at the university	42	47	26
Previous experience as employee and as entrepreneur	42	47	37

Table 5.14 presents the elements that the alumni recognized as support activities to their entrepreneurship roles. Again the entrepreneurship course at Icesi and in the industrial engineering program at the Universidad del Valle are given the highest recognition. It is important to observe that the marketing and management course had also a significant level of recognition.

Table 5.14
Academic Activities Supporting Entrepreneurship Role

Academic Activities	Icesi (%)	Javeriana (%)	Valle (%)	
			Business Administration	Industrial Engineering
Finance and accounting courses	33	13	20	31
Marketing courses	38	33	25	23
Entrepreneurship trade shows and fair	14	13	10	4
Production courses	15	13	10	8
Entrepreneurship courses	43	–	–	39
Management courses	38	27	50	27
Systems courses	6	–	–	–
Activities of the Center for Entrepreneurship Development	17	–	–	–
Seminars about entrepreneurship	17	–	–	–
Creativity workshop	18	–	–	–
Latin American Congress on Entrepreneurship	16	–	–	–
Others academic activities	8	47	36	19

In Table 5.15 the basic factors for the growth of the business are analyzed, and even though there are many variables here, it is interesting to note the effect of management capacity, dedication, relationship with clients and products, managerial formation, and opportunity identification. The ranking of entrepreneurship orientation and business plan development varies greatly among universities.

In terms of other academic activities that may have affected the growth rates, Table 5.16 indicates a wide range of results. Only Icesi entrepreneurs give the entrepreneurship course and the Latin America Congress on Entrepreneurship special consideration. In the industrial engineering program at Universidad Del Valle, the starting a new business course gets special recognition from the students.

Table 5.15
Basic Factors for the Growth of Business

Basic Factors	Icesi (%)	Javeriana (%)	Valle (%)
Entrepreneurship orientation	57	20	33
Managerial capacity	74	73	54
Dedication	78	60	74
Relationship clients/product	72	80	72
Creativity and innovation of product/services	57	47	44
Opportunity identification	68	73	44
Expert counseling	19	13	11
Updated business plan	28	13	16
Strategic planning	46	47	26
Managerial formation	70	60	39
Managerial education	36	33	17
Graduate studies	20	27	17
Other	8	13	9

Table 5.16
Academic Activities Useful in the Growth of the Business

Academic Activities	Icesi (%)	Javeriana (%)	Valle (%)	
			Business Administration	Industrial Engineering
Finance and accounting courses	60	40	40	62
Marketing courses	54	27	45	35
Entrepreneurship trade shows and fairs	11	13	10	4
Production courses	19	20	20	23
Entrepreneurship course	37	–	–	–
Management courses	53	47	60	39
Systems courses	12	–	–	–
Latin American Congress on Entrepreneurship	15	–	–	–
Other courses	7	33	40	4
Other factors	–	27	30	–
Starting a New Business course	–	–	–	50

Table 5.17 and Table 5.18 present the main recommendations that the alumni made to their universities in order to improve the percentage of entrepreneurs among the future alumni. Practical workshops; hands-on experiences; adviser, consultant, and mentor support; and more contact between students and entrepreneurs are the main recommendations.

Table 5.17
Entrepreneur's Recommendations

Entrepreneur's Recommendation	Icesi (%)	Javeriana (%)	Valle (%)
Real support	22	47	18
Practical workshop	67	41	80
Student-entrepreneur contact	39	12	64
Hands-on experiences	41	18	56
Advisers, consultants, mentors	35	18	42
Identification of new opportunities	11	18	29
Creativity seminars	7	24	13
Seminars	5	6	4
Entrepreneurship extension	5	18	2
Follow-up to new enterprises and entrepreneurs	20	0	40
No answer	5	18	–

Table 5.18
Non-entrepreneur's Recommendations

Non-entrepreneur Recommendations	Icesi (%)	Javeriana (%)	Valle (%)
Real support	8	36	9
Practical workshop	39	13	72
Student-entrepreneur contact	33	19	68
Hands-on experiences	23	13	70
Advisers, consultant, mentors	17	13	38
Identification of new opportunities	27	7	26
Creativity seminars	6	29	21
Seminars	8	3	23
Entrepreneurship extension.	11	26	4
Follow-up to new enterprises and entrepreneurs	22	23	–
No answer	13	6	–

One important point of the research was to learn the main reasons why alumni have had to close their businesses. As shown in Table 5.19, in many cases alumni ended their entrepreneurial careers for reasons not associated with business failure. Few cases were bankrupt or bad businesses, as such. It is interesting to observe that 60% of the Javeriana alumni ended their entrepreneurial pursuits for a change of activity.

Table 5.20 shows in more detail the reasons for closing a business. It is important to observe that the economic environment and the change in governmental policies (which in many cases are too drastic to overcome)

Table 5.19
Reason for Ending Role as Entrepreneur

Reasons	Icesi (%)	Javeriana (%)	Valle (%)
Business sale	11	20	31
Change of activity	25	60	31
Bad business	25	0	0
Bankruptcy	11	20	0
Other causes	43	0	44
No answers	18	0	6

Table 5.20
Reasons to Close a Business

Reasons to Close a Business	Icesi (%)	Javeriana (%)	Valle (%)
Bad opportunity identification	14	20	13
Erroneous business plan	25	20	31
Managerial mistake	18	40	44
Lack of expert advise	7	0	6
Change in governmental policy	18	20	6
Charge in the economic environment	46	40	38
Smuggling	21	20	13
Open market economy	18	40	6
Drug-related business	21	0	0
Lack of dedication	25	20	50
Lack of entrepreneurial orientation	18	40	6
Lack of management formation	4	0	6
Others	11	40	33

are two of the leading factors. When the Colombian economy opened to the international market in the early 1990s, foreign competitors entered the Colombian market and wiped out many Colombian businesses that were not ready for the change. However, Table 5.20 shows that many other factors were involved in the closing of businesses. Some of them are very much related to the development of a better entrepreneur.

The research also studied the time at which the entrepreneurs started their first businesses, and it found significant differences in this matter. For example 31% of Icesi entrepreneurs, 7% of Javeriana entrepreneurs, and 4% of Universidad Valle's entrepreneurs started their businesses before graduation.

In terms of gender the research indicated that 44% of Icesi entrepreneurs were women, in contrast to 24% at Javeriana and 28% at Valle. It is possible that the population of women in the total alumni may explain these differences.

A very important statistic is the survival rate for the businesses, especially considering the difficult political, economic, and social environment that Colombia in general, and the Valle del Cauca state in particular, has suffered. At Icesi, the business survival rate was 71%, at Javeriana 71%, and at Valle 65%.

One of the research interests was to find the main support activities required by non-entrepreneurs to becomeentrepreneurs. In Table 5.21 they are present, and a project bank from which they could pick new ventures is the most important one for all the groups. At Icesi, alumni support in business plan development is also a very important support activity.

As indicated by Table 5.22, the originality (O), efficiency (E), conformity of rules (R), and total (T) results of the Kirton Adaptation Innovation Test (KAI) were applied to the entrepreneurs and the employees of each one of the universities. The originality component did not provide any significant difference, and in the case of Valle alumni none of the dimensions measured differences.

Table 5.21
Main Support Activities

Main Support Activities	Icesi (%)	Javeriana (%)	Valle (%)
Managerial consultants	30	36	28
Support in business plan development	52	32	32
Technical consultants	30	19	36
Project bank	55	42	47

Table 5.22
Correlation Analysis

Variable	O	E	R	T
Valle (Entrepreneurs)	38.7	22.4	34.6	95.7
Valle (Employees)	38.7	22.1	34.2	94.9
Javeriana (Entrepreneurs)	38.7	22.1	36.5	97.4
Javeriana (Employees)	38.5	21.4	33.1	93
Icesi (Entrepreneurs)	38.9	22.4	35.3	96.6
Icesi (Employees)	38	21.7	32.1	91.7

The Personal Entrepreneurial Characteristic test did not allow the identification of significant differences among programs, universities, or groups (entrepreneurs, intrapreneurs, and employees).

Third Stage

In the third stage (which, as mentioned before, had some difficulties in keeping representative samples for program and university) in-depth interviews were done with 49 entrepreneurs in an attempt to identify and carefully document their entrepreneurial career paths. Data about family, educational experiences, hobbies, jobs, values, convictions, support facilities, motivations, business ideas, sources, business development, managerial policies, and so forth were collected. At this time that database has not been deeply analyzed, and hopefully next year a research project will be done about the database.

Conclusions

1. This study developed a methodology to evaluate many variables related to the entrepreneurial and non-entrepreneurial activities of alumni of different universities and programs. It is the first time that a study like this one has been carried out in Latin America, and it provides some benchmarking figures for all the programs in entrepreneurship development at the university level.

2. The finding that in many cases more than one-third of the alumni had been able to become entrepreneurs brings some additional support to the efforts being made at the universities in terms of developing entrepreneurship.

3. More courses, more seminars, and more support systems are the actions that the university should take to increase the conversion rate of university students into entrepreneur alumni.

4. It is clear that there has been a change in the career path of university degree holders and that many of them are considering entrepreneurship as a correct and fruitful alternative for their professional, personal, and social development.

5. Even though the business survival rate is quite high for the difficult economical, political and social environment, the universities will have to improve their training in areas such as business planning, opportunity identification, SME management, and entrepreneurial orientation.

6. Support from family and friends was a very important factor in the decision to become an entrepreneur, which indicates the need for more intensive actions in family-managed business and in-network development.

7. In the programs where entrepreneurship courses had been established as required courses, the alumni considered them more important than other business-related courses. However, finance, accounting, marketing, and management courses also had significant importance.

8. For the growth of a business, management capacity, dedication, close relationships with clients/products, and managerial capacity are more important than the other factors.

9. For the growth of a business, the finance, accounting, marketing, and management courses are generally the most significant academic activities.

10. The psychological tests were not discriminatory tools. More research will have to be done in order to identify a better test for future research.

11. It is necessary that every university keep the alumni database updated and that extensive research studies, such as this one, be conducted.

12. It is necessary to repeat this research in 5 years to figure out if the situation is changing, and in what sense. It will be also very useful if research projects like this one could be done in different universities to have a significant basis for comparison.

13. Many other variables should be included in research like this: distribution of number of years after graduation before starting a business, duration and growth rate of every business, financing of the start-up and growth stages, and relationship between the business and the formation process.

Acknowledgments

The financial support of Fundación Corona and Universidad Icesi and the cooperation of academic personal of Universidad Icesi, Universidad Javeriana, and Universidad del Valle were fundamental in the development of this research. The excellent work of Erika Xibille, Elsa Maria Infante, Alejandro Rincón, Andrea Romero, Diana Micolta, Monica Franco, Carlos Fajardo, María Isabel Velasco de Lloreda, and Olga Lucia Bedoya, who helped in different stages of the research, made this research feasible. Also the willingness to cooperate of the alumni of the three universities is duly acknowledged by the authors.

Reference

Jiménez, J. E., and R. Varela. 2001. "El espíritu empresarial en tres universidades de Cali." Informe final de investigación, Universidad de Icesi, Cali, Colombia, April.

CHAPTER 6

Incubating Innovative Start-ups: Some Lessons for Chile[*]

Germán Echecopar

The last decade has witnessed a worldwide increase of interest in entre-preneurship. In Latin America this trend has brought new training pro-grams, especially at universities, focused on developing entrepreneurial spirit and capabilities. Latin American governments are also redesigning their legal frameworks and publicly funded programs to promote the development of a local venture capital industry and proper incubation environments. These changes will take some time to produce the desired results, and probably more learning is needed before the appropriate framework for each country or region is set up.

This chapter makes a contribution to this process by showing what has been learned among a group of leading innovative Chilean firms about how to promote successful start-ups. Its main purpose is to help entrepreneurs and incubator managers make better decisions and increase the success rate of innovative start-ups. Although any start-up may find some of the following ideas useful, this work is focused on start-ups with some technological emphasis. The data used were

[*] Their support is appreciated. Any remaining errors are the responsibility of the author.

obtained through semi-structured interviews with 15 leading firms from the electronics, biotechnology, and wine sectors.

As a secondary objective, the chapter also discusses how these findings can be used by business incubators to improve start-up survival. Particularly, it raises the question of why incubators are usually financed by local or national governments, and what can be done to improve the survival odds of private for-profit incubators. These findings should also be useful for policy making to promote a better environment for innovative entrepreneurship.

The next section will briefly review the critical variables for start-up success according to the business incubation literature, and will contrast these variables with the results of interviews with 15 leading entrepreneurs in Chile. The final section presents the conclusions of the study.

Business Incubators

The renewed interest in innovation and entrepreneurship has prompted greater attention to business incubation. In 1996 the Science Park and Innovation Center Association (SPICA) counted about 1000 business incubators and 280 science and technology parks worldwide. These numbers increased to 2500 incubators and 600 science and technology parks in the year 2000 (Heinz 2001). In the United States, business incubator programs grew from 12 in 1980 to 800 in 2002 (NBIA 2002). Although these are gross numbers and should be taken with care, they nevertheless suggest strong dynamism in business incubation, especially those linked to innovative activities.

In Latin America, data from Chile, Argentina, Mexico, and Brazil suggest that entrepreneurial activity is among the highest in the world, although most of it falls under the category of "necessity entrepreneurship" (Reynolds et al. 2002). A recent study shows that incubators have been increasing at an annual rate of 30% in Brazil since 1998, reaching 135 incubators in the year 2000 (Almeida and Botelho 2001). In Chile, business incubation is a very recent phenomenon and only a handful of incubators have appeared in the last 2 years.

The National Business Incubation Association (NBIA) in the United States defines business incubation as "a dynamic process of business enterprise development. Incubators nurture young firms, helping them to survive and grow during the start-up period when they are most vulnerable. Incubators provide hands-on management assistance, access to financing and orchestrated exposure to critical business or technical support services. They also offer entrepreneurial firms shared office services, access to equipment, flexible leases and expandable space, all under one roof." The order in which these services are listed is not accidental. As we will see, the main services required by start-ups are not shared office services, but rather quality advice and access to networks.

Business incubators have traditionally been created as not-for-profit institutions, either within government, nongovernmental organizations (NGOs), or universities, but lately there has been an important surge in for-profit incubators. In the United States, a few venture capital firms, angels, corporations, and entrepreneurs are experimenting with for-profit business incubation. They also offer space, funding, and services, but usually in exchange for equity stakes (Hansen et al. 2000). Brazil also has seen the appearance of private incubators. Business incubation started in 1999, and by 2001 there were 12 private incubators (Almeida and Botelho 2001). Although several of these incubators were strongly focused on Internet incubation, and thus have suffered from the burst of the Internet bubble, nevertheless these incubators are refocusing and continuing business. This small surge in private incubators raises the question of why public support for incubators is necessary and under what conditions can private incubation be successful.

Public support may be warranted when markets fail to provide an optimal solution. In business incubation this could be due to the presence of positive externalities in new firm formation. For example, innovative new firms introduce new products, services, or processes that can be imitated by incumbent firms and other new entrants. Usually the innovative firm does not fully reap the benefits of its innovation, thus producing a positive externality for the industry and its consumers. The presence of these positive externalities can justify public support for innovative incubation activities, if these activities will not happen without public support and if the externalities generated are greater than the cost of public action.

Even though the presence of positive externalities may justify public support for incubation of innovative firms, this does not imply that incubators have to be publicly owned or not-for-profit.

The NBIA suggests that there are two general principles that characterize effective business incubation.

- The incubator aspires to have a positive impact on its community's economic health by maximizing the success of emerging companies.
- The incubator itself is a dynamic model of a sustainable business operation.

The second principle highlights the importance of cost effectiveness, and experience shows that private firms tend to be more cost effective than public firms. Heinz (2001) also draws from the experience of SPICA to assert that "Business incubators can fulfill political tasks, but they should be understood and operated just like their clients—as enterprises." Thus, even if incubators have public funding, they should be managed as any private firm, with a clear business model that creates resources for sustainable operations.

Lessons from Foreign Start-Ups

The increase in business incubation efforts during the last two decades has allowed for some formal studies on what are critical variables for success in business incubation, and a few conclusions are already emerging.

Peña (2001) worked with a sample of 114 start-ups in the Basque region of Spain and found that previous management experience of entrepreneurs, organizational learning capacity, flexibility to adapt to changing market conditions, and the existence of a founding team are all variables positively associated with business growth. These findings are consistent with management theory that stresses the importance of building internal resources for innovation in order to generate competitive advantage (Chesbrough and Teece 1996).

Angelelli and Listerri (2001) in a study of Latin American entrepreneurship found that the probability of success increases when entrepreneurs have prior work experience, have a core team with complementary capabilities, place their start-up in a very competitive environment, and can rely on a network of successful business people for cooperation. Close cooperation is especially critical with customers and suppliers. Cooperation is useful for solving critical problems in the early stages. During this period, attendance at commercial fairs is suggested as a good investment because it provides new ideas for products, markets, and technologies, as well as new opportunities for networking. Among the main hindrances to firm growth in the early stages were difficulties in expanding the client base, and connected to this, scarcity and unbalanced access to financial resources. Additional problems were difficulties in hiring adequate managers and access to technology and reliable suppliers.

This study highlights that in addition to building internal resources for competitive advantage, new firms need also to rely on strong networks. This conclusion agrees with several authors who argue that networks are increasingly important in the new economy (Hansen et al. 2000; Kelly 1998).

Empirical evidence from other countries also supports these connections. Lee et al. (2001) found that employment growth in Korean technological start-ups was strongly correlated with firms' internal capabilities and with some external networks (especially ties to venture capital firms), while they found weak effects of linkages to universities and no effect of government-sponsorship linkages. They also found strong inter-action effects: multiplicative terms of internal capabilities and partner-ship-based linkages were positively correlated with firm performance. Yli-Renko et al. (2001), in a study of 180 entrepreneurial high-technol-ogy firms in the United Kingdom, found that social interaction and net-work ties are associated with greater knowledge acquisition. In other words, external networking also contributes to firm performance by enabling the acquisition of internal capabilities.

The importance of networks may explain the attention recently received by networked incubators, such as Idealab (Hansen et al. 2000). As the next section will show, the experience of Chilean knowledge-intensive Chilean ventures reinforces the importance of networking.

Innovative Start-ups in Chile

Chile has experienced a remarkable transformation in the last 20 years, both in terms of economic growth and institutional development. Exports of natural resources, and some low value-added processing, led the economic expansion until the mid-1990s, but in the last few years growth has slowed considerably. This current lack of dynamism in the economy has generated an emerging interest in opinion leaders on how to design an environment more conducive to the development of higher value-added products and services. In 2001, the Ministry of Economics started a major initiative to promote innovation and entrepreneurship in Chile, while press coverage for these topics has increased significantly in the past 2 years.

The Chilean government has created funds to finance research and development at universities and industry, as well as technology transfer for industry. CORFO, the government-funding arm for industry, has developed several new funds for seed capital, early stage research, and venture capital. It has also revised legislation to promote the develop-ment of venture capital and deepen the financial system by enabling the supply of a wider array of financial instruments and increasing competi-tion. Even though some of these efforts were started more than 10 years ago, there are only a few signs that a knowledge-intensive sector is start-ing to emerge.

After growing rapidly during the first half of the 1990s, export growth almost stopped in the second half, growing only 8.7% in the period from 1995 to 2002, or about 1% per year. Within this stagnant export situa-tion, growth has come from wood, salmon, wine, basic chemicals (mainly methanol), and fuels (mainly in refueling of ships and planes). Of these products probably only wine could be considered a high value-added product and currently wine accounts for only a little over 3% of Chilean exports. In total, less than 10% of Chilean current exports could be considered high value-added.

In order to provide some understanding of what is holding back the development of knowledge-intensive sectors in Chile and what steps can be taken to promote their growth through entrepreneurial activities, interviews were undertaken with 15 entrepreneurs and managers who had been successful in producing and exporting high value-added products. Eight of these entrepreneurs worked in the electronics industry, one in biotechnology and resource-intensive industries, one was working in both areas, and five worked in the wine industry. This imbalance in sectors reflects the nature of biotechnology as an emerging sector in Chile, with few firms competitive at international levels, but a sector that nevertheless has great potential in Chile given that a great share of university research in Chile goes into chemistry and biology. In addition, interviews were performed with managers of public institutions and technology centers linked to these sectors.

Firms in the Chilean electronics industry are usually small. They tend to focus either on the design and implementation of engineering solutions to particular problems of medium and large firms, or on manufacturing knowledge-intensive niche products. None of these electronics firms produced mass products. The biotechnology firm was large and had interests in several resource-intensive sectors, but not in electronics.

The interviews were semi-structured. First, an interview guideline was designed with the main variables found in the literature on innovative start-ups. The guideline was then refined after each interview to add issues that were considered important by entrepreneurs. For the interview guideline, we divided the process of creating a start-up in its different phases and asked how they performed those phases and what were the main hindrances they found on each phase. At the end we had open questions about their general perception of the process of creating a start-up in Chile and what suggestions they had to improve it.

Following Levien (1997) and Ryan (2001), the start-up process was divided into the following phases: generation of idea, formalization of the idea (the prototype in electronics), commercial evaluation, business planning, creation of company, initial operations, and growth.

From the interviews we found the following results.

1. Generation of the idea: Entrepreneurs didn't find a lack of interesting ideas–they perceive that many students of engineering schools come out with creative ideas. What they found difficult was to discern which ideas had strong commercial potential. In addition, they did perceive

a shortage of entrepreneurial spirit to take risks and commit to their projects.

2. Formalization of the idea: In electronics this phase refers to the generation of a prototype that could be manufactured for markets. Electronic entrepreneurs found two main difficulties in generating quality prototypes. First, funding was not easy to find. There are few angels, and public funding for technology projects is only available for established companies. Lack of early funding contributes to the generation of poor-quality prototypes that are not adequate for presentation to investors.

   A second problem is that there is no components industry in Chile. Electronic components have to be imported, while plastic boxes and other non-electronic hardware have to be produced by labor-intensive techniques, or also imported. Lack of local availability of components also contributes to generate poor-quality prototypes because many of the parts have to be produced by hand and lack professional look and performance.

3. Commercial evaluation: This phase includes researching the market (competitors and customers), creating a business model, and testing the prototype with at least one qualified (beta) customer. Few entrepreneurs go through this phase, but those that go through it find that commercial evaluation is extraordinarily important for success. The most successful entrepreneurs suggest that in electronics you can start with a local market niche, but you can not avoid thinking and planning globally. This implies that market research and the business model have to be international, while the beta customer has to be as sophisticated as an international customer.

   Successful firms in wine and biotechnology also started with a clear idea of who were their clients and what they needed. Firms that first built the product and then looked for markets were not doing so well.

   There are several problems in this phase. First, local high-tech entrepreneurs are technologically oriented, usually do not realize the importance of commercial evaluation, and seldom think globally. Second, there is no funding for market evaluation at an international level at this stage of the project. Third, it is not easy to find people with the specific industry knowledge to appropriately evaluate the commercial potential of the idea.

4. Business planning: Again, only a few entrepreneurs actually do a business plan. Usually high-tech entrepreneurs don't find business planning useful or have never made one and don't know where to start. However, business planning can be a very profitable investment for would-be entrepreneurs. One of the successful Chilean firms hired the

UCLA Anderson Business School in the United States to help develop a business plan for its idea. The business plan was well evaluated in a contest of business plans and afterwards the firm found very easy access to venture capital funding. The firm did not implement the business plan to the letter, but that is not uncommon in high-tech start-ups because markets change rapidly.

What seems critical about business planning is that the entrepreneurs have to perform a process of thoroughly thinking about the implementation of the idea, which allows them to see the big picture. After markets change, they have learned to think in terms of the big picture and can reshape their strategies, taking the most relevant variables into account. Even though the plan is useful in itself, it seems that more important than the plan itself is the exercise in planning and the assurance to investors that this exercise has been done in a serious manner. This expertise should be developed at home.

5. Creation of the company: Two are the main problems in this phase are finance and team building. The venture capital industry is not developed in Chile. The government has provided legislation to promote the creation of venture capital funds, but so far the main results are investment funds for established firms with new projects, that is, merchant venture capital. Traditional angels in Chile usually do not work in high-tech sectors and in the sectors where they work, they have had a control-minded strategy, looking for ownership of more than 50% of the company. Entrepreneurs, on the other hand, had been reluctant to share ownership, preferring love money (family and friends), whatever bank funding they could get, and other bootstrap financing. Lately angels and high-tech entrepreneurs have become more open to sharing ownership and control. In this regard, the legal agreement between the venture capitalist and entrepreneurs can be a key issue for preventing future conflicts.

   Entrepreneurs usually are technologically oriented, and team-building needs are generally seen to be solved by referring them to sales and marketing partners, or managers.

   Entrepreneurs also find it difficult to recruit workers with manufacturing skills, but because many electronic firms are niche-oriented, manufacturing capability is not a critical variable for competition. Most firms say they can easily train their workers in-house because skills for their operations are not that sophisticated yet.

6. Initial operations: After starting operations, the main problem becomes securing and expanding the client base. This leads to irregular cash flow and difficulties in retaining the firm's human capital. At this stage, flexibility is critical and firms need to constantly adapt their product to customer needs and create new products to provide for

smoother work activity and cash flow. Working closely with customers is important, and in foreign markets this also means constant monitoring of trade and technology fairs.

7. Growth: Few electronics firms in Chile have entered the growth phase. Those that have highlight the importance of strategic alliances and venture capital funding. Strategic alliances are key for accessing new markets, especially foreign markets, and for acquiring critical technology to develop new products. Venture capital is better suited for strong growth, but if it isn't available, bank financing provides resources for growth at a slower rate.

Lessons for Incubators

From the literature on business incubation and the interviews with Chilean entrepreneurs, some lessons can be drawn for business incubation in Chile.

At the design level, the incubator should produce a sustainable business model for itself. Traditionally, incubators have provided several services to start-ups: office space, professional services (accounting, lawyers) on a shared basis, basic management training, and guidance regarding where to look for financial resources. Although in some incubators supported by public funding these services have been offered for free, a sustainable operation requires that start-ups pay for these services in cash or shares. If they do not show profitability prospects when these costs are included, or if entrepreneurs cannot find a minimum funding from private sources, probably they should not be incubated.

The incubator should develop its business model by focusing on variables that have been found critical for success in the experiences of other countries (Bizzotto et al. 2001; NBIA 2002) and of local entrepreneurs.

1. The incubator should commit to maximizing start-up wealth and community impact. Because networking is increasingly important and local partners can be most helpful, it is important to maintain good relationships with incubator graduates and local partners.

2. The incubator should focus on areas where the partners can provide internationally competitive technical and market knowledge, and preferably in areas where firms can produce synergies among themselves. Incubators should always try to incorporate international best practice in start-ups.

3. The incubator should build a network with experienced business people in all critical areas for business success: technology providers and brokers, research and development institutions, training institutions, suppliers, business management, international distribution

channels, and financing. Each new firm may have critical demands in any of these areas, and the incubator should be able to provide some opportunity for solution.

The size of the network can be increased by nurturing close ties with incubator graduates. This can be done by keeping a small number of shares of the graduating firm or by incorporating the graduated entrepreneurs in the board of directors of the incubator or on industry-specific advisory boards. Graduated firms are potential venture capitalists for other start-ups.

4. Find a mechanism to attract ideas in a continuous way and have an external evaluation at some point of the process before committing major resources. External evaluation is useful to ensure realism in the business plan.

5. Help start-ups develop internal capabilities to manage markets. Particularly, provide entrepreneurs with opportunities to visit internationally sophisticated potential customers and competitors to obtain a clear understanding of the nature of the market and of potential trends. This should be done even before making a prototype.

6. Help start-ups develop internal capabilities to manage innovation. The new firm should have a structure that includes responsibilities for knowledge brokering activities: technological antenna, internal diffusion and discussion of new ideas, and continuous testing (Hargadon and Sutton 2000).

7. Provide a technology advisor and a business advisor for each start-up. The advisor will help the new firm develop the management and innovation capabilities of points 5 and 6.

8. The incubator should provide opportunities for formal training in specific topics that can be critical to a start-up success. This can be done through partnerships with educational institutions.

9. Maintain a management information system and collect statistics and other information necessary for ongoing program evaluation. Constant monitoring should improve the program's effectiveness and allow the start-up to evolve with the needs of the clients. Start-up performance should be evaluated at the end of the first year to assess if progress is fast enough to warrant continuing support. External advice should be requested for this evaluation in order to increase objectivity.

10. Define an expected graduating date at the time of admitting the start-up, and respect it. Some flexibility can be allowed by continuing to provide some services, but not all, for a determined amount of time after graduation. This may be warranted when the start-up has not consolidated its

technology and its selling capability. Graduation can start in a gradual and scheduled way sometime before the graduation date.

11. Design incubation models appropriate for different types of entrepreneurs, sectors, and projects. Better yet, focus only on some combination of these.

Conclusions

From the interviews performed with leading business people in the electronics, wine, and biotechnology sectors, we obtained several suggestions for creating a more effective business incubation environment. Business incubators should design incubation models appropriate for the type of firms they incubate, provide opportunities for early and sophisticated market feedback, help to create internal capabilities rather than achieve certain short-run objectives, provide an extensive network of internationally competitive contacts, define clear objectives with each firm, and monitor its achievements.

References

Almeida, M., and A. Botelho. 2001. "Incubadoras privadas: perspectivas no Brasil." Proceedings World Conference on Business Incubation, Rio de Janeiro, October 23–26.

Angelelli, P., and J. J. Listerri. 2001. "Algunas consideraciones sobre la experiencia del Banco Interamericano de Desarrollo (BID) en la promoción de la empresarialidad." Proceedings World Conference on Business Incubation, Rio de Janeiro, October 23–26.

Beibst, G., and A. Lautenschläger. 2001. "Networks for Innovative Company Start-ups." Proceedings World Conference on Business Incubation, Rio de Janeiro, October 23–26.

Bizzotto, C., O. Dalfovo, M. Hoffmann, and A. Sena. 2001. "Preincubation: Overcoming Barriers to Success." Proceedings World Conference on Business Incubation, Rio de Janeiro, October 23–26.

Chesbrough, H., and D. Teece. 1996. "When Is Virtual Virtuous: Organizing for Innovation." *Harvard Business Review* (January–February): 65–74.

Hansen, M., H. Chesbrough, N. Nohria, and D. Sull. 2000. "Networked Incubators: Hothouses of the New Economy." *Harvard Business Review* (September–October): 74–84.

Hargadon, A., and R. Sutton. 2000. "Building an Innovation Factory." *Harvard Business Review* (May–June): 157–166.

Heinz, F. 2001. "Business Incubation Globally–The State of the Art." Proceedings World Conference on Business Incubation, Rio de Janeiro, October 23–26.

Kelly, K. 1998. *New Rules for the New Economy: 10 Radical Strategies for a Connected World*. New York: Viking.

Lee, C., K. Lee, and J. Pennings. 2001. "Internal Capabilities, External Networks, and Performance: A Study on Technology-Based Ventures." *Strategic Management Journal* 22: 615–640.

Levien, R. 1997. *Taking Technology to Market*. Menlo Park, CA: Crisp Publications.

National Business Incubator Association (NBIA). 2002. http://www.nbia.org/resource_center/bus_inc_facts/index.php.

Peña, I. 2001. "Effectiveness of Business Incubators as a Policy to Promote New Firm Survival and Growth." Proceedings World Conference on Business Incubation, Rio de Janeiro, October 23–26.

Reynolds, P., W. Bygrave, E. Autio, and M. Hay, M. 2002. *Global Entrepreneurship Monitor*. Wellesley, MA, and London: Babson College and London Business School.

Ryan, R. 2001. *Entrepreneur America: Lessons from Inside Rob Ryan's High-Tech Start-up Boot Camp*. New York: HarperCollins.

Yli-Renko, H., E. Autio, and H. Sapienza. 2001. "Social Capital, Knowledge Acquisition and Knowledge Exploitation in Young Technology-based Firms." *Strategic Management Journal* 22: 587–613.

CHAPTER 7

Inception Characteristics of Companies Through the National Entrepreneurship Contest

Ricardo Aguilar Diaz

Juan Carlos Leiva

Entrepreneurship is a topic of great importance nowadays. According to several authors and institutions, for example, Reynolds et al. (1994), Gibb and Ritchie (1982), and the Inter-American Development Bank (IBD 2002), the creation of new companies is a fundamental part of developing economies in this global economy.

A country like Costa Rica cannot escape from this global tendency. One event making a great impact is the National Entrepreneurship Contest, held by the Technological Institute of Costa Rica (ITCR). It has been held four times since 1997. In this contest, we look at ideas and business projects that are evaluated by an expert panel of judges. The winners are awarded special incentives to start new companies. This contest goes through three stages: (1) evaluation of new ideas, (2) training for new business plans, and (3) presentation to the judges.

This chapter looks at the impact this contest has on starting new businesses. Our general goal is to understand the creation of companies in Costa Rica. The specific goals are to:

- Measure how many companies were created by the influence of the National Entrepreneurship Contests.

- Understand the characteristics new enterprises and their owners have, and compare these owners with the people who have not started new companies after the contests.

- Describe the previous inception of companies and the relevance of the National Entrepreneurship Contest in this process.

Our intention is not to generalize about the processes, but to come up with first-hand information and present new research opportunities for the future. This chapter is organized in five sections: (1) literature review, (2) survey design, (3) contest systems and data collection, (4) analysis, and, finally, (5) main conclusions.

Literature Review

The economic view has historically focused on analyzing the impact of economic conditions on stimulating new business creation, and the impact of new business creation on the economic system. Although this provides key insights, it focuses on demand aspects only, leaving out the whole side of entrepreneurial supply—the characteristics that motivate entrepreneurs to act—which can be quite independent (Mason 2000; IDB 2000). It was not until recently that some authors have set out to explain what the entrepreneurial phenomenon is about. A recent analytical perspective (Audretsch and Acs 1994) proposes that business creation is a product of specific facets that include marketing (strategy and innovation of firms), segmentation (scope and scale economy, R&D, market share), and macroeconomic factors (business life cycle, unemployment levels, capital gains, general economic performance).

There are also non-economic views that are important in describing how the process of creating companies really works. The non-economical views have two aspects: psychological, and processional (Gartner 1988).

The psychological way, historically, concentrates on the inner characteristics that define an entrepreneur. Some examples of those characteristics are

- The necessity for success;
- Autonomy;
- Desire for control; and
- Instinct and orientation thoughts (Gibb and Ritchie 1982).

Another non-economic analytical method considers that the entrepreneur is made by environmental factors (family, culture, education, and others). Those analysts consider that the entrepreneurial process is very varied, with contexts that determine the decisions made by the entrepreneur (Gartner 1988; Shapero 1984; Gibb and Richie 1982; Reynolds et al 1994).

Additionally, networking is considered as an alternative of the entrepreneurial process. In this analytical method, the basic variable on which the trend studies are based is the integration of the networks and the use that the person gives them (Johannisson 1998).

The predominant focus in the present research will be eclectic in the analytical components (taking into consideration the contributions and disadvantages that they have), but guided by a processional view.

Survey Design

The survey was based on questions and answers and their prospective results.

1. How many companies did the National Entrepreneurship Contest create by motivation or because of its influence? Prospective results:
   a. Number of enterprises created by contestants.
2. What kind of demographic characteristics are present in owners and their enterprises. Are there differences between entrepreneurs and non-entrepreneurs? Prospective results:
   a. Enterprise characteristics such as:
      • Date of start up;
      • Employees;
      • Economical sector (industry, services, technology, etc.).
   b. Personal characteristics:
      • Age, gender, city, and social class;
      • Team working tendency;
      • Education;
      • Age at the time of starting company and when they decided to become entrepreneurs;
      • Motivation to participate in the contest.
3. How were the inception stages of the new enterprises?

This survey about inception was based on the theoretical approach of the Inter-American Development Bank (IDB 2002). This model was based on a theory revision, such as an in-depth interview series with key informants of the Latin American context (see complete survey www.iadb.org). According to many papers (Gibb and Ritchie 1982; Reynolds et al. 1994), the entrepreneurship event is internal and influenced by the environment, and because of that this model contains three stages: inception (starting motivation), start-up (business turning point), and early development (first 3 years of operation) (see Table 7.1).

The main events–those that are tangible and identifiable in the opening process of a new company–were defined inside each stage. These main events came from a combination of internal and external factors of the context on which the enterprises are developed. According to Audretsch and Acs (1994), Reynolds et al. (1994) and Gibb and Ritchie (1982), there are many factors that affect an entrepreneurial process. According to this approach, the model contains internal factors and external factors related to psychological aspects, processional aspects (Gartner 1988), and networking (Johannisson 1998). Specific internal factors that are considered primarily are: expertise and objectives; the external factors are the market and resources.

At the same time, there are other indirect issues that could influence the entrepreneurial process, such as indirect factors that could alter or modify the four main issues. The present research focuses in the first model stage, inception.

The results for the inception stage were described by the following characteristics.

1. Gaining motivation and competence:
   - Personal motivation;
   - Main source of enterprise knowledge and experiences (family, education, work experience).

Table 7.1
Analytical Framework for the IDB Study

Stages of the Process	Main Events	Factors
Inception	Gaining motivation and competence Identifying a business opportunity and ideas Business planning	Culture and education system Structure and productive dynamics
Start-up	Final decision Access and mobilization of resources	Economy and market conditions
Early Development	Market entry Birth of the enterprise	Regulatory framework Personal factors

2. Identifying a business:
   - Main sources of business opportunities;
   - First clients.
3. Business plan:
   - Financing start-up;
   - National Entrepreneurship Contest role;
   - Evaluation and advice for National Entrepreneurship Contests.

The National Contest and Data Collection

National Entrepreneurship Contest

This national contest is organized by the ITCR each year and is started with innovative business ideas. The contest has three categories: (1) electronics/software, (2) biotechnology/agro-industry, and (3) manufacturing and services. Its budget is approximately $10,000; usually the ITCR gives 10%, and the rest of it comes from sponsors. The winner in each category receives $1,500 and is incorporated under the university Incubator Center of Enterprises (CIE).

The people interested in participating must present a paper with the following information:

1. Personal:
   - Training and education;
   - Personal, academic and entrepreneurial experience;
   - Personal motivation.
2. Business ideas:
   - Innovation;
   - Competitive advantages;
   - Entry barriers.

The first panel of judges (ITCR professors) reviews these papers, and those that receive at least 70 points pass to the second stage and receive a weekend workshop (six weekends) on how to make a business plan. Then they present their business plans to the final panel, which is made up of professors, sponsors (see Table 7.2), former ITCR entrepreneurs, and prior competition winners.

Ninety persons formed the total sample. Out of 82 phone interviews, only 20 people were selected for a second interview: 10 people who decided to start their own companies (after the panel considered them entrepreneurs), and 10 who did not. This second interview was in two

Table 7.2
Sponsors of the National Entrepreneurship
Contest in 2002 Data Collection

LA REPUBLICA
MAS POR MENOS
FLORIDA BEBIDAS
INTEL
AMANCO
ARTINSOFT
BANCO NACIONAL
CISCO SYSTEMS
MICROSOFT
SIEMENS
94.7 RADIO STATION
PRONAMYPE
BAXTER

parts. First, written information was collected, and then all participants were gathered for an oral interview directed by a psychologist. It is possible that this panel did not accurately represent all Costa Rican people, in that it was made up only of people from the contest who were very interested in becoming entrepreneurs. On the other hand, it did have the advantage of including people who wanted to become entrepreneurs but could not continue in the contest, which gave a different perspective that most of the other studies did not consider.

Analysis

This section presents the results obtained in the field study.

- Eighteen companies have emerged influenced by their participation in the enterprise competition.

    Out of these eighteen companies, eleven are operating and seven are inactive. The National Entrepreneurship Contest has been held four times since its beginning in 1995. During this period, 82 ideas or business projects were received. Fifty-nine of them presented a business plan. Eighteen companies were founded from these plans. The creation rate is around 21%, and the surviving rate is nearly 12%. It is interesting to compare this data with other surveys. For example,

Durham University in the United Kingdom obtained 15% for creation and 12% for surviving (Gibb and Ritchie 1982).

We found that 50% of the companies are associated with the information and technology sectors. However, 100% are thought to have gotten their competitive advantage in relation to these sectors.

- The people who created their own companies were typically between 25 and 34 years old, all were university graduates, and the majority were men from middle class families.

   These data did not differ from that of the people who did not create their own companies; they are very similar to other research at a Latin American and Costa Rican level (IDB 2002; Leiva 2001).

   The usual age when people begin their businesses is between 25 and 34 years old, when they are mature and have resources and support available. The high percentage of professionals is due probably to the university sponsoring the contest. The data that is interesting to highlight is that 63% of the people polled in this category decided before the age of 25 to become entrepreneurs. This fact shows a group of people with professional vocation defined from an early age, and indicates that they take advantage of their studies and advancement opportunities (such as competitions) that nurture their future emerging skills.

- The motivations that influenced the participants in the contest are not the same between people who opened their own company and those who did not.

   The main motivations mentioned by people who opened their own company were desire to start their own company (38%), to interchange experiences and/or contacts (25%), and to promote their own business ideas (25%).

   Those that did not start their own company also mentioned these reasons, but to a lesser degree. They had been urged by the professor during the course at the ITCR (23%).

- The previous experiences of people who founded their own companies were different from those who did not.

   This point is an interesting difference because it shows how people with business experience were predominant among those who had opened their own companies (51%) versus employees (26%).

   In the case of people who did not start their own businesses, the data shows that for those who were predominantly employees, the majority came from small and medium enterprises (SME) (76%). Another approach pays attention to the absence of people from large enterprises (LE) among contestants, especially those who opened their own companies (just 13% were employees of LE). We note from this survey that the majority of people who opened their own businesses were more likely to be from SMEs rather than LEs.

• Two of the principal motivations for becoming an entrepreneur were to fulfill personal ambitions and to develop personal abilities.

From these series of possible factors, economic and non-economic (see Table 7.3), the people polled mentioned their personal fulfillment and knowledge-use as the most important.

On economic issues, the number of people who mentioned "to improve income" as a very important motivator was relatively low (15%). An additional 31% mentioned economic aspects as an important factor—not as the most important one, but worthy of consideration. The responses of the people who did not start a company are very similar to the people who did.

An additional element is the low importance of two factors, role model and social recognition. There is a lack of importance in these factors among people who started their companies and those who did not. For example, among people who opened a company, none considered that looking like an entrepreneur was very important or just important, and only 23% mentioned it as an important factor of their improved status.

• Work experience and university studies are the main sources of enterprising capacities and motivation.

Work experiences and university studies are the most frequently mentioned factors in providing enterprising abilities. Work experience appears as the best context rated by the poll, because none of the enterprising abilities decreased from the 38% mentioned. Specifically, work experience seems the best supplier of communication abilities, negotiation skills, and the ability to motivate other people. The university is seen as an important supplier of technical knowledge (marketing, engineering), but does not provide knowledge or skills in business vocation, risk tolerance, and others previously mentioned. It is strong in technical skills but deficient in business-world competencies.

The two most important sources of business opportunity identifiers were the interaction or discussion with other people (100% of the opinion polled) and the experiences at work and previous activities (88%).

To identify business opportunities, the entrepreneurs came up with personal sources like networks and their own past experiences, over other sources like the Internet, magazines, the media, trade fairs, newspapers, and academic papers.

There were eight persons who gave valuable information in identifying their business ideas. This indicator denotes that the use of personal networks is active, although such networks are not profuse in

Table 7.3
Motivation to Start a Business

Motivation Factors	Not Important	Medium Important	Important	Very Important
To be your own boss	0%	5%	19%	29%
For self-fulfillment	0%	5%	5%	52%
To become like an entrepreneur you admired (parents)	14%	5%	10%	0%
To become like an entrepreneur you admired (friends)	19%	5%	10%	0%
To become like an entrepreneur you admired (somebody in your town)	19%	5%	5%	0%
To become like an entrepreneur you admired (somebody in the media)	14%	14%	0%	0%
To contribute to society	0%	5%	14%	43%
To obtain social status	14%	29%	10%	5%
To follow family tradition of being in business	19%	5%	10%	0%
Because you were unemployed	19%	0%	5%	0%
Because you could not go further in education	19%	0%	5%	0%
To become wealthy (stock)	33%	0%	24%	0%
To improve income (flow)	14%	14%	19%	14%
To use your knowledge	0%	10%	10%	43%

comparison to other results at the Latin American level, and to other contexts that define that network as the largest (Kantis 1999; IDB 2002).

Most of the companies began selling to final consumers, while selling to other companies was not considered as important. It seems that the companies that emerged from the National Entrepreneurship

Contest had focused on the final consumer, in very specific and small-scale markets.

- Most of the people who opened their own company structured a business plan.

    About 70% of the people mentioned had done some kind of planning themselves, or had asked third parties to help with their plans. This result is related to the characteristics of the population in the study, so it refers to a dynamic competition.

- Outside or foreign capital is not available either for starting or continuing a new business.

    According to our survey and in concordance with other studies, (IDB 2002; Castillo and Chávez 1999; Leiva 2001) there is an absence of venture capital for financing the start up of companies, and the majority of the capital comes from personal savings and family and friends' resources.

- A high percentage of contestants considered their participation in the National Enterprising Competition very important, and the main contribution they consider they have received is motivation.

    About 88% of the people considered that the national contest was very important for the competitors and the main contribution was motivation. There were three general contributing categories: motivation, technical training (business plans, strategic, planning), and vision (networking, entrepreneurial experiences).

Conclusions

We found that 18 companies have emerged, supported and influenced by their participation in the enterprising competition, and that there are differences between preliminary motivation and the experiences of people who had started their own companies after participating in the competition versus those who did not. The data, according to some theories, indicates that people with experience from SMEs are more likely to start their own companies because they come from more encouraging backgrounds.

On business motivation, the participants have a very good assimilation of the non-economic factors (self-fulfillment, personal development, social contribution, among others), but do not underrate the economic issues. In order to encourage the enterprising spirit, we must consider these kinds of motivating factors as important elements to encourage the starting of companies in society—in other words, to work from the demand side (conditions that encourage people to set up companies) to the supply side (trained and motivated people).

Two principal sources of business opportunities were the interaction or discussion with other people and the experiences of work and previous activities. This means that business opportunities that appeared in the context of the entrepreneur and networking are key factors for the future entrepreneur.

Last, there are undeveloped and latent needs in the Costa Rican environment for supporting new entrepreneurs. It is necessary to acquire more venture capital, improve instruments such as the National Entrepreneur Contest, gain more university involvement, supportg entrepreneurs, encourage more collaboration with corporate enterprise, and receive more coordination among environmental institutions.

References

Audretsch, D. and Z. Acs. 1994."New Firm Startups, Technology and Macroeconomics Fluctuations." *Sloan Management Review 6,* no. 6 (December).

Castillo, G. and L. F. Cháves. 2001. *PyMEs: Una oportunidad de desarrollo para Costa Rica,* San José, Editorial FUNDES.

Gartner W. 1988. "Who Is an Entrepreneur? It Is the Wrong Question." *American Journal of Small Business* 12 (spring): 11–32.

Gibb, A. and J. Ritchie.1982. "Understanding the Process of Starting Small Businesses," *European Small Business Journal* 1, no. 1: 26–46.

Inter-American Development Bank (IDB). 2000. *Comparative Study on Entrepreneurship: Final Report.* Washington, DC: BID.

Inter-American Development Bank (IDB). 2002. *Entrepreneurship in Emerging Economies: the Creation and Development of New Firms in Latin America and East Asia.* Washington DC: IDB.

Johannisson, B. 1998. "Designing Supportive Context for Emerging Enterprises." Discussion paper, Vaxjo University.

Kantis, H. 1999. "Casos de redes y desarrollo local en América Latina." *Globalización, desarrollo local y redes asociativas.* IPAC and Ministerio de la Producción y el Empleo de la provincia de Buenos Aires. Buenos Aires, 18–19 may.

Kantis, H., I. Masahiko, and K. Masahiko. 2002. *Entrepreneurship in Emergent Economies: Creation and Development of New Companies in Latin America and East Asia.* Summary report. Inter-American Development Bank, Washington, DC.

Leiva, J. C. 2001. "El proceso de creación de empresas en Costa Rica durante los años 90." Tesis de Maestría, Universidad Nacional de General Sarmiento, Buenos Aires.

Mason, Collin. 2000. Panel discussion presentation, Entrepreneurial Event Conference. Universidad Nacional de General Sarmiento, Buenos Aires, IDES, September 13.

Reynolds, P., D. Storey, and P. Westhead. 1994. "Cross-National Comparisons of the Variation in New Firm Formation Rates." *Regional Studies* no. 28.

Shapero, A. 1984. "The Entrepreneurial Event." in *The Environment for Entrepreneurship,* ed. C. A. Kent. Lexington, KY: Lexington Books, 21–40.

CHAPTER 8

Teaching Entrepreneurship in Chile: The UDD Case

Pedro Arriagada Stuven

Teaching entrepreneurship is an issue of academic debate. Is there a way to teach such a thing called *entrepreneurship*? Many people think that the spirit of creating new business ideas and the ability to start new projects is something embodied in a few and cannot be taught to people without this natural gift. Others feel it has been proven that entrepreneurial capacity is not an innate ability to create something new, but also the motivation to introduce changes, to find new ways, to look for new business models, and so on, and that everyone has this potential. Entrepreneurship is therefore something that can be generated and motivated in almost everybody. This chapter outlines the efforts of the Universidad del Desarrollo (UDD), a relatively new academic institution in Chile that strongly believes in the importance of generating an entrepreneurial capacity in their students.

I have had the privilege of leading this effort on the UDD side. My more than 20 years of teaching business economics at the graduate and undergraduate levels, both in Chile and in the United States, had given me a lot to think about, which is the best way of teaching. At the same time, my exposure to business operations and several start-ups in the last 10 years has given me the background to insert the academic concepts and thoughts into a practical framework.

Diagnosis

The Traditional Way of Teaching Business Administration in Chile

Since the 1950s business administration has been taught in Chile, first within departments of commerce and later as a separate field leading to an academic degree known as *Ingeniero Comercial.* What started as a novelty in traditional universities, such as the Universidad Católica and Universidad de Chile, is today taught in more than 50 universities in Chile. Its beginnings are related to a cooperation agreement signed between the University of Chicago and the Universidad Católica and Universidad de Chile. Due to this, several Chilean professors went the Department of Economics at Chicago and later reorganized the programs in Chile.

It is important to note that the degree *Ingeniero Comercial* reflects very well the spirit of the education: very demanding in math and science. In addition to that, the two universities that started the program had it under the Department of Business and Economics, and it was mainly oriented toward training in formal economics. It was not until the 1970s that within the same programs a special degree in business administration was granted. This denomination has created some resentment on the part of civil engineers.

The teaching during all these years has been characterized by a demanding and formal training in quantitative analysis and by a traditional structure where the building blocks are around the basic functional areas. Later the students get exposed to more advanced topics related to specific areas, and, finally, to strategy issues.

In the last 10 years, the soft areas and more liberal arts aspects have been integrated into the process but always following the same methodological structure. The students have only recently accepted this innovation, because at the beginning many considered these second-class courses.

In order to summarize the main characteristics of the traditional way of teaching business administration in Chile, we can say it is:

• Quantitative and rigorous;
• Functionally oriented; and
• Easily replicated.

As a result, the programs produce an *Ingeniero Comercial* very strong in techniques and instruments. In the process, the students have mastered lots of information not knowing much of what to do with it. Also, given their ages (17 to 24 years old) and lack of business experience, many of the material they have received goes much beyond their capabilities to understand and personally relate. On the other hand, the students have strong analytical capabilities that allow them to work with models. The process of learning is mostly cognitive and rationally oriented.

Experiments of Teaching Entrepreneurship in Chile

At the time of writing, formal teaching of entrepreneurship does not exist in Chile. There is a lack of understanding of what this really means, and it is not well respected in the traditional academic environment. When the wave started around the teaching of entrepreneurship, it was outside the university system. Instead, it was new institutions like Young Entrepreneurs that started a very down-to-earth and practical approach with high school students. These are motivational approaches, very light in content, that intend to plant the seed in young people and present them with the issues of starting a small business.

This mode has been growing with time but is not yet regarded as formal education. Most of the programs are limited in terms of time, oriented toward crafts and skills, and intended for students with no easy access to the formal educational system.

Conclusion: The Existence of a Wide Gap

There is certainly a big gap between the two worlds, with almost no possibility to converge. They are absolutely different both in roots and purpose, with different objectives. This is certainly a problem because the entrepreneurship approach is diminished in terms of rigor and quality.

The UDD Hypothesis

The UDD approach is to introduce the entrepreneurship flavor inside the formal programs at the university level: fill the existing gap and transform the traditional way of teaching business administration in Chile by introducing a formal and more academic-oriented way of teaching entrepreneurship.

The UDD approach starts from the assumption that entrepreneurship can be taught within an academic structure. This approach is a big bet in Chile, because it goes completely against the current and leaves UDD in unknown territory. Also, UDD is a rather new academic institution in Chile. It started its work in Concepción, the second-largest city of Chile, 12 years ago, and moved to Santiago only 4 years ago. This means that it has to compete with the traditional universities in Chile, some of them with more than a hundred years of existence. The entrepreneurial flavor is a way to differentiate its product, and a way to become number one in the field. With not more than 2 years in the field from the teaching and research point of view, UDD already has become a reference in the field and a focal point for students with this set of preferences.

On the other hand, UDD is a very good example of entrepreneurial capacity. It makes a lot of sense, then, for it to become an important place for the teaching of this field. The fact that in a few years the UDD has become an important player in the industry of university education in Chile gives this project a lot of credibility.

Given the little experience that existed in Chile on the subject matter, UDD looked around the world for the best practices. Babson College, a small business school in Wellesley, Massachusetts, came to UDD's attention. They were listed as number one in the field in most rankings, and did that despite being small compared to the traditional business schools in the United States. A process of interactions began, through which UDD learned Babson's teaching model and the process of implementation. It took almost a year of work and interactions for UDD people to understand the key elements of Babson's model and adapt it to UDD reality.

Key Elements of UDD Approach

Our approach stresses the following elements.

- Multifunctional approach. Real-life business problems are multifunctional by nature;
- Integrated approach. Business issues have to relate to other aspects of the organization and people involved;
- Problem-oriented approach. The techniques and business instruments are better exposed while related to a business problem and with a decision-making process; and
- Strategy up front. Strategic decisions involve the three aspects already mentioned.

These elements turn the traditional teaching pyramid upside down. Instead of putting strategy at the very top, we put strategy at the bottom. Consequently, the multifunctional approach and integration is crucial, given that strategic dilemmas are like that by nature. The students are learning the techniques and instruments only in relation to the strategic dilemma that they are facing.

This approach also requires of a different way of teaching. This goes far beyond using or not using cases. It has to do with the nature of the professor. In that sense, the principle of teaching with cases does become more important only if they translate their experience with academic support, which is not always easy.

The UDD Experience: Planning and Launching

To create this new, integrated course structure, we considered the following factors.

• Start at the MBA level. There were two advantages of starting at the MBA level. First, the program is quite new, and, second, it is more self-contained than the undergraduate program. Also, the approach of the program fits very well with the characteristics of the students involved, most of them with years of business experience and no formal training in the area. It must also be said that in Chile there is very strong competition in MBA programs. The UDD program started in Concepción and was quite new in Santiago, only 2 years old. This meant that the new approach could give us the possibility to compete and differentiate.

• Reorganize content in the methodology of the business life cycle. Following Babson's business life cycle approach, we organized the first 9 months of the program around four modules. The first module was organized around starting a business, the second around the dilemmas faced on the first stages of growing and conquering a market, the third around control and structure, and the fourth around the dilemmas of maturity. Instead of having courses, each module includes topics strongly interrelated and with a common purpose. From six to ten different professors participate in a given module.

• The role of the module coordinator and of the professors. There is one professor coordinating each module. His task is crucial because he has to monitor the content of each class very closely and enforce every step possible for integration. For example, in the second module strategy is the key and every single aspect taught in the module has to be oriented toward strategy: marketing issues, economic and pricing issues, financial and accounting issues, and also quantitative-oriented issues such as how to work with data. This goes against the traditional way, in which each professor is autonomous in his or her class. Here everyone teaching in the module is doing it with the same objective in mind.

• The students' expectations. In Chile the vast majority of MBA candidates are engineers of different specializations that at a given stage in their professional career require formal training in management. Most of the students are looking for content and tools that are needed to assume tasks on their jobs. They typically have experience in technical matters and are now trying to move to more general managerial positions.

- Hard time selling the program to potential students. Given that the MBA market is quite mature in Chile and that almost every program available replicates the same model, it was not easy to sell this new approach to potential candidates. The message is not easily transmitted through a newspaper ad or in a brochure. It requires a one-on-one explanation and discussion with the potential student, and for that a direct marketing campaign was needed. Once the right potential target was reached, the selling message was very strong.

- Easy time selling the program internally. In the UDD case, analysis of the Babson model was very strong in terms of signaling what we needed and wanted. There was a strong agreement that this was the right thing to do, and that this way of teaching also had great potential to improve significantly the quality of Chilean human resources. It also helped that the number of faculty is small, very well-integrated, and not at all divided into specific functional departments.

- Looking for the right professors. As was already said, we understood from the very beginning that this kind of a program requires very talented professors that are not easy to find in the normal academic environment. Fortunately enough, the UDD structure, its founders, and its philosophy have naturally attracted the kind of professors required for this kind of program: people with a solid academic background but with solid professional experiences in the business world. That is why it was very easy to sell the program to the former professors, who without much resistance embraced the new model.

- The importance of recognized academic support. Both for internal and external selling purposes, it was extremely useful to have Babson's academic support. For 6 months we studied the way the program was executed at Babson, then analyzed ways to incorporate its main characteristics in our context. Finally, once the decision was made, we incorporated the advice and teaching support of four Babson professors who had vast experience not only teaching but also implementing the program at Babson.

The UDD Experience: Work in Progress

The program started in April 2002, which means at the time of writing this chapter we only are 20 weeks into the program in Concepción and 18 weeks into the program in Santiago. Both programs are identical, and each is already on module three, the one devoted to general management. They have already finished module one, where most of the soft elements of teamwork, leadership, personal motivation, and other related topics are addressed, and module two, which concentrated on strategy. So far, and with limited experience, we can make the following observations.

- Student motivations. We have a small program of 22 students per class in Santiago and the same number in Concepción. This class size is proper for the objectives followed and methodology used in the program.
- Practical and applied orientation. On average, our students are 32 years old and have 8 years of work experience. This means that they are expecting a very applied and down-to-earth orientation. They fear theory and lecture-style teaching.
- Evolution toward general management positions. At this stage of their professional careers, students are evolving to more general management and strategic positions. They expect learning skills that can be used in that perspective.
- Experience of coordinators. The task of coordinators is not easy. They have the ultimate responsible for their modules. Apart from the always-difficult task of coordinating schedules and other administrative issues, it is crucial to coordinate content and styles of teaching. It is my personal experience that it is easier to find common objectives every 2 weeks in the module than constantly communicating with the different professors about them. In that period of time, the students are exposed to most of the professors of the module at least once.
- First module. This takes the student from a business idea to a business project. We devoted 5 weeks to this stage, and it was very well-received by the students. We included here all the soft aspects of management, and went from personal to group motivation. The students found it very motivating but felt as thought the program had not yet started, because they did not have much to study yet in terms of readings, case preparation, and so on. Every one of them had to prepare a personal manual related to what was learned in every single exercise and group discussion. They also participated in a teamwork experience held during a two-day field trip.
- Second module. The students started facing challenges in terms of the traditional demands of the study load in this module. A focus on strategy was crucial to the success of this module. Every topic, including statistics and accounting, evolved around strategic issues. This module included marketing, statistics, accounting, and

microeconomics, and every one of them was highlighted by the professor in charge of strategy.

- Third module. Here the students got into the traditional topics of management and control. The first two modules gave them the right focus and perspective in order to relate these issues to strategic considerations. They understood the why of things and the ability to look at the details of management in the right perspective.

- Fourth module. As of the end of November, 8 months after the beginning of the program, the students are analyzing the macro challenges faced by mature business organizations. Issues like internationalization, disinvestments, and strategic alliances are the ones that call their attention.

- Evaluations. It has not been easy to create evaluation procedures and standards for this method of teaching. Our students are very much oriented toward grades, and become very competitive in these terms. We had just one evaluation in module one, and that was the analysis of the personal "module diary," in which each student outlined what he or she had achieved in the module. In the second module, we had two evaluations plus a class participation grade. Each evaluation was fully integrated in the sense that none of the professors asked specific topics of his or her concern alone, but instead integrated their questions around a common case. The case was chosen from the strategy point of view, and the rest of the topics used it as a common ground in which to position their own questions.

- Professors' motivation. This was a big concern when adapting the new model into the program. As said before, our traditional system gives each professor almost full autonomy over his or her course. It was feared that the coordination and overlapping needed by the new method could cause friction among professors that could affect their motivation. On the contrary, the experience demonstrated that the new method was fully accepted by the professors involved, and highly improved their motivation in teaching. The only concern expressed by some of them was that sometimes they were required to sacrifice specific content for the sake of integration and coordination.

Next Steps

The experience until now (as of November 2002) leaves us with unresolved matters, the most important of which follow.

- How to evaluate the change and monitor its progress. Here again the task of each module coordinator is crucial. Evaluating students' performances is not easy. We have planned two formal evaluations per module that are wholly integrated. It is crucial then to have a clear common denominator or anchor to what links the different subjects involved. In module two, for example, this anchor is clearly strategy design, and every other aspect taught in the module has to relate to strategy design. The preparation of the two formal evaluations is a challenge to the program.

- How to translate the experience into the undergraduate education. We have not yet decided how to translate the MBA experience into the undergraduate education. It has been decided that in the freshmen year an integrated one-year long course in entrepreneurship is going to be included, which is going to somehow replicate the four MBA modules. This will give our freshmen students an overall perspective of what they will find later on and will give a perspective to the functional areas.

- How to extend the experience to the other disciplines within UDD. So far this experience has been incorporated and designed inside the management school. The question is how to translate this experience into the other faculties of the university, given that the entrepreneurial spirit is a paradigm not only of management. Entrepreneurship is to become a keystone at UDD; therefore, it makes sense to include that same flavor, whatever the program of study involved.

Final Remarks

UDD is very pleased with the new format and with the new methodology of the MBA program. The best way to finally evaluate the change is with the experience of the coming graduates, still 9 months away. The process of change has been smooth. The experience of the four Babson professors involved in the program has also been quite good, not only in terms of teaching but also in regard to the way UDD has handled the process.

CHAPTER 9

Educating Entrepreneurs

Edward G. Cale, Jr.

There is an old saying that entrepreneurs are born, not made. If this is true, then universities all over the world—where there is a growing focus on entrepreneurship research and education—are wasting their time and money. However, although there are born entrepreneurs who need little if any help from higher education to inspire their achievements, I firmly believe that universities can help to promote and develop the entrepreneurial capabilities of many students who would not otherwise be drawn to entrepreneurship. The trick is to find methods to awaken the entrepreneurial spirit, which often lies dormant, and then to give the students the tools, experiences, and environment that allows them to successfully act on their newfound dreams.

To better understand what universities can do to help develop entrepreneurs, we must first understand just what it is that we are trying to create. To do so, I would like to start by giving an overview of how we conceptualize the entrepreneurial process at Babson College. But before I do so, I should make a few comments about Babson College.

Founded in Wellesley, Massachusetts in 1919 by Roger Babson, an entrepreneur himself in the financial services sector as well as a candidate for president of the United States, Babson College is a private college providing undergraduate and graduate degree programs as well as executive education services, all in the area of management and business administration. With slightly more than 3,000 students, roughly equally divided between the undergraduate and graduate programs, Babson College has been known for many years as a leader in research about and teaching of entrepreneurship. During the 1990s, Babson College was consistently recognized as one of the top two or three leaders in entrepreneurship education by a variety of ranking organizations.[1] Although these rankings have surely meant that Babson College has attracted a disproportionate number of entering students interested in entrepreneurship, the vast majority of students are pretty typical of the normal students entering highly selective schools of management in the United States. In other words, despite our reputation, the majority of students entering Babson College do not come to us with the specific goal of starting their own businesses upon graduation.

And now on to how we conceptualized entrepreneurship at Babson College. Although there are many definitions of entrepreneurs, entrepreneurship, and the entrepreneurial process, Jefffry Timmons, a pioneer in the study of entrepreneurship, developed one of the seminal models for thinking about the entrepreneurial process. In one simple illustration, Professor Timmons captured the essence of the entrepreneurship process, as shown in Figure 9.1.[2]

The entrepreneurial process involves identifying an opportunity for an entrepreneurial venture, building a team capable of executing the opportunity, and obtaining the resources necessary to carry forth the venture. The proper shaping of the opportunity by the team requires creativity in envisioning a new product, new market, or a new distribution channel for an old product. Obtaining the resources for the venture, which usually come from external sources, requires strong skills in communicating the potential of the opportunity to those in control of the resources. Building the team and uniting it with the resources requires leadership skills on the part of the entrepreneur. Finally, at the core of the whole process is the business plan: the conceptual model for the pro-

Figure 9.1
Entrepreneurial Process

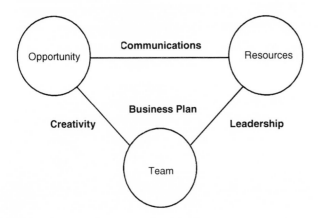

duction, marketing, distribution, human resources, alliances, funding, and other requirements to drive the venture forward.

At Babson, we sometimes summarize the above process with a one-sentence definition of entrepreneurship. "Entrepreneurship is a way of thinking, reasoning, and acting that is opportunity obsessed, holistic in approach, and leadership balanced."[3] Although the process model of entrepreneurship talks to analytical skills that one would expect to see in a business program at a university, this one-sentence definition of entrepreneurship interjects human qualities, such as the passion of obsession and ways of thinking and acting.

Taken together, the process model and definition of entrepreneurship seem to require a complex set of human attitudes, approaches, and skills. The list certainly includes the following qualities.

- The ability to analyze the market, human resource, financial, and production requirements of an opportunity;
- Leadership skills;
- Communication skills;
- Teamwork skills;
- Creativity;
- Passion;
- Action orientation; and
- Holistic, cross-functional thinking.

Traditionally, schools of management have prided themselves on and have typically emphasized the analytic skills they build into their graduates in such fields as marketing, finance, operations, accounting, human resource systems, and information technology. Some schools, particularly in recent years, are paying some attention to leadership, teamwork, and communications skills. However, for the majority of schools, the teaching of analytic tools and frameworks remains as the core educational thrust.

Table 9.1 summarizes the components of entrepreneurship that are normally addressed and not addressed in "traditional" business programs. Obviously, any given undergraduate or graduate program will fall somewhere between emphasizing only the traditional skills and covering all skills, both traditional and entrepreneurial in bent. One characteristic that does not appear either in the process model or in the definition of entrepreneurship, but which most people would associate with entrepreneurship, is the required willingness of the entrepreneur to take substantial risks in pursuing his or her venture. Therefore, I have added that characteristic to the table.

Table 9.1
Entrepreneurial Traits versus Management Education Programs

| | Touched on in Some | Focus of Traditional |
Not in Traditional Programs	Traditional Programs	Programs
Creativity	Leadership	Analysis of finance, marketing, production, human resources, etc.
Passion (obsession)	Communications	
Action orientation	Teamwork	
Holistic, cross functional thinking		
Risk taking		

I have placed three issues in the middle category. Leadership, teamwork, and communications surely receive some attention in traditional business programs, but are typically treated as subjects to study, not activities to practice and hone. One caveat is necessary: Table 9.1 is a static table but the situation in schools of management is always in a state of flux. It is a fair statement to say that 20 years ago, most schools of management in the United States emphasized only the analytical skills addressed in item one. Since then, schools have generally been bringing in, with varying speed and energy, the nontraditional skills on the left-hand side of the table.

Thus, it would appear that some schools of management are increasingly paying attention to the wide array of skills that support an entrepreneurial student. Babson College, however, can be distinguished from most other schools of management in our whole-hearted embrace of *all* of these skills. Starting in 1992 with a radical redesign of our MBA program and then in 1996 with a similar reengineering of our undergraduate program, the faculty and administrators at Babson College sought to create the most innovative, entrepreneurial environment that we could. Ten years into the process we are still constantly questioning and refining what we have created, but we appear to be approaching our goal of creating the overall environment we were seeking.

In the following sections, I describe the programs we have implemented, and which we continually try to improve, to help our students become more entrepreneurial. However, what makes Babson College rare, if not unique, is the emphasis we place on entrepreneurship throughout the college. Entrepreneurship is:

• A way of thinking and acting which we build into our core courses;

- A part of the greater Babson environment of student life and co-curricular activities; and
- A discipline in which students can major by taking specific entrepreneurship courses.

Thus, a student who is majoring in entrepreneurship at Babson is benefiting from the synergy of three overlapping forces. Pictorially, the entrepreneurial environment at Babson might be represented by the Venn diagram in Figure 9.2.

Historically, entrepreneurship first emerged at Babson as an elective major in which students could take courses. At this time, the overall environment of the college, and certainly the core curricula, were not particularly supportive of entrepreneurship. With time, however, the broader Babson community began to realize the power of entrepreneurial thinking, whether a student planned to start his or her own business or not. With this realization, both core courses and the overall environment have evolved, particularly in the last 10 years, to be directly supportive of the entrepreneurial approach.

I have divided the rest of the chapter into three sections. In the first, I describe the various ways in which we have created an environment conducive to entrepreneurial thinking, as well as the inclusion of entrepreneurship into the core curricula. In the second section, I list and briefly describe the specific courses we offer in entrepreneurship. To my way of thinking, creating the environment is at least as important as the specific courses. The last section contains a brief overview of Babson College's programs in Latin America.

I do not present Babson's program as a model or ideal program—it works for us in our environment with our students. It can certainly be improved upon. Parts of it would not work in other contexts. However, it does show

Figure 9.2
Synergies from Three Overlapping Forces

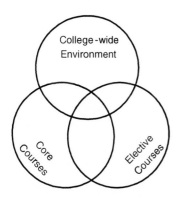

the type of thinking and program that can play a role in increasing the entrepreneurial interest and capabilities of a group of students.

Creating an Entrepreneurial Environment

Case Studies Approach

For several reasons, we strongly believe in the case studies method for business education. The purpose of our business courses is to give students the tools, inclination, and desire to make real and difficult management decisions. Business cases, in presenting students with real business problems, focus both the faculty and the students on issues that are relevant to solving actual business problems. Superfluous material, which may be of academic interest but is not useful in business decision-making, quickly falls by the wayside.

More importantly, the case method puts responsibility squarely on the students. Their grades depend on their ability to understand, analyze, and communicate their recommendations on a daily basis. In making the class student-centric, not faculty-centric, the case method both challenges and empowers students to take control and action in difficult situations. In most cases, the student must go beyond an analysis by proposing and justifying a recommended action plan.

Finally, the case method sharpens the students' oral communication skills. They must justify their analyses and recommendations both to their faculty and to their fellow students. In a well-run case classroom, students will learn from each other as well as from the faculty member. With its emphasis on decision-making and action orientation, the case method clearly supports valuable entrepreneurial skills.

Foundation Management Experience

All first-year undergraduates at Babson take a yearlong course called the Foundation Management Experience (FME). The course covers a general introduction to management concepts (accounting, marketing, finance, production, human resources) as well as the use of information technology to support these business functions. Running throughout the course is a 20-part case on the start-up and growth of an entrepreneurial venture. The students learn their business concepts as those skills are needed in the case company they are studying. However, a vital central element of the course is that students must develop and propose a start-up venture of their own. Through a series of presentations and class votes, each class of 60 students winnows the potential ventures down to two proposals, which the students will then launch with financial support from the college. For a 4-month period, the students run their businesses, for which they develop accounting, control, marketing, and human resource systems. At the end of the year, the students shut down their businesses, repay their start-up costs to the college, and then turn over all proceeds to a charity of their choice. In the 8-year history of FME, the more than 100 student business have never failed to repay their start-up costs and transfer some sum of money to their charity organization.

Clearly, the FME student business gives all undergraduate students at Babson a first-hand experience of being entrepreneurs. They are responsible for putting together a team, their business plan must win the approval of their classmates, they must justify their start-up resources to the faculty, and then they must successfully manage their business through the inevitable challenges and problems they encounter. Beyond teaching the basic business skills, FME requires students to be creative in initiating their companies, it hones their communications skills (they make roughly 20 presentations during the course), and it gives them a first-hand experience in teamwork.

Intermediate Management Experience

All of the traditional core management courses are presented to students in a three-semester sequence called the Intermediate Management Experience (IME). What separates IME from traditional business programs is that the experience is highly integrated. Business functions are not taught on a stand-alone basis. Through cases, students are confronted with real and complex business problems that involve the need to make decisions across functions. When a student makes a marketing decision, he or she is forced to deal with the financial, human resource, and production implications of that decision. Thus, the central thrust of IME is to make students think in a holistic, integrative method, as befits an entrepreneur.

Most traditional business programs do not integrate functional thinking until students take a business policy course in their final year. IME, with a strong focus on strategy from the beginning, forces the students to think of the big picture from the beginning of their experience. Also, as with FME, there is a strong reliance on case analyses, class participation, and student-centered activities.

Founders' Day

Every year, Babson sets one day aside to focus on and honor entrepreneurs. Typically, three entrepreneurs are invited to campus, regular classes are cancelled, and the students spend the day listening to talks by all three entrepreneurs and then attend seminars for give and take with their entrepreneur of choice.[4] Faculty, business leaders, the media, and other outsiders are invited to attend all activities. Thus, during the inter-active sessions, the discussions can become quite lively, with students, faculty, and others asking the entrepreneurs for their insights or posing, at times, other challenging questions. In dedicating the day to entrepre-neurship, we are sending a strong message to our students about the importance that Babson places on entrepreneurs. We hope that both the talks as well as the seminars will inspire our students to follow in the steps of the honorees.

Student Businesses

Babson has a strong history of encouraging student-run businesses, and provides low-cost space for students wishing to develop their own ideas. Students businesses have included Web-page development, laundry pickup and delivery, video rental services, storage space rental, vacation planning and scheduling services, and a range of other goods and services. Just last year, the business of one Babson student collected more than $20 million in revenue running a telephone calling card business targeted at international students who attend U.S. universities (www.nobelcom.com). Obviously, in encouraging students to start and run their own business, Babson both attracts and develops potential entrepreneurs. There is no doubt that the entrepreneurial ventures of the few also whet the appetite of their less-entrepreneurial classmates.

Business Competitions

Whereas the introductory undergraduate and graduate courses in entrepreneurship both have at their core the requirement that students develop and present a business plan for starting a new venture, there are also two free-standing business plan competitions on campus.[5] Graduate students can compete in the Douglass Foundation Graduate Business Plan Competition. Undergraduates may enter the John H. Muller, Jr. Undergraduate Business Plan Competition. In either case, the plans pass through a series of faculty and outside evaluations, narrowing the num-ber of plans to a final few. The finalist plans are then judged by a panel of entrepreneurs, venture capitalists, and faculty, who award cash pay-ments to the best plans in each class. The winning graduate plan receives a $20,000 cash award as well as $40,000 work of in-kind services (legal and patent fees, communications, etc.). The second place plan receives $10,000 in cash and the third place plan receives $5,000 in cash. The winning undergraduate plan receives $5,000. It is not uncommon for the winning plan, particularly in the case of the graduate student plan, to receive substantial additional start-up funds from angel investors or ven-ture capitalists.

In addition to the formal business plan competitions described above, Babson also holds an open annual competition called the Rocket Pitch. Entrepreneurs are invited to pitch their company or concept in 3 minutes or less to a large audience of students, faculty, entrepreneurs, investors, and service providers. While the Rocket Pitch does not require the same level of development as the formal business plan competitions, they provide the entrepreneurial student with a venue for early testing of the concepts. The purpose of the Rocket Pitch is to force the entrepreneur to focus his or her opportunity, and to teach him or her to quickly and succinctly deliver the critical differentiating elements of the business idea. The event also provides an excellent opportunity to meet and network with a large group of quality entrepreneurs, investors, and service providers. We believe that by involving the extended Babson entrepreneurial community early in the development process of these business opportunities we can provide important feedback and advice to each entrepreneur.

Field Experiences

Babson has a number of ways in which we require or encourage students to have active field experiences where they work in or for existing businesses. In spending time in actual businesses, the students are forced to develop an action orientation, to sharpen their communication skills, and to further develop their team-building capabilities. As with the use of the case method in their classes, field experiences help the students to focus on those skills and capabilities that are most important in a business environment. Fieldwork also gives the students valuable real-world experience, which they can use to build their resumes, as well as provides them with an opportunity for networking. Although there is no requirement that students seek field experiences in entrepreneurial companies, many do. Babson's field-based activities include the following.

- *Internships:* We strongly encourage all students to engage in employment internships during the summer breaks between academic years. Fully 97% of the MBAs in the full-time, two-year MBA program obtain internships between their first and second years. Of those students, more than 40% intern in small start-up organizations. Undergraduate participation in internships is, similar to the MBA participation, nearly 100%. Because the undergraduates have three summers in which to intern, they will often have experiences in both start-up as well as established organizations.
- *Mentor Companies:* Closely related in benefits to internships, all first-year MBA students have a year-long relationship with a Boston area

business, called a Mentor Company. Working in teams of five or six, the students use their Mentor Company as a source for data to be used in their marketing, finance, and accounting classes, which helps to make the learning process more grounded in reality. In addition, the students perform a competitive analysis of their Mentor Company as well as their Mentor Company's closest competitor. Out of this analysis, the students develop an action-oriented strategic plan for their company's future.

- *Management Consulting Field Experience:* Both undergraduate and graduate students are offered management consulting field experience (MCFE) opportunities. In a MCFE course, a team of four to six students and one faculty member engage in a semester-long consulting experience with a real business. Typically, the students are brought into the business at the beginning and presented a problem that the business is facing. The students will then schedule additional meetings with personnel from the business, conduct research, interview customers, consult with other faculty members, and, over the semester, develop an analysis and recommendation package for the business client. At the end of the semester, the students present an oral and written report to their client with their recommendations and findings.

In a typical MCFE project, the faculty serves only as a resource to the students, and do not play the role of primary consultant. MCFE projects have a strong impact on students, requiring them to display high professional standards and assume full responsibility for their recommendations. The students learn teamwork, action orientation, and communications skills, all the while gaining experience in a real business environment. Usually, client satisfaction plays a substantial role in the grade that students receive for the project. Most students at Babson take at least one MCFE project during their program.

Creativity Training

First year undergraduates as well as MBAs are required to participate in exercises designed to improve or free up their creative instincts. At the undergraduate level, corporate creativity trainers engage in a multiple-day process of encouraging students to think creatively about the FME business they will be proposing. At the graduate level, the students are required, in the first month of their MBA program, to develop a team creativity project. With projects ranging from painting to poetry and from dance to theatre, the students are often engaging in such acts for the first times in their lives. Although they are usually resistant to the project at the beginning, they often report a real sense of achievement and teamwork when they are through. Although there can be no proof that the activity improves their creativity, it is our hope that it does so.

The Coaching Program for Teamwork and Leadership

To help them develop as managers and entrepreneurs, all undergraduates go through two coaching experiences, where Babson alumni spend time interacting with the students and then give them constructive feedback and coaching. The purpose of the First Year Coaching Program is to build the students' awareness of effective leadership, teamwork, decision-making, listening, and oral communications and to give them some sense of how they are doing in relationship to those competencies. On the other hand, the Advanced Coaching Program, which takes place during their third year, is designed to help the students prepare for and think about their future professional lives.

Willingness to Take Risks

Although Babson College does not have a formal program to encourage our students to be risk-takers, one could argue that the encouragement of risk-taking is college-wide. Clearly, by placing entrepreneurship at the center of what we do in the college, we are paying homage to risk-takers in general. In the classroom, faculty will often value a creative or novel approach of one student over the more mundane approach of another. We continually urge students in teams to work on their weaknesses, not their strengths—to take risks for the reward of bettering themselves. At the graduate level, after several years of tinkering and analysis, we have settled on a grading system that does not penalize students for taking risks; rather, we hope, it encourages them to do so. Significantly, more than half of our entrepreneurship faculty have start-up business experience, many of them having failed once or more before finally succeeding. We teach both the failures and the success, to learn from both and to not fear the former.

Admissions Policy

One of the purposes of our admission policy at Babson is to ensure that all entering students meet our rigorous requirements. However, of equal importance, we want to assemble a student body of well-rounded people who have a high potential for teamwork, creativity, and leadership. Thus, we require all students applying for admission, both at the undergraduate and graduate levels, to complete an interview with admission staff or Babson alumni. Thus, we often decide to reject an applicant with high academic standards who doesn't possess the attitudes and inclinations that we deem essential to our community.

Courses in Entrepreneurship

The following courses are offered to undergraduate students at Babson College. I have not listed graduate courses, which, for the most part, are similar but more intense then their undergraduate counterparts.

- Entrepreneurship and New Ventures concentrates on how new businesses are started. Objectives are understanding entrepreneurs, seeking and evaluating opportunities for new ventures, and gathering resources to convert those opportunities into businesses. There are two projects: each student interviews an entrepreneur, and teams of students write a business plan for a new venture they have chosen.

- Financing Entrepreneurial Ventures covers various aspects of financing an entrepreneurial venture. Major topics include attracting seed and growth capital from sources such as venture capital, investment banking, government, and commercial banks. Among the issues discussed are valuing a company, going public, selling out, acquisitions, bankruptcy, different legal forms of organization, partnerships, and taxes.

- Managing Growing Business focuses on building and managing a firm from the day it opens for business until it is relatively mature. Through readings, cases, and guest speakers, students analyze case studies on companies as they progress from birth to adulthood. The case analyses require the students to understand the range of challenges and problems facing growing companies, and to develop an action orientation toward addressing those problems.

- Entrepreneurship: The Key to Family Business Success is designed for students interested in the issues, problems, and unique concerns of family business involvement and management. It is intended for those who are affiliated with family firms or interested in doing research on a family firm. The course draws heavily on the personal experiences of students in the class. Cases, videos, readings, and guest lectures focus on critical aspects of family business management. The course is organized around the following themes: understanding the family business systems theory, culture, and stages of evolution; individual development and career planning; management of family structure, conflicts, and relationships; and organizational issues including succession and estate planning, strategic planning, and formalizing the firm. All students write papers based on family business research.

- Entrepreneurial Field Studies is a practical course in which students work in the field, individually or occasionally in pairs, on real entrepreneurial projects. Students will apply concepts that they have learned in class by either implementing their own business plan or working with an entrepreneur on a specific project. Students are guided by the instructor, but are expected to provide most of the initiative to complete the project. Contact time for this course will be split between in-class sessions and out-of-class individual meetings with the instructor.

- Corporate Entrepreneurship explores the challenge of maintaining or re-igniting an aggressive, opportunity-driven entrepreneurial spirit within complex established organizations. The course deals with such issues as corporate venturing, creativity, and aggressive growth within large organizations.
- Venture Capital, Angels, and Incubators concentrates on developing knowledge of the early-stage private equity markets: venture capital in seed and early stage, the rapidly growing angel marketplace, and professional incubators both nonprofit and for-profit. Most of the class is taught from the entrepreneur's perspective. Materials provide future entrepreneurs with a detailed understanding of how private investors analyze, think and behave so that the entrepreneurs can understand the founding, fund-raising, and strategic assessment process of the investing entities. The venture capital portion follows the traditional venture life cycle, that is, fund raising, investing and liquidity. Course materials describe venture capital history and trends, the inner workings of a venture firm, choosing the right venture capital partners, valuation, and deal structure. The section of the class on angels covers how to find the right angel, the investing process, and the relationship between the entrepreneur and the professional accredited private investor. Several classes focus on incubators and their strengths, weaknesses, role in the funding chain, and a review of both physical and virtual incubators.
- Introduction to Social Enterprise Management is about the opportunities and challenges of using students' managerial skills and entrepreneurial talents creatively and appropriately to help solve social problems and to make a difference in the lives of others. To that end, we focus on organizations with an explicit civic mission or social purpose, from well known nonprofits like Habitat for Humanity, National Foundation for Teaching Entrepreneurship, and City Year to widely regarded for-profits like Ben & Jerry's, Newman's Own, and Timberland. Course materials include readings, cases, and films (where relevant). Periodically throughout the semester, leaders of social enterprise organizations will join the class to explore the subject matter in more detail and from a practitioner's perspective. The chief aims of this course are to (1) provide a historical context for considering social

enterprises, (2) engage participants in institutional efforts to create a good society through direct exposure and experience with the work of these organizations, (3) develop the skills and competencies necessary to respond positively to the managerial challenges faced by these organizations, and (4) prepare participants for leadership roles in their communities. Entrepreneurship Comes of Age: Introduction to Social Enterprise Management is offered as a four-credit entrepreneurship elective to upper-level students who have completed all management core requirements.

- Marketing for Entrepreneurs provides an in-depth study of entrepreneurial marketing stratifies and techniques. The course examines how start-ups or small to medium sized businesses with distinct needs market within limited budgets. The course compares conventional marketing to "guerilla" marketing where hands-on, creative methods are key to survival. These unconventional marketing tactics also can serve to revitalize larger businesses. Classes focus on case discussion and guest speakers; assignments include a team project.

Latin American Programs

In recognition of our leadership position in the teaching of entrepreneurship, Babson College has for years been running the Price-Babson program to help train interested faculty from around the world on the development of entrepreneurship education. In January 2003, Babson College sponsored a similar program, the Babson Fellows program in Santiago, Chile, to share with colleague from throughout Latin America our differing views and experiences on entrepreneurship education. More than 60 entrepreneurs and educators from Argentina, Brazil, Chile, Colombia, Ecuador, Mexico, and Peru attended. In the near future, we intend to run case-writing and case-teaching workshops throughout Latin America, as well as encourage the building of an academic network throughout the hemisphere for research and teaching on entrepreneurship.

Notes

1. *U.S. News and World Report's* "America's Best Colleges" named Babson College's undergraduate program number one in entrepreneurship in 1995, 1996, 1999, 2000, and 2001, Babson's graduate program number one in entrepreneurship 1994–2001; *Financial Times* ranked Babson College number two in the United States in entrepreneurship in 2002; *Success* magazine ranked Babson College number one in entrepreneurship in 2001.

2. Timmons, Jeffry A. *New Venture Creation: Entrepreneurship for the 21st Century.* New York: Irwin/McGraw-Hill, 1999.

3. Ibid.

4. See http://www2.babson.edu/babson/Babsoneshipp.nsf/Public/members for a list of entrepreneurs honored in the past.

5. For more information, see http://www2.babson.edu/babson/Babsoneshipp.nsf/Public/muller.

CHAPTER 10

The Application of Project-Oriented Learning on the Development of the Entrepreneurial Spirit in Undergraduate Students: The Case of ITESM in Mexico

Alexandra Solano, Angélica Mora,

and Pedro Márquez

During the last decade and since the abandonment of a centralized economy and the adoption of a free market development approach, Mexican universities have emphasized to their students the development of business-oriented skills, attitudes, and values. Specifically, the Instituto Tecnológico y de Estudios Superiores de Monterrey (ITESM), the largest private higher education institution in Mexico, has encouraged the development of entrepreneurial spirit in students of all degrees (graduate and undergraduate) by constantly transforming its business curricula into making entrepreneurship one of its institutional trademarks.[*]

---

[*] For ITESM, *entrepreneurship* means the development of those skills, attitudes, and values required for the successful launch and administration of business projects at the small and medium-size enterprise level.

Although ITESM's first organizational effort to emphasize the formation of entrepreneurs appeared in 1988, 45 years after its foundation, when it introduced entrepreneurship courses as electives for most of its undergraduate programs, it was after a large consultation with stakeholders conducted in 1995 that ITESM increased its relevance and renewed its instructional profile. Overall, it modified its entrepreneurship instruction model and made entrepreneurship more than an elective course–it became a compulsory element of all its engineering and business programs. In order to adapt its strategic entrepreneurship programs to the changes seen in Mexican society (new educational approaches and the recent technological advances in information systems and telecommunications), in 2000 ITESM incorporated the project-oriented learning (POL) approach as its central pedagogical strategy for the development of its students' entrepreneurial education.

This chapter describes the ITESM experience in redesigning the traditional theory-based entrepreneurship course into an innovative course supported by a hands-on teaching pedagogy, such as POL. It is suggested that POL has led to a more effective learning process and an improved entrepreneurial spirit among the student population, particularly with those students previously skeptical of the entrepreneurship program's added value. It is also argued that the self-motivation, education, and confidence that support a POL-based course design are appropriate for the instruction of future Latin-American businessmen.

In order to set up the context under which entrepreneurship education becomes strategic for a developing country, this chapter initially describes the current socio-economic conditions prevailing for small and medium-size enterprises (SMEs) in Mexico. Next, ITESM's origin, evolution, and commitment to innovative higher education are reviewed. The chapter also describes the most important features of its new educative model and the process under which different didactical techniques were introduced into ITESM curricula. Thereafter, it focuses on the introduction of POL in the entrepreneurship program and signals the initial results obtained from a first generation of POL-formed entrepreneurs. Finally, the implications and future research agendas for the use of POL to form entrepreneurs in Mexico are discussed.

The Small and Medium-Size Enterprise in Mexico

Mexico's abandonment of the import substitution industrialization development strategy in the mid-1980s and the adoption of a frank free market paradigm have been widely studied during the last decade (Weintraub 1992; Urquidi 1997). The new development strategy, adopted since the administration of president Carlos Salinas (1988–

1994), transformed the manufacturing sector from a group of heavily regulated factories focused on satisfying the local demand while enjoying the protection of enormous trade barriers against foreign competitors into one suddenly exposed to diverse economic pressures such as globalization, domestic open markets, and increased competition.

According to official figures provided by the National Institute of Statistics, Geography and Informatics (INEGI), small and medium-size enterprises (SMEs) (firms with fewer than 100 employees and annual revenues up to $250,000), made up 97.1% of the manufacturing industry companies in 2001 (INEGI 2001). For the same report, SMEs averaged 4.9 employees, in contrast to the 642.3 employees averaged by large-size enterprises. Within the SME sector, the small enterprise (SE) (fewer than 15 employees and annual revenues of $25,000) sector had the largest participation in the industrial (92.2%), commercial (93.7%), and service (97.5%) sectors. Approximately half the SMEs are concentrated around seven cities located at either the Mexico-U.S. border or around Mexico City.

Due to its economic relevance as a source of employment (53%), GDP contribution (42%), and regional development (INEGI 2001), the importance of SMEs has a strategic role on the country's development. However, as Beltran and Leroy (2001) discuss, Mexican SMEs have been losing ground to transnational corporations on the basis of larger economic efficiencies and stronger strategic management. Arroyo and Erosa (1999) concluded their study on SME competitiveness by identifying two concrete challenges faced by the Mexican SME after trade liberalization. First, SMEs require the rapid modernization of their production processes and development of economic efficiencies. Second, they need to transform their administration from traditional family-based empirically trained management into one conducted by trained professionals skilled in administrative disciplines, such as strategic management, marketing, and accounting.

ITESM Origins and Historical Evolution

ITESM is a private higher-education institution established in 1943 with the objective of providing innovative top-quality technical training to the industrial city of Monterrey in northern Mexico. Since then, it has evolved into the largest and most prestigious institution of its kind in the country, with a current total student population of 100,000 students enrolled in over 60 undergraduate and graduate programs in fields ranging from of engineering, business, and humanities to medicine and marine and agricultural sciences. In a short period of 6 decades, ITESM counts 150,000 alumni and has grown into a complex array of 34 campuses covering all regions of the Mexican geography. At present, it provides medium-high, higher, and continuing education through traditional (also known as in-person learning) and virtual (long distance and online) programs in approximately 50 cities in Mexico and Latin America. By 2002, it had developed exchange, dual, and joint degree programs with approximately 100 universities worldwide, holding at some of its schools international accreditations such as ABET (Accreditation Board for Engineering and Technology), AACSB International (Association to Advance Collegiate Schools of Business), IFT (Institute of Food Technology), NAAB (National Architectural Accrediting Board), and SACS (Southern Association of Colleges and Schools).

Through the years, the number of students, professors, and programs has grown at a rapid pace, adapting to the constant socio-economic changes seen in Mexico during the twentieth century. At its core, it has kept its commitment to Mexico's national and regional development. Although an important number of graduates have assumed important public roles such as governors, cabinet members, congressmen, and congresswomen, the largest share of alumni have turned to the private sector by either participating as executives of large commercial firms, by assuming control of their families' own businesses, or by having founded and succeeded at their own enterprises (Perez 2001). Although ITESM has introduced new programs in the humanities and social sciences during the last decade, it remains as a purveyor of highly trained individuals interested mostly in private sector ventures.

The Stakeholder Consultation and the New Educative Model

According to its president, Rafael Rangel (Perez 2001), after a successful 50-year-long educational experience employing a traditional approach (mostly based on lecturing), in 1995 ITESM decided to undergo a serious reevaluation of its raison d'être. Its institutional commitment to educative innovation suggested pondering the new environmental and educational trends, evolving student needs, and the possibilities that technological progress in information systems and telecommunications produced. A nationwide consultation with approximately 10,000 representatives of its major stakeholder groups was carried out, requesting the input of hundreds of students, alumni, teachers, employers, intellectuals, and federal and local authorities among others. The consultation explored diverse issues such as ITESM's role in the nation's development, its educational objectives, and its appropriate pedagogical strategies. As a result, four central challenges were identified and incorporated into its mandate: the need to create jobs, increase Mexico's international competitiveness, participate in the national democratization process, and improve its educational model. The resulting mission commands it to "educate individuals who are committed to the social, economic and political improvement of their communities and who are internationally competitive in their areas of specialty; and to carry out research and extension relevant to Mexico's sustainable development" (Perez 2002).

At the core of the strategies conceived to reach its mission was the restructuring of the teaching-learning process across all its academic programs, based on two major principles: constructivist learning and experiential learning (Brooks and Brooks 1993; Wilson 1996). The constructivist paradigm assumes that knowledge cannot be transmitted from one individual to another, but instead has to be built by the student. According to this model, the teacher assumes a different role from a simple transferor of knowledge into a much more complex facilitator of the learning experience. A professor then becomes a designer of learning experiences, processes, and environments. The student becomes responsible for his or her own education by building meanings through the discovery, comprehension, and application of such knowledge to problems, projects, experiences, and so forth. Through constructivist learning students improve their cognitive structure and modify the attitudes, values, and principles that guide their behavior and professional performance. In a nutshell, for the ITESM educational model, "the student's learning is not based on the isolated development of its cognitive capacities, but the total change of its social-affective cognitive system" (Perez 2001).

This innovative student-centered educational model is based on five features.

1. Advocates self-study (the gathering of information from different sources) as the most important student attitude toward a life-long learning experience.

2. Adds explicit formative objectives to the learning objectives included in traditional syllabi. Learning is meant to be significant for each student and evaluated according to its formative impact.

3. Provides access to a technological platform through which students can access up-to-date international information banks and networks.

4. Focuses the instructional process on the students, particularly on the development of specific abilities, attitudes, and values required to perform as individuals conscious of the national reality, while remaining competitive internationally.

5. Cultivates collaborative learning through innovative didactical techniques such as POL, problem-based learning (PBL), and case studies.

The educational model is supported by four didactical techniques that are employed according to the nature and objectives of each course. Although PBL was generally adopted by engineering courses, POL and case teaching have spread throughout the business and social science programs. POL is an adapted model of PBL developed by Aalborg University and Twente University (Kjersdam and Enemark 1997). Both PBL and POL represent a constructivist approach to instruction, requiring students to articulate through the development of projects and the solution of custom-designed assignments, an interdisciplinary array of skills from math, language arts, fine arts, science, and technology (Green 1998). Through POL and PBL, the theoretical contents of traditional courses such as accounting, project planning, or marketing strategy are combined with other practical forms of education to motivate students to work collectively on projects or problem solution.

> This approach allows students to become actively engaged in their learning experience. The instructor takes a back seat while students initiate, facilitate, evaluate, and produce a project that has meaning to them. Instead of creating and directing exercises for passive students, instructors become coaches, facilitators, and sounding boards for student ideas (Green 1998).

Consequently, these pedagogical approaches reduce the gap between theory and practice, a dilemma frequently faced by business schools, particularly entrepreneurship programs, throughout the decades. As Terry Thode (2002) from the George Lucas Foundation concludes, students who learn about the real-life added experience provided by POL education become more skilled to analyze, comprehend, and solve personal and professional problems at hand. Simply put, students enjoy their learning process if such a process makes sense. Consequently, POL lends itself to many disciplines. It provides participants the opportunity to become active in what and how they learn, while building intrinsic motivation and specific problem-solving skills and attitudes. Based on the successful introduction of these pedagogical approaches, ITESM adopted POL as the most appropriate didactical technique for the instruction of its entrepreneurship program.

Project-Oriented Learning and the Entrepreneurship Curricula

As described earlier, the entrepreneurship curricula assumed a strategic role for the new educative model. An improved formation of entrepreneurs demanded the introduction of pedagogical techniques and instructional approaches capable of efficiently providing students with the capacity to identify, analyze, and endeavor on new business ventures.1 Through the new POL-based entrepreneurship program, ITESM attempts to generate creators of a new society instead of passive spectators, and concentrate its education efforts in the production of agents of social, economic, and political change.

Before the instructional redesign process initiated in 1995, undergraduate students could register in an entrepreneurship course as an elective course toward their business degree. Such a course required students to put together a business plan under the guidance of a general management instructor. The course design did not attempt to bridge theoretical and pragmatic knowledge, focusing instead on the development of specific managerial (planning, directing, executing, controlling) and communication (group work, conflict solution, collaboration, persuasion, public relations) skills. Throughout the course, students spent long hours building small projects. Projects were presented at a fair and evaluated before a jury of invited businessmen. Awards were given to the best projects in different categories. Frequently, student projects consisted of minor spin-offs of existing products already in the market, remaining forever unrealized.

Then, during the consulting process of 1995, a significant issue was raised by the academic community: What can be done for the entrepreneurship students to make their experience a learning process nearer to reality, capable of awaking the entrepreneurial spirit in them and helping them produce feasible and sustainable projects? The obtained result aimed at a complete overhaul of the entrepreneurship program.

In order to develop a pedagogical experience throughout so that students could learn-as-they-do and induce an entrepreneurial spirit, a new entrepreneurship course was designed. The new course was initially tested as a pilot project at the Mexico City campus in 2001. The structure of the course was based on eight key elements:

1. Aimed at developing a particular set of skills, attitudes, and values for the whole student population, regardless of their academic programs;
2. Guided by instructors employing coaching techniques;
3. Organized through teamwork and collaborative-learning pedagogical techniques;
4. Grounded on the circumstance of the small and medium-size Mexican enterprise;
5. Centered around strategic decision-making;
6. Based on solid but simple theoretical content;

7. Backed upon the systematic assessment of qualified teachers;
8. Strengthened by a technological platform such as Lotus Notes/Learning Space or Blackboard.

Having the professor act specifically as a tutor, the course was focused on developing managerial skills, technical abilities (investigation, analysis, synthesis, and problem solution), and communication skills (teamwork, public resolution of conflicts, collaboration, persuasion, and relations). For it to become possible, student independence was emphasized by allowing them to select their own teammates, type of project to develop, and collaboration processes. They were also requested to elaborate the team's project plan, indicating phases, responsibilities, and strategies according to their own learning styles and needs. During the development of their plans, limited assessment was provided by their tutorial professor. At no time did the professor remind students of their commitments; he kept to the role of a close and experienced adviser, providing feedback only at student request.

On the first class day, a custom-made student's guide was distributed to each participant. The manual contained the course objectives; basic rules such as evaluation percentages and handout dates; activity schedule; satisfaction conditions; and legal regulations to be observed by the students. Despite the large set of project and supervision liberties, business plan assessments were frequently requested and working schedules closely followed by the participants.

In order to ensure all the course's content be covered by all students, a minimum content in the structure of the business plan was requested as compulsory. The contents were reviewed during assessments with teachers, who assumed a consultant role by providing suggestions instead of instructions. A series of workshops, case studies, and conferences with additional contents were conducted in parallel to support the self-directed learning process. These support activities were designed to further advance specific abilities and skills, such as selling, product development, and negotiating. These activities were completely elective for the teams. When accepted, one restriction had to be obeyed: only one of the team members could participate in each event. During evaluation periods, all teammates shared the grade obtained by their group member. Evaluations were based on each business plan, inducing equal member commitment and collaboration. To reduce the possibility of free riders, a share of the grade was given by teammates through co-evaluation.

Due to the whole course's nature, teamwork (and not work division) became, through the students' own experiences, compulsory. Inconsistencies along the business plan's different stages were strongly penalized among teammates. Students forced themselves to work coordinately and cooperatively throughout the whole project. Consequently, pressure increased and conflict became common, as so many people interacted so closely and constantly.

Throughout the course, students had access to three technological platforms. First, Blackboard offered a technological tool for communication and consulting. It contained all the curricular contents of the subject and allowed communication between students and teachers as well as among rival teams. Second, the entrepreneur program's Web page was destined to provide specific information on workshop logistics, Web conferences, and special events. Finally, the Incubatec WebPortal, allowed access to the external world, mostly through a selection of national and international advisers, including teachers, entrepreneurs, investors, and governmental and nongovernmental organizations.

Once business plans were finished, the best projects were chosen by the whole student group to represent them at a larger competition with other groups. This phase turned out to be central for the pedagogical process because several issues became relevant. Do the students believe their projects have market potential and sustainability? How committed have they become with them? Are they capable of articulating and conducting a fierce defense of their projects? Are they capable of accepting the superiority of other projects? How well do they handle defeat or triumph when exposed to the community?

Both the WebPortal and the project Web sites allowed for an entrepreneur forum, through which the students exposed their projects before selected judges (commonly executives belonging to the entrepreneurial environment), who selected the 10 winners. The winners of this last stage qualified to participate at a formal business dinner with potential investors. The Entrepreneurship Program Gala allowed the best students to expose their projects and establish direct contact with diverse sources of funding, both private and public. At the gala, 10 projects received recognition as "Best Enterprise and Business Plan" for the term. Only a few carefully selected projects entered the next stage: formal business incubation supported by ITESM resources.

As it may be observed, the balance is very positive in favor of the technique's application to stimulate the entrepreneurial spirit of youngsters. The latter leads to questions about assessment (evaluation method in POL); students' work load in relation to other subjects; teachers' training to accomplish their role as tutors; and the previous definition of a life and career plan that defines a series of objectives, generating the expectation in the students of making them materialize in a real enterprise. However, other issues come into play, such as the impact that business plans developed with this technique will have over the nation's SMEs.

Conclusion

Continuity of business plans carried out by the students in the academic course has been realized in the application of the POL technique, which is intended to stimulate them to create businesses and become active generators and motors of economic growth. To grow is to change, and to promote this change is what the entrepreneurship program of ITESM seeks. However, transformation implies breaking paradigms in the educational model, from the perspective of the administrative structure, as well as from the teacher-student relationship inside the classroom. For many years, it has been spoken about the change from *teachers* to *tutors,* and from *receptive students* to *proactive* ones. But these changes mean a slow process of learning and adaptation. POL experience can act as an excellent catalyzer to achieve the desired change.

Motivation and enthusiasm are key attitudes for POL to reinforce students' knowledge. It is expected that, with such attitudes, they feel stimulated not only to create new enterprises, but also to prepare themselves by developing managerial, technical, and communicative skills. Equally, with the knowledge obtained using this technique, the quality of the business plans clearly surpasses that produced by students who learn under a traditional didactical program. Direct contact with experts, businessmen, and investors is another element that helps alumni's expectations in relation to the entrepreneurship program to be highly positive. Considering the carrying out of the project as a race that will take them to the creation of self-owned enterprises constitutes an additional motivator that has been integrated into the technique in its adaptation to Mexico.

Taking into account that over 90% of Mexican enterprises are micro and medium size, it may be considered that the impact in the mid and long term will be the development of students who are successfully integrated into society as the future entrepreneurs of the country, generating employment and national wealth. Mexico, as an emerging developing economy, has a wide horizon of opportunities to elevate the competitiveness of new enterprises, which are capable of surviving in an environment of constant change. By the end of the development of the entrepreneurs course, students have the capacity to work under pressure, in teams, and to challenge themselves to create the needed opportunities. Goethe said "Success is about being prepared to take advantage of opportunities when they appear."

References

"Active and Productive Learning in Higher Education: Students and Producers vs. Consumers." 1995. SEFI seminar proceedings, Curriculum Development Group, November 1–3.

Aebli, H. 1991. *Factores de la enseñanza que favorecen el aprendizaje autónomo.* Madrid: Narcea.

Arroyo, P., and V. Erosa. 1999. "Micro and Small Mexican Firms: Survival, Subsistence or Global Competitiveness?" Working paper, University of Texas at Austin.

Beltran, O., and C. Leroy. 2001. "Las MiPyMES, reflexiones desde una perspectiva de management." Unpublished paper, ITESM–University of Miami, Mexico.

Brooks, J. G., and M. G. Brooks. 1993. *In Search of Understanding: The Case for Constructivist Classrooms.* Alexandria, VA: Association for Supervision and Curriculum Development.

Bruner, J. 1988. *The Process of Education.* Cambridge, MA: Harvard University Press.

Fierro, C., B. Fortoul, L. Anad Rosas. 1999. *Transformando la práctica docente: una propuesta basada en la investigacion-accion.* México: Paidos.

Green, M. 1998. "Project-Based Learning and the GED." *Focus on Basics* 2, Issue B, (June). Available online at http://gseweb.harvard.edu/~ncsall/fob/1998/anson.htm.

INEGI. 2001. *Anuario estadístico de los Estados Unidos Mexicanos.* Aguascalientes: Instituto Nacional de Estadistica, Geografia e Informatica.

Kaufman, R. 1990. *Planificación de sistemas educativos.* México: Trillas.

Kjersdam, F., and S. Enemark. 1997. *The Aalborg Experiment: Project Innovation in University Education.* Aalborg, Denmark: Aalborg University Press.

Oblinger, D., and S. Rush. 1997. *The Learning Revolution: The Challenge of Information Technology in the Academy.* Bolton, MA: Anker.

Thode, T. *The Power of Project-Based Learning.* San Rafael, CA: George Lucas Educational Foundation, 2002

University of Kansas. 2002. "Project Based Learning: What Is It?" at http://www.4teachers.org/projectbased.

Urquidi, V. *México en la globalización; condiciones y requisitos de un desarrollo sustentable y equitativo.* FCE. Mexico DF: Fondo de Cultura Economica.

Weintraub, S. 1992. *Transforming the Mexican Economy: the Salinas Sexenio.* The National Planning Association, Washington, DC: National Planning Association.

Wilson, B. 1996. *Constructivist Learning Environments.* Englewood Cliffs, NJ: Educational Technology Publications.

Note

1. For ITESM, *entrepreneurship* means the development of those skills, attitudes, and values required for the successful launch and administration of business projects at the small and medium-size enterprise level.

CHAPTER 11

Promoting Entrepreneurship: The Successful Experience of the Universidad Del Pacífico, Peru

Sergey Udolkin Dakova, Adriana Paredes and Veronica Pardo

The purpose of this chapter is to show the impact of the decision made in 1985 by the university authorities to replace traditional teaching methods with more practical ones. The results of this decision are reflected in the positive change in the profile of the business administration and accounting school graduates. The new methods aimed to motivate students, through programs and courses, to become future entrepreneurs and visionary professionals, to be flexible, organized, proactive, and socially responsible, so that they become capable of creating job opportunities for themselves as well as for others.

Structures Promoting Entrepreneurship

Background on the University

The Universidad del Pacífico is a private, nonprofit university created in Lima, Peru, in 1962 by a group of businessmen. The Company of Jesus assumed the direction of the university since its inception with the cooperation of the Asociación Fomento de la Investigación y Cultura Superior (Association to Further Research and Higher Culture) (AFICS) entrepreneur group. The organization later changed its name to Asociación Civil Pro Universidad del Pacífico (AproUP).

We are reputedly the best university in Peru for the three major areas of concentration that we offer: business administration, accountancy, and economics. In the last semester, 2002-II, we had 1,494 students: 605 in business administration, 116 in accountancy, and 773 in economics.

School of Business Administration and Accounting

The School of Business Administration and Accounting was born in 1969, when the Universidad del Pacífico decided to separate the single program in economic sciences into two academic programs: the Academic Program of Economics and the Academic Program of Business Administration. Later, in 1976, it created the Academic Program of Accounting, and in 1984, with the combination of these two last programs, the School of Business Administration and Accounting was born. The School of Business Administration and Accounting has different ways of fostering interaction between the academic and the business world and promoting enterprise creation.

1. The Business Management and Development Center (CGDN) was created as an agency to stimulate business. It targets business persons and investors both in Peru and abroad with the aim of providing them with information, developing business contacts, networking, and supporting the development of strategic alliances. Through its business portal on the Internet (www.upbusiness.net), the CGDN provides up-to-date information on investment projects, business opportunities, international competitive bidding, export fairs, and a directory of alliances. It has established important strategic alliances with major international networks such as the Pacific Basin Economic Council[1] (PBEC) and the International Center for Entrepreneurship and New Ventures[2] (ICEVED).

2. Recognized business persons working for Peru's major companies comprise an advisory committee. They advise the Dean of the School of Business Administration and Accounting in matters related to the study programs and the students' training. By means of this committee, the school keeps up and tightens the bonds established with the business world, in order to enhance the study program with real-life experience and to keep abreast of the needs of the business environment.

3. A Program of Integration and Visits to Companies (PIVE) was designed with the purpose of expanding student knowledge on the state of affairs of companies and let them be aware of the potential of business firms in provinces as well as in the international environ-

ment. The program seeks to enrich and to complement the academic education of the student with the practical knowledge provided by the companies.

4. A management-consulting center provides services to companies in the public and private sector. It was created to assist government agencies and private enterprises and other institutions requiring temporary advisory services from experts in analysis and problem solving in the areas of strategic planning, management, and business development. The center provides assistance in the areas of strategic planning, management, finance, accounting, market research, production, applied information technology, human resources, internal control, total quality, and process reengineering, among others.

5. At the Research Center at the Universidad del Pacífico (CIUP), the professors and students of the School of Business Administration and Accounting carry out research on current, interesting subjects to cooperate in the generation and communication of knowledge.

6. Through the Integrator II course, students are connected with a real company to attain advising and consultancy work. Upon completion, students will have an integrated vision of all the areas of the accounting profession based on practical experience.

7. By means of an entrepreneurship course, the school seeks to develop in students the abilities to create and innovate, as well as the capacity to integrate all the knowledge acquired during their university careers, and put it to use in the preparation and support of a business plan. Business plans developed by our students are submitted to investor groups in order to promote their implementation.

8. The Enterprising Spirit Promotion Office acts as an agency linking investors and alumni, leading to the creation of new companies. It has a database containing about 500 business plans developed by students since 1991. Throughout the year it organizes various activities such as fairs of business ideas, business plans competitions, and presentations by alumni at investment forums.

Entrepreneurial Experience

In this section, we explain how the School of Business Administration and Accounting of the Universidad del Pacífico develops the entrepreneurial spirit in students.

Management Training Program

During the 1980s, there was a national concern about the future of university students because of the serious economic and social crisis that

Peru was going through. The economic situation in 1985 was the following: unemployment rate, 12%; underemployment rate, 54%; inflation rate, 158% (it reached 7,649% in 1990). Besides, the country was beleaguered by lack of foreign currency for importing inputs, equipment, and reserves; constant increases in costs; continuous blackouts caused by terrorist attacks; and catastrophic damage due to natural phenomena.

Under these circumstances, the School of Business Administration and Accounting made the decision in 1985 to include the Management Training Program (PEG) that required students to set up a company, individually or in association with another student. At the end of the program the measurable results yielded by the new company were evaluated in order for students to obtain the bachelor's degree.

The PEG was a tool to promote entrepreneurial spirit, which facilitated the creation and development of an entrepreneurial project that made it possible for students to become part of the decision-making process, while simultaneously being involved in administrative, legal, social, cultural, and economic aspects.

The PEG intended to verify the proper absorption of the knowledge acquired by students during their education, as well as to measure their ability to apply it in a complete and efficient manner. Likewise, the PEG sought to evaluate the students' creative, promotional, and managerial skills, appraising their skills as professional administrators or accountants, and their teamwork skills.

In order to achieve such goals, the students had to conceive and execute a business project. Thus, the participants were required to launch a company under any of the legal forms and in any economic activity sector. Upon 6 months' operation of the business, it had to produce verifiable results, even though this did not mean that the business should produce economic benefits for the operation period. In addition to the economic results, the evaluation took into consideration criteria such as the company's portfolio of products; its position with regard to competition; its management, operation and internal organization; and the social impact of the activities performed, as well as its forecasts. The evaluation was based on the following factors:

- Adequate combination of initiative;
- Promotion, management, and direction abilities;
- Operating efficiency demonstrated in terms of the input-output ratio;
- Viability and verified possibility of success of the company in the future;
- Anticipation of eventual effects of unforeseeable political and legal factors and the handling of these;
- The verified social impact of the project.

The PEG was in effect until 1991, when the new national government launched the automatic baccalaureate, and later on it became an option for obtaining the professional degree. From 1985 to 1999, the PEG realized the following achievements:

- One hundred ninety-five former students enrolled in the PEG and incorporated 150 enterprises;
- Seventy-five percent of these former students are still managing those enterprises or have set up other companies;
- The PEG was an effective contribution that contended with, within its possibilities, the professional unemployment and underemployment problem;
- The PEG contributed to the improvement of the curricular structure of the business administration and accounting programs and to the enrichment of their contents by linking academic projects and the business world;
- The PEG improved the professional qualifications of students since participation in the program was a general requirement.

Course on Entrepreneurship

Because the School of Business Administration and Accounting did not want to lose its drive to encourage students to set up their own businesses, the course on entrepreneurship was included in 1991 as a requisite for obtaining the bachelor's degree. Until the end of 2002, 463 business plans were prepared in the following economic sectors: agriculture, agricultural-based industry, production, tourism, services, fishery, commerce, and technology.

The students of the School of Business Administration and Accounting must take the course on entrepreneurship during their last semester. This 16-week course, which demands from students the preparation and defense of a business plan, is aimed at developing their innovative and creative skills, and their capacity to integrate the knowledge acquired throughout their career. Throughout it, students learn to detect and evaluate business opportunities in the different sectors of the economy. Table 11.1 outlines the topics covered in the course.

Groups of students develop the business plans. Throughout the course, students receive guidance from the professor in charge of the course, in addition to the advice of other professors specializing in different areas such as operations, marketing, foreign trade, human resources, market research, agribusiness, e-business, and tourism, among other subjects. The investment involved in these business plan proposals from 2000 to 2002 ranges from $6,505 to slightly over $24,000,000.

Table 11.1
Entrepreneurship Course Structure

Topics	Classes
Analysis of the business idea (6 hours)	Class 1: Techniques for detecting business opportunities (3 hours) Class 2: Presentation of business plan per group (3 hours)
Analysis of the business sector (9 hours)	Class 3: Theory (3 hours) Classes 4 and 5: Presentation of the analysis per group (6 hours)
Market research (21 hours)	Class 6: Market research techniques (1.5 hours) Class 7: Estimating demand (1.5 hours) Classes 8 and 9: Presentation of market research design (6 hours) Classes 10 and 11: Presentation of estimating demand per group (6 hours) Classes 12 and 13: Presentation of market research results (6 hours)
Strategic plan (6 hours)	Classes 15 and 16: Presentation of strategic plan per group (6 hours)
Marketing plan (6 hours)	Classes 17 and 18: Presentation of marketing plan per group (6 hours)
Operating plan (6 hours)	Class 19 and 20: Presentation of operating plan per group (6 hours)
Accounting and financial evaluation (21 hours)	Class 21: Costs, budget and taxes (theory) (3 hours) Class 22: Finance–Cash flow statement, income statement, balance sheet, funds required (3 hours) Classes 23 and 24: Presentation of budgets (6 hours) Classes 25 and 26: Presentation of financial evaluation per group (6 hours)
Advice (6 hours)	Classes 27 and 28: Advice on presentation (6 hours)
Total hours = 81	

The evaluation of business plans is conducted by a board of judges comprised of three professors from different specialties. The aspects considered in the evaluation are creativity and innovation in the proposed business and the ability to sell and defend the proposal; the benefit and impact of the business on society; and the business skills required by the project.

The following figures show the economic sectors in which business plans were developed between 1992 and 2002. According to the graphic, in every year except for 2000, service was the economic sector with the greatest number of business plans, followed by production until 1996. However, it is important to note that since 1995, agricultural-based industry and tourism started to increase, obtaining more business plans that offered development areas outside Lima. In 1995, agricultural-based industry absorbed 9% and tourism got 16%, whereas in 2002 the first one obtained 23% and in 2001 the second one 23%. In 2002, the most important economic sectors were agricultural-based industry, 23%; services, 21%; production, 19%; livestock, 16%; tourism, 7%.

From the time when the Office of Entrepreneurial Spirit was set up at the end of 1999, some business plans were made by request of a third party that suggested students prepare business plans in tourism and agricultural-based industry. These economic sectors, together with services, became two of the most important being developed as of the year 2000.

Figure 11.1 shows the percentage of agriculture-based business plans developed from 1995 to 2002. Regarding the agriculture sector, there are three reasons that explain the increase in the number of projects developed in recent years. The first reason is related to the lack of support provided to the development of this sector by the Peruvian government under President Alberto Fujimori during the 1990s. Second, seminars on agribusiness were incorporated into the curriculum of the School of Business Administration and Accounting in 1999. Finally, that same year, the Agribusiness Consultative Council was created. This

Figure 11.1
Business Plans Developed for Agriculture-Based Industry

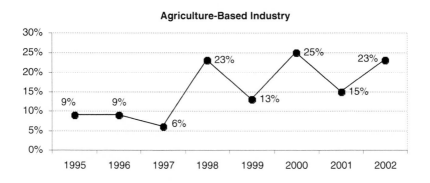

Figure 11.2
Business Plans Developed for the Tourism Industry

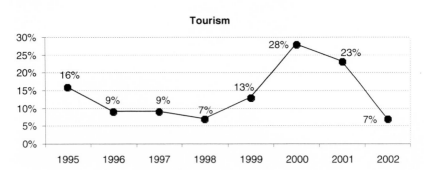

council was founded by leading Peruvian businesses in this field, and it is headed by the Universidad del Pacífico.

Many students that enrolled in the agribusiness seminar worked on a market research project that they could then use as input for the business ideas they would develop later in the entrepreneurship course. Likewise, real ideas that could be developed in the course were presented through the Agribusiness Consultative Council.

As Figure 11.2 indicates, the number of business plans developed for the tourism industry increased in 2000 and 2001. The main explanation for the increase in business plans was the rise in the number of foreign tourists coming to Peru due to the eradication of terrorist activities in the country. It is worth mentioning that Peru is highly valued in the international market for its history, its landscapes, and the opportunities it offers for those interested in enjoying adventure holidays. Another determinant was the fact that the government-decreed laws that favored the development of this sector. In 2002, there was a decrease in the number of business plans related to this sector because of students' preference for agriculture industry with relation to exporting.

Finally, Figure 11.3 shows a decrease in the development of business plans in the service sector. This is because students prefer to develop plans in the sectors mentioned earlier.

Office of Entrepreneurial Spirit

In 1999, the School of Business Administration and Accounting created the Office for Entrepreneurial Spirit Promotion (OFEE) with the purpose of connecting students with the business sector for exchanging experiences, sharing knowledge, and achieving strategic alliances that may lead to the setting up of investment projects. In order to achieve this goal, the OFEE carries out various events or activities every 6 months.

Figure 11.3
Business Plans Developed for the Service Industry

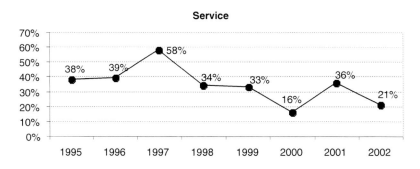

The OFEE has 463 business projects available to students and alumni of the university, as well as listings of local and foreign investors. This information may be found in the university's business Web site at www.upbusiness.net. The OFEE also stores and publicizes business information prepared by various institutions on sectors such as tourism, industry, and commerce, among others. The OFEE performs the following activities.

1. The business fair: At the beginning of each academic semester, the university invites governmental and nongovernmental organizations, enterprises, and private investors to the Fair of Business Ideas. At this fair, future investors present their business ideas to the students so that those who become interested can develop them into business plans during the entrepreneurship course. The investors finance the elaboration of the plan, giving approximately $750 to each group. About 20 people present their ideas to students each semester. The governmental organizations, nongovernmental organizations, and companies for which students have made business plans are shown in Table 11.2.

2. The business plan presentation: The best business plans of the entrepreneurship course are presented to a selected group of businessmen at the end of each academic semester. The purpose of this activity is to look for investors interested in joining, financing, or buying the projects.

The Virtual Exhibition of the Business Plans

At the end of each academic semester, the best business plans are shown through the Internet business portal of the School of Business Administration and Accounting, at www.UPBusiness.net, in search of investors who are interested in joining, financing, or buying the projects.

Table 11.2
Companies Participating in the Business Fair

Type	Name	Function
Governmental Organizations	MITINCI	Ex-Ministry of Industry, Tourism, Integration, and International Commercial Negotiations.
	PROMPERU	State entity in charge of making Peru's image and reality known through the promotion of investment and tourism.
	PRISMA	Reinforces capacities of poor groups of people so they can reach their own economic and social development.
Nongovernmental Organizations	Care Peru	The poorest Peruvian communities solve their most threatening problems.
	Save the Children	Save the Children Sweden works in Peru for protecting and promoting the rights of children and teenagers.
	Instituto de la Montaña	Develops ecosystems in mountains.
	Convenio Unes	Promotes activities that contribute to improving the lives of people from Junín.
	Instituto Rural Valle Grande	Contributes to the professional and human development of farmers and livestock farmers from the Peruvian central coastal region and highlands of Yauyos.
	Caritas del Peru	Belongs to Caritas International, which is a confederation of 154 Catholic relief, development, and social service organizations present in 198 countries and territories.
	Cosude–Peru	Swiss Agency for Development and Cooperation is Switzerland's International Cooperation Agency within the Swiss ministry of foreign affairs. The aim of development cooperation is to alleviate poverty by helping people in partner-countries help themselves.

Table 11.2 (Continued)
Companies Participating in the Business Fair

Type	Name	Function
	PROSOYA	Association for the promotion of Support to Youth and Community Development, which has the following main objectives: the protection of the environment, the provision of support to children and youths who are orphans and in a difficult economic situation, and the promotion of production and ecology.
Companies	Yanacocha Mining	Yanacocha Mining is a prestigious mining corporation with an important place in the history of mining investments. Newmont is the world's leading gold producer, with operations in the five continents, and Buenaventura is Peru's leading producer of precious metals. In 2001, Yanacocha reached a production of 1,902,489 ounces of gold.
	Quimica Suiza	Quimica Suiza has the strongest market share for pharmaceutical products and dyestuffs, and it is a leader in other mass consumption and industrial products in Peru.
	Sonesta	Sonesta Posada del Inca belongs to Sonesta International Hotels Corporation with lodges in four departments of Peru.
	Rainforest Expeditions	Rainforest Expeditions is a Peruvian ecotourism company founded in 1992 with the objective of combining tourism with environmental education, research, and local sustainable development to support the conservation of the areas where they operate.
	Clinica San Pablo	Private clinic that specializes in people with nervous system problems, alcoholism, and drugs.

Business Plan Contests

Contests are organized to encourage undergraduate and graduate students who have successfully finished the entrepreneurship course to develop business plans and to obtain funds to finance them. Examples of these contests are the ones organized by the Santander Bank and Union Vida Pension Fund Administration, among other national and international contests. Since this course is for the last semester of the Business Administration and Accounting Program, some participants have already graduated and others are still studying at the university.

Media Strategy Involving Entrepreneurs, Students, and Alumni

The university coordinates with different media (newspapers, radio and television) for publicizing business plans, with the purpose of obtaining financing for implementing them. During the years 2000 to 2002, the business plan trends were the following:

- Ten percent of the business plans were set up by former students themselves;
- Services, agricultural-based industry, and tourism are the economic sectors with the greatest incidence of business plans, with a percentage of 23%, 19%, and 19%, respectively;
- All the business plans incorporated the social impact of the project;
- Thirty-two percent of the business plans were elaborated for a third party;
- The remaining plans stemmed from the students' own ideas.

It is important to highlight that 71% of the business plans developed refer to the coastal zones, 20% to the mountains zones, and 9% to the forest zones (see Table 11.3). The increase in the number of business plans in the mountains and forest is important because these two regions have the highest percentages of poverty according to the national surveys done by INEI. Students' projects represent the creation of potential development centers in these regions.

Successful Business Plans

Management Training Program Results

The La Viga S.A. Company constitutes a real example of the good results obtained through PEG. Diego de la Torre, Diego de la Piedra and Carlos Marsano organized this business on November 14, 1988, under the legal form of a corporation, which began operations on February 14, 1989. At the start, the company was engaged in the distribution of

Table 11.3
Business Plan Development by Region and Economic Status

	Coastal Region	Highland	Rainforest
Extremely Poor	6%	46%	40%
Poor	33%	26%	29%
Not Poor	61%	28%	31%
Total	100%	100%	100%

Source: INEI

cement for one of the five largest cement factories in Peru, Cementos Lima S.A. This activity is regularly carried out in two forms: cement delivered to the work site, and cement delivered to the plant.

La Viga S.A. rapidly positioned itself among the companies with larger sales, thanks to the development of an innovative strategy which involved providing a differentiated service to its clients, based on punctual deliveries and better customer care.

This company offered clients additional benefits, such as advisory services, discounts, and financing facilities, among others. In less than a year, the company became the market leader and was ranked among the 5000 top companies in Peru.[3] As a growth strategy, the partners decided to diversify the range of products offered, thus initiating the marketing and distribution of other construction materials such as bricks, iron, dry concrete mixtures, and construction aggregates. In 1997, it became one of the largest construction steel distributors of the Peruvian market.

A point worth noting in La Viga's business strategy is the special effort displayed by the partners to develop among their 53 workers a corporate culture based on quality and excellence, with special emphasis on the social responsibility of businesses. At present, La Viga has a 12% share of the Peruvian market and a 33% share of the Lima market, and its average annual sales exceed 50 million dollars. La Viga is ranked among the 30 socially responsible Peruvian companies. This honor is supported by the systematization of social responsibility strategies and policies, actions in the internal environment, and social actions in the external environment.

Entrepreneurship Course Results

One of the results obtained by the entrepreneurship course is the Inka's Garden company, which trades herbs and spices, mainly with the United States. Miguel Rosales Sepulveda, a former student of business administration, found this business opportunity through the National and International Integration and Visits to Companies Program, and substantiated the competitive advantages of Peru in this sector.

His initial idea was to export oregano into the American market. He developed the business plan in the entrepreneurship course during the second semester of 2001. At the beginning of 2002, he set up the business with a partner; both of them invested their own money. The most important strength that made the company accepted by the foreign market was the confidence transmitted to its clients through its competent post-sale service and their timely filling of the orders. In the long term, this venture is expected to become a recognized trading company.

Currently Inka's Garden is exporting paprika and planning to trade other products like basil and parsley. It has three full-time employees and has generated 25 new employment opportunities. Its monthly sales are $30,000.

Conclusions

The educational approach of the Universidad del Pacífico since 1985 represents an innovative approach in the Peruvian university educational system.

Experience showed that the PEG was better than a thesis or an exam for assessing graduates, because it connected students with the real settings in which they would later have to develop professionally, considering the social and economical situation of the country at the time.

The results of the entrepreneurship course show that graduates master both theoretical and practical information. This is reflected during the course when students integrate and apply the knowledge acquired during their careers in the development of their business plans.

It is also important to mention that thanks to the Office of Entrepreneurial Spirit some students develop projects that are requested by businesses and investors. These projects have more chances of being implemented, and students often participate in carrying them out. Students have also demonstrated that during their research they often develop alliances with persons or institutions that are key to the implementation of the business plan.

In an economically unstable country like Peru, the programs and courses offered by the School of Business Administration and Accounting have become an effective contribution to help solve the country's unemployment and underemployment problems, given that they help form professionals capable of building their own businesses and becoming successful business persons.

Notes

1. For more information about the PBEC, see www.pbec.org.
2. For more information about ICEVED, see www.iceved.com.
3. Peru: The Top 5000, 1990.

CHAPTER 12

Prospects for Teaching Entrepreneurship Online: A Focus on Latin America

John R. Bourne

Interest in entrepreneurship is growing rapidly worldwide, as is interest in online learning. This chapter describes the prospects for teaching entrepreneurship online, with a specific emphasis on what types of delivery mechanisms might be employed. Our discussion will be in the context of the possibility of teaching entrepreneurship in Latin America. In this chapter, the intersection of opportunities in information technology, online learning, and entrepreneurship are examined.

A brief background for the three major areas that relate to the ability to offer entrepreneurship education online in Latin America is provided first.

Background

Information Technology in Latin America

The information technology infrastructure of Latin America has grown rapidly during the last decades. A doubling of the Latin American online population from 10.7 million in 2000 to 25.3 million in 2001 has occurred, and more rapid growth is projected.[1] Prospects for growth are high, especially in Argentina, Chile, Mexico, and Brazil. Jupiter Media

Metrix estimates[2] that by 2005 more than 50 million Internet users in Latin America will connect to the Web through wireless devices. PC sales in the region may well benefit from slumps in the United States and Western Europe. Growth in Info Task adoption in Latin America, including increased computer sales, numbers, and quality of Internet connections, as well as a decrease in telecom costs, is likely to push Latin America toward becoming much more wired in the coming decades despite limitations posed by economic underdevelopment. Given this projection, Latin America will soon be in a position to be able to provide online education to large populations.

Entrepreneurship

The number of new ventures created in the United States is estimated (Spinelli 2001) as engaging perhaps 12 million potential entrepreneurs (Figure 12.1). If one maps the same percent of potential entrepreneurs in the proportionate Latin American market, one finds some 25 million potential entrepreneurs. In fact, the percentage of the population engaged in entrepreneurial activities in Latin America has been estimated to be higher than in the rest of the world. The 2001 Global Entrepreneurship Monitor summary report (Reynolds et al. 2001) indicates that Mexico has 18% of the population engaged in entrepreneurial activities, while only 5% are engaged in Belgium, for example. Hence, the estimate of 25 million entrepreneurs in Latin America could easily be quite conservative. The hypothesis of this chapter is that these numbers create the possibility of their being a robust market for teaching entrepreneurship online. Why online? Because an extensive backbone for teaching entrepreneurship in not in place in Latin America, a suitable way to supply the region appears to be growing the number of instructors and providing linkages with entrepreneurship instruction in North America and Europe. In fact, little is known currently about the potential for online education in Latin America.[3] Various hints have appeared that suggest that online learning will grow rapidly—for example, in Mexico, robust examples of online learning have become active, and specialty education in some areas in Argentina have appeared.[4] Figure 12.1 illustrates the potential number of entrepreneurs in the United States, and Figure 12.2 shows the prospective (conservative) number that might exist in Latin America. As indicated in the figure, if only 1% of the entire market was reached by online learning, that number could approach a quarter of a million people.

Online Learning and the Sloan Consortium

Online learning has become rather well developed in the United States during the last decade, growing from virtually nothing to well over

Figure 12.1
Entrepreneur Market in the United States (Spinelli 2001)

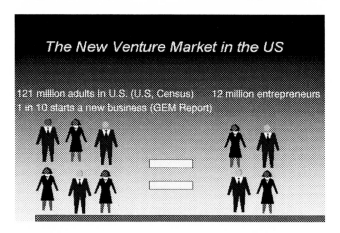

Figure 12.2
Entrepreneur Market in Latin America (Spinelli 2001)

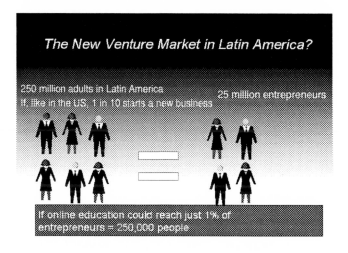

2 million online learners in 2002. Consisting of over 200 institutions, the Sloan Consortium (Sloan-C) is the leader in coalescing knowledge about online learning and promoting quality online education. The mission of Sloan-C[5] is to make education a part of everyday life, accessible and affordable for anyone, anywhere, at any time, in a wide variety of disciplines. Sponsored by the Alfred P. Sloan Foundation,[6] Sloan-C is primarily a consortium of accredited higher education providers and organizations that supply equipment, tools, and infrastructure support to

Figure 12.3
Growth Rate for Online Learning in the United States

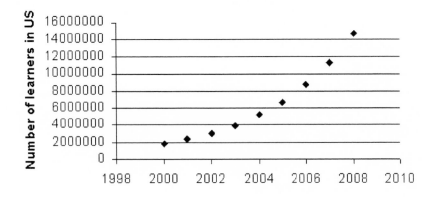

higher education. Sloan-C encourages collaboration, sharing of knowledge, and effective practice to improve online education in the areas of learning effectiveness, access, affordability for learners and providers, and student and faculty satisfaction.

Recent projections for growth in online learning populations by Sloan-C have been at the 30% per year level.[7] Figure 12.3 demonstrates a projection for online learner populations in the United States after several years. Of course, the exponential growth projected in this figure will likely decrease in the last part of this decade due to limiting factors in population. However, in Latin American, one can readily imagine a similar growth chart—but starting at close to zero at the current time. Thus, we hypothesize that there are opportunities in this area that can be taken advantage of.

The Methods

In order to take advantage of the potential for online learning in the teaching of entrepreneurship in Latin America, we will first discuss some basic characteristics of online learning and then discuss which models of online learning may prove most suitable for teaching entrepreneurship online in Latin America.

Figure 12.4 shows the typical organization of an online course. Web pages usually include a syllabus, a goals statement, and materials including case studies, laboratory exercises, homework, and other background materials. Of most importance is the discussion area that

Figure 12.4
Typical Organization of a Course

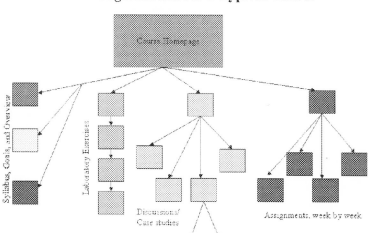

permits students to discuss problems with their instructor. Sloan-C views interaction among people as one of the most important aspects of online education.

Figure 12.5 shows a typical homepage, as viewed from a browser. The benefit to having a page of this type is to organize materials and provide a place for students to return to. Many institutions currently use course management systems that provide this type of interface without having to build the page in HTML. Among the more popular course management systems are WebCT (www.webct.com) and Blackboard (www.blackboard.com).

Figure 12.6 demonstrates how course materials can be organized by having a page that points students to what to do each day of the course. A key finding in online education is that good organization of materials online will help students to not become confused.

Figure 12.7 shows the different types of technologies that are useful for implementing online courses. These include Web pages created with HTML, slides (with audio), simulations, and streaming media (both video and audio). Streaming technology is used for implementing audio and video presentation over a slow communications link (e.g., a telephone line). Microsoft (www.microsoft.com) and Real (www.real.com) make systems for delivery of such presentations.

Figure 12.5
A Typical Homepage

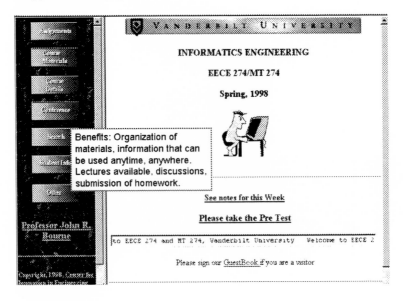

Figure 12.6
Assignments

Assignments by Week

Laboratory Assignments
Listing of Cold Fusion Assignments |
Grading | **Assignment Notes** | *Student Responsibilities*

Go To This Week's Assignment: | 1 | 2 | 3 | 4 |

Benefits: High level of organization; homework submission, immediate feedback, conferencing, extends classroom significantly, examples, presentations

Week of Semester	Reading Assignment: Cold Fusion Textbook and other readings	Assignment
Week 1: Getting Started: Lecture: • Overview • Basic ideas • Conferencing • Demos	CF Reading Assignment: Chapters: 1, 2, 3 (the above chapters are in the Cold Fusion book)	ASSIGNMENT #1: • Review Internet 101 (http://www.aln.org/internet101/) if you feel you have the need. Do not submit anything. • Complete Lab 1 **Submit what is requested in the lab.** Continue working on assignment for the next three weeks, or until the project groups have been formed. • Complete CF Reading Assignment 1 • Begin setting up your own web server, if you have a

Figure 12.7
How Online Materials Are Organized with Technology

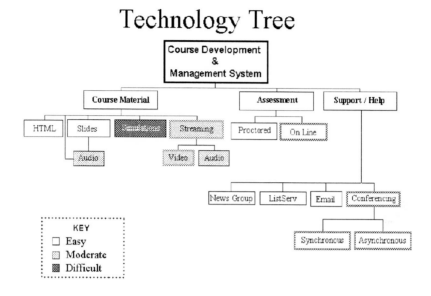

Asynchronous Methods

Probably the most important technology that should be used in online learning is the course conference in which people can rapidly interact. As shown in Figure 12.8, students can reply to each other's messages. The useful contrast is how this method differs from standard e-mail. With e-mail, the instructor is often the locus of questions; in contrast, the course conference provides a way to view all communication among all participants in a course. Students often answer each other's questions, thus saving time for the instructor.

Synchronous Methods

Many people getting started in online learning wish to promulgate tried and true classroom methods, and hence opt for using synchronous methods, as shown in Figure 12.9. Although many systems exist for communication using synchronous tools, most utilize large amounts of bandwidth. Point-to-point synchronous communication between two people usually works relatively well; however, adding many people often reduces communication to a crawl. Pictures become jerky and audio desynchronized. For populations in which high-speed communication is not available, synchronous communication is not recommended. This

Figure 12.8
A Course Conference for Asynchronous Communication

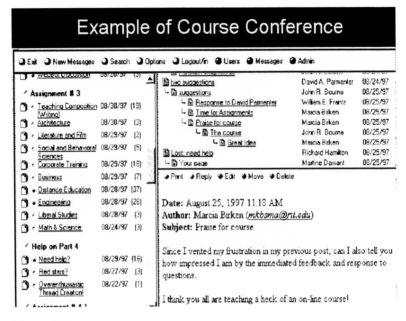

Figure 12.9
Examples of Synchronous Communication (Near Real Time)

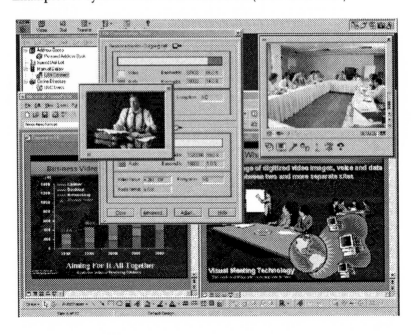

situation would likely occur in Latin American where phone lines are still used in many places for Internet communication.

Finally, we should mention the utility of simulations. Figure 12.10 shows an example of a simulation of an electronics laboratory. Students can use the simulation prior to going to a physical laboratory. Reductions in the amount of time needed in the physical laboratory were demonstrated in this work.

URLs

The Web site with the most relevant information about online learning is at http://www.sloan-c.org. The journal of Asynchronous Learning Networks can be found at http://www.aln.org.

Examples of Methods Needed for Teaching Entrepreneurship

Based on the basic information provided above, we will next address the best ways to provide entrepreneurship education online.

Figure 12.10
Simulation of an Online Laboratory

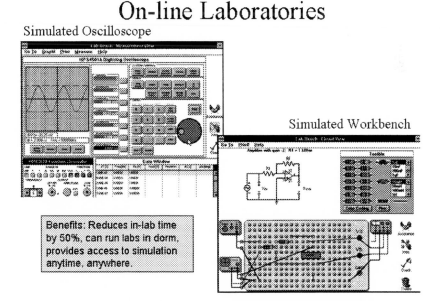

Basic Method

A suitable first step is to build a basic Web page similar to those shown above. An alternative is to purchase a course management system. Due to the high cost of course management systems, our recommendation for neophytes in the area is to try making a simple page using HTML first. This can be done on a PC using an Internet service provider (ISP) with little expense. Many ISPs provide helper systems so that you can accomplish this task with little or no programming required.

Once you have completed a simple page or set of pages for a course, you are ready to populate the course with materials for teaching entrepreneurship. The types of pedagogical constructs that we recommend including are:

- Case-based teaching
- Simulations
- Multimedia
- Discussions with experts

Case-Based Teaching: How Are Cases Best-Used Online?

The case method is synonymous with business education and, indeed, entrepreneurship education. However, teaching cases online is a relatively undeveloped concept. Cases taught face-to-face require intense interaction between a facilitator and a class. Interaction and questioning is a hallmark of the traditional case method. To capture the same face-to-face immediate response interaction is not as possible online, generally due to the lag times for posting responses in an asynchronous conference. Synchronous methods could work for non-collocated groups if the bandwidth would be high enough–this is generally not the case, however, due to the difficulty of supporting groups of 10 to 30 or more. One potential solution is hypothesized below for use in teaching cases.

1. Simulations: These are always good for teaching. For teaching entrepreneurship, team-oriented modules could be written that use materials similar to the Venture Opportunity Screen Guide of Timmons (1999) or the similar materials provided by Kauffman Foundation (see http://www.fasttrac.org).

2. Multimedia: Streamed lectures are especially suitable for use for teaching entrepreneurship. Taking videos of lectures and providing them via streaming media would be a useful method for providing U.S.-derived lectures in Latin America. The cost of providing the lectures is minimal; the cost of producing them is high.

3. Experts at a distance: The teaching of entrepreneurship benefits from visits and discussions with CEOs of successful (and not so successful) new ventures. Although such visits can be secured easily in a major city, access to CEOs is not so easy in remote areas. Hence the bringing of experts from a distance is a useful idea to consider. Experts can be connected via point-to-point video media at long cost and low bandwidth with some success (e.g., using Windows Media, a Microsoft product).

High-Cost Versus Low-Cost Solutions for Online Learning

Do you need really hi-tech solutions for teaching online? The answer is almost certainly no. However, scaling is a problem that must be understood and overcome. Course management systems provide a way to get started with little technical hassle; however, costs are higher than producing Web pages on a small server. There are several high-cost course management systems available for purchase. Two that are used around the world are WebCT and Blackboard. Both require a fairly significant investment in hardware, software, and administration of the systems. Both would work well for you; however, your financial models should demonstrate that the added expense is really justified.

A second expensive solution is the use of streaming video–that is, video that can be viewed over low-speed connections. Various solutions for streaming video are available and work modestly well for low numbers of viewers over good connections. However, is it worth producing streaming video? The following are arguments against it.

- There is little pedagogical value in streaming a "talking head;"
- With streaming video any interaction is essentially nil;
- Interaction is discouraged;
- Cost to produce is very high.

Instructor-led solutions seem to work best for online education. Next, we will examine ways that online education, specifically for entrepreneurship, could be implemented.

Suitable Methods for Starting Online Education in Entrepreneurship in Latin America

A list of things that are likely desired for teaching entrepreneurship in Latin America follows:

- The ability to discuss cases;

- Discussions with entrepreneurs;
- The capability of submitting documents for review (e.g., position papers, business plans);
- Class voting on different scenarios;
- The ability to take positions and argue scenarios;
- Financial presentations.

What are the constraints that limit our ability to achieve these types of activities in the same ways that we do in the classroom? Dominantly, these constraints are:

- Bandwidth—that is, the speed of communications among non-collocated people taking a course in entrepreneurship;
- Limitation number of multiple participants in synchronous communications online;
- Lack of maturity of synchronous method.

Multiple potential solutions exist. Traditional asynchronous conferencing (e.g., using a discussion board such as Vbulletin (www.vbulletin.com) or other similar tools) will work fine for most cases in which voice is not needed. By using a traditional discussion board, one accrues the following advantages:

- Very, very low cost;
- High reliability;
- The ability to accommodate many people.

The disadvantage to the solution is that no voice is included. However, another solution is to use a product called Wimba (www.wimba.com) that provides a voice asynchronous conferencing system. With Wimba, participants can post voice messages, even from a computer connected to the Internet by phone. Figure 12.11 demonstrates the look of the system. In Wimba, to post a message you speak into your microphone and the message is sent to the server where others can listen to the message. Although there is some delay, the fidelity is excellent and should be able to tie together learners with low-speed and high-speed connections. Some delay occurs, but it is hypothesized that such a system would work well for implementing case study discussions.

To teach cases using a combination of methods would likely be a good solution. A written case could be posted on a standard discussion board and something like the Wimba voice system used to discuss the case.

Figure 12.11
Wimba Audio Discussion Board (www.wimba.com)

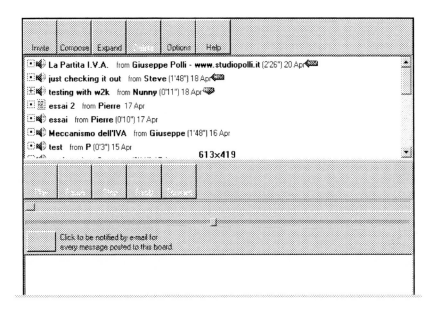

The standard discussion board would capture written comments and voting, while the Wimba system would capture the voice interactions. Writing of business plans would work nicely in the asynchronous collaborative environment provided in Vbulletin, for example.

Discussion

Approaches for methods of teaching entrepreneurship in Latin America are many and varied. The methodology described previously is the author's choice; others would choose other approaches based on preference. The set of techniques described in this chapter have the advantage of creating a simple and inexpensive delivery platform that can be used to try out markets without a large investment. Starting with only a Web server and a few page-creation tools, a conference system, and perhaps streamed audio or video will enable trying out teaching online with a modest investment. The alternative approach of investing in a course management system should likely be taken only when scaling to teaching more than a few hundred people. Above this level, economics of scale begin to appear when course management systems are used.

The Sloan Consortium is ready to assist international schools that are interested in starting online programs.

Acknowledgments

The support of the Alfred P. Sloan Foundation for the Sloan Consortium is hereby acknowledged.

References

Reynolds, P. D., S. M. Camp, W. D. Bygrave, and E. Autio. 2001. *Global Entrepreneurship Monitor.* Summary report. Wellesley, MA: Babson College.
Spinelli, S. 2001. Director of Blank Center for Entrepreneurship, Babson College. Personal communication.
Timmons, J. 1999. *New Venture Creation: Entrepreneurship for the 21st Century.* New York: Irwin McGraw-Hill.

Notes

1. U.S. Internet Council Report, November 2001.

2. U.S. Internet Council Report, November 2001.

3. The author is editor of the Journal of Asynchronous Learning Networks and Director of the Sloan Consortium. Few inquiries about the consortium and fewer papers are received. Currently, only 0.5 percent of the consortium membership is in Latin America (2002).

4. For example, Escuela de Tecnologia Pianistica de Buenos Aires offers piano tuning online.

5. Web access to the Sloan Consortium is available at www.sloan-c.org. On these pages you will find listings of courses offered by Sloan-C members, and you can join the consortium as well. The Sloan Consortium offers an online journal (*Journal of Asynchronous Learning Networks*), workshops, an annual conference, effective practices Web site (www.sloan-c.org/effectivepractices), a listserv for members, and consultation services.

6. Sloan Foundation: www.sloan.org.

7. Study conducted in 2002 via an online survey.

CHAPTER 13

Index for Creation and Development of Knowledge-Based Firms[*]

Gonzalo Jiménez

Scott Tiffin

Repeated studies in the Global Entrepreneurship Monitor Project by international teams led by Babson College and London Business School (Reynolds et al. 2001) have demonstrated that entrepreneurship plays a major role in national economic growth, generation of employment, and the creation of new firms. Porter (2002) has demonstrated the close relationship between a country's entrepreneurial capacity and the Gross National Product (GNP). He estimates that almost 40% of GNP growth in the United States during the period from 1996 to 1999 is due to entrepreneurship. Furthermore, it has been clearly shown that innovation is a key to the success of firms in economies that are growing and changing at an accelerating pace (Stevenson, 2000).

---

[*] This work was financed by the Institute for Latin American Business at Babson College. The research assistance of Macarena Carmona and Gonzalo Muñoz is gratefully acknowledged. Profesor Héctor Hevia provided valuable statistical analysis and suggestions. The authors remain solely responsible for this work.

Innovation based on knowledge—and in particular, scientific and technological knowledge derived through research and development—has a major impact on human development. On one hand, it directly improves human capacities through the improvements it delivers to peoples' lives; and on the other, the innovations constitute an indirect means to attain greater levels of human development through the economic growth and productivity improvements they create.

In developed countries there are many data and empirical studies that analyze the innovative and entrepreneurial activities of firms, but in Latin America this is not the case. There is an urgent need to raise the right questions and generate data about the real extent and dynamics of new firm creation across Latin America. For this reason, we have created an index that attempts to measure the capacity of Latin American cities to create and grow new knowledge-based firms. This index measures some important features of the capability of a city to compete in national, regional, and global marketplaces. It can also be used as a tool of immediate practical utility to analyze how to improve its situation, set up its strategic agenda, and define priorities by helping orient the actions of investors and strengthen the strategic vision of municipal or regional authorities.

Most of the attention of public policy and research for innovation and competitiveness has tended to focus on the national level of countries. However, there is a growing recognition that, especially for entrepreneurship and the creation of knowledge-intensive firms, a great deal of the action occurs in local innovation clusters. (Acs, 2002; Heitor, Gibson and Ibarra, 2002). Promoting such clusters is done most effectively by regional, and, especially, city governments. Our intent with this index is not only to generate data at the urban level that will measure relative performance against best-case benchmarks, but also to create rivalry and competition among cities that will result in new awareness and new investments to improve their capabilities in this critical area.

The idea of highlighting knowledge-based firm creation is a new concept for most cities in Latin America. With dependent economies structured around resource extraction and export, little history of linking university research to the productive sector, and a modest stock of researchers and entrepreneurs skilled in innovation, it is obvious that outside the national (or to a lesser degree, provincial) capitals, many cities will not view themselves as likely candidates for such transformation. It is our contention, however, that cities can be as entrepreneurial in a collective form as individuals can be in starting up their new firms—both can create productive organizations out of very scarce initial resources. The sparking of tremendous local collective energy that creates industrial, artistic, and technological progress in communities has been demonstrated with great clarity by Peter Hall in his massive book *Cities and Civilization* (1998). We hope, with the knowledge that this index provides and the unleashing of a natural instinct for competition, that cities across Latin America will be able to take action that will initiate major changes.

In this chapter, we summarize the model that underlies the index, the methodology of data gathering and analysis, and the principal results obtained by applying the tool to five cities in Chile. The chapter briefly summarizes our work on the first iteration of the index, which we hope to refine and deploy more widely in the near future.

The Model

From the extensive literature that exists on the topic of entrepreneurship, a strong consensus stands out on the identification of the principal factors that bear on the enterprise creation process: opportunities and resources. In addition, it is possible to see in the vision of many experts and institutions a third element that influences the creation of firms, which we conceptualize here as preconditions for change, or the facility of undertaking entrepreneurial action.

The model underlying our index incorporates these three dimensions, hypothesizing that their interaction ultimately determines the capacity of a city to generate firms based on new knowledge. In defining new knowledge-based firms, we have gone back to the original description made by Schumpeter (1934). He highlights the innovation of a product, an industrial process, materials inputs, the creation of new markets, and industrial reorganization. In Figure 13.1, we present a summary illustration of the model, in which are shown the three factors and several principal subcomponents that constitute them. Our design for an indicator strives to balance several different factors. To have any utility, it is essential to choose a structure that is theoretically sound, and indeed provide a realistic measure of the desired phenomena. However, theoretical complexity must not be at the expense of the ability to find the right data in the field that are identical across many countries and regions of Latin America. We have to attain a common data level that allows cities to compare among themselves and against best-practice benchmarks. Furthermore, the index has to be constructed in such a way that it can be easily and quickly understood by busy and nontechnical city councilors, or it will never enjoy wide diffusion. Last, it has to be capable of being created at a cost that is within the ability of most cities in the region to pay for the data gathering and analysis. These successive design criteria definitely result in a product whose value is not based in being at the cutting edge of theory, but, as we will show in this chapter, does provide a good working measure upon which valuable action and further field work can proceed.

Figure 13.1
The Model

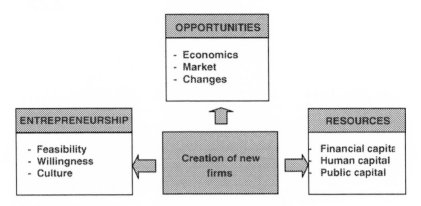

Each of these three major indicator components is built on a hierarchy of subcomponents. First, let us briefly examine opportunities. Opportunities arise from a group of indicators measuring both local and national capabilities. We chose three subcomponents. Economic opportunities reflect the characteristics of the surrounding economy that influence the process of creating new firms. Market opportunities identify the more specific characteristics of local markets, in terms of their ability to generate potentials for commercial exploitation. Opportunities for change (written as simply changes in the diagram) summarize a series of factors that measure the degree of readiness and openness of a locality to sustain a knowledge-based economy.

The second component is resources. This segment of our model describes what is needed to create and grow firms, and is modeled by three principal subcomponents as well. First is financial capital, which attempts to measure the availability, capacity, and quality of the local financial system. Second is human capital, which evaluates the availability and qualification–both real and perceived–of local human resources. Third, we consider public capital, which measures the quality and quantity of physical infrastructure available to support the creation and growth of firms.

Third is the component measuring the ability to create new firms, which we summarize as entrepreneurship. This is made up of feasibility, which evaluates the characteristics of opportunities in the city to develop and grow projects, and also includes the quality of public management and the tradition of cooperation among stakeholders. Willingness measures the current interest or viewpoint on the desirability of new commercial initiatives. Culture is a subcomponent that consists of a series of subjective elements about the city or region and which influence, either in a positive or negative manner, the development of innovative projects in the city.

We now explain the process of measurement and data gathering, and then show how these three main components are weighted to bring them together into a single measure.

Gathering Data for the Index

The index is built on two basic types of data. In the first instance, it is made up of secondary quantitative data gathered principally from public sources. These data include such things as regional economic indicators, infrastructure, and technological capacity. In the second instance, the index is made up of primary information gathered through surveys of stakeholders in each city.

With respect to the quantitative information, indicators were selected that yielded an overview of the economy, the market, and the demographics of the study area, putting special emphasis on variables that are common in similar studies and available in public data sources. In parallel, the questions for the survey were chosen with the objective of obtaining the overall perception of the various social, political, and economic stakeholders in the city, particularly on topics and variables that were not available from other sources. The interviews also supplement the scarce and, at times, nonexistent data from published sources.

To test the theoretical soundness of our model, a group of experts in the fields involved was interviewed to obtain their suggestions about the indicators that should be included and to determine the relative weights of the different components that made it up.

All the variables (71 in total) were normalized to a scale of 1 to 7. In some cases it was necessary to standardize some data to a percentage or per capita scale, in order to measure intensities and not just the results of scale. In this way, we end up with a final numerical value of 1 to 7 for each of the index components. Next, we applied the weightings resulting from the suggestions of the pool of experts, in a simple linear model. A value of $I = 1$ represents the least possible capacity of a city to develop new knowledge-based enterprises, while a value of $I = 7$ denotes the highest capability.

Once the component and weighting interviews had finished and the index finalized in its first complete form, we began qualitative and quantitative data gathering in each city. We interviewed academics, businesspeople, and public managers about their perceptions on the more qualitative or missing data. Eighty-three people were interviewed in person. They were selected in light of their expertise in providing the best possible answers, and by their immediate availability. This highly opportunistic selection of key informants obviously has the potential to contribute a significant bias to our results. However, as will be seen later in this chapter, our results do correspond very closely to actual published material that can be interpreted as showing similar rankings, so we consider the bias in this instance to have been probably not too significant. We asked them about such things as the local market characteristics, dynamism, opportunities, human capital, financial capital, and relevant cultural indicators. Obviously these data will be exceptionally useful in supporting a much wider variety of research and actions if the index were to diffuse across many cities in the region and be carried out on an annual basis.

Application of the Index in Five Chilean Cities: Results

We gathered data and carried out analysis in five cities in Chile: Arica, Iquique, Concepción, Valdivia, and Puerto Montt (see Figure 13.2). They constitute most of the regional population outside the capital city, Santiago, which in a typical Latin American manner is by far larger and concentrates most of the business and intellectual resources of the country. These five cities are, roughly speaking, of the same size and have roughly comparable intellectual and business resources. The results of our first study are summarized in Table 13.1.

As the table shows, the city of Concepción obtained the highest value in the index, which would indicate this is the location that should have, comparatively, the highest capability to create new technology-based enterprises. Following this city, in descending order, are Valdivia, Iquique and Puerto Montt (tied), and finally, Arica.

Concepción is the second largest city of Chile and benefits from eight universities of good quality, and other institutes of higher education. For these and other reasons, it has generated an environment more favorable to the promotion of entrepreneurship. The second place ranking of Valdivia shows the importance again of the existence of universities, which stimulate innovation and entrepreneurship. In fact, this is probably one of the factors that has the greatest influence on the relatively low showing of the city of Arica, which has only one small university.

Next, we examine the values for the three principal subindices constituting the overall single ranking number, as shown in Table 13.2. In interpreting the data, the first point that appears is that the difference in the capability of the cities to generate innovation and new enterprises is not explained by one component alone rom our model, but the combination of all the components, which all have an important role to play.

Figure 13.2
Map of Chile

Table 13.1
The Ranking

City	Index
Arica	3.46
Iquique	3.80
Concepción	3.93
Valdivia	3.87
Puerto Montt	3.80

Table 13.2
Subindex

City	Opportunities	Resources	Entrepreneurship	Index
Arica	3.61	3.37	3.36	3.46
Iquique	4.08	3.59	3.64	3.80
Concepción	3.69	4.04	4.12	3.93
Valdivia	3.81	3.71	4.07	3.87
Puerto Montt	4.05	3.39	3.83	3.80

For example, in the case of Concepción, it is obvious that the principal strength consists of the greater ease of entrepreneurship, which means an environment that is propitious to develop new commercial initiatives and an open disposition of its inhabitants to support and participate actively in such initiatives. It is surprising, however, that this is the city that portrays the least opportunities, significantlybelow cities such as Iquique and Puerto Montt, which both show, relatively, the highest opportunities. In this way, our index begins to supply key directions for further analysis and palliative action, by focusing attention on specific characteristics that support innovation and entrepreneurship. For example, in Puerto Montt, the most important frestriction for the creation of new enterprises is related to the scarcity of resources, since in the other dimensions the city is relatively well endowed. This is probably due to it being the center for Chile's dynamic salmon farming industry, which is now the second largest in the world. Something very similar is happening with Iquique, which presents a high level of opportunities, but these end up being diluted in the final index due to the comparative disadvantage of this city in terms of entrepreneurship. Arica shows low values in all threecomponents of the index, and entrepreneurship appears as the weakest.

The principal strengths and weaknesses of each of the five cities are summarized in Table 13.3. In these data, the relevance of culture and the value framework stand out in Concepción, which facilitate the development of an entrepreneurial spirit. At the other extreme, the relatively low involvement of the people of Arica in terms of interest in new business stands out. This city shows weakness in the willingness factor, which

Table 13.3
Summary of Strengths and Weaknesses

City	Strengths	Weaknesses
Arica	Culture	Willingness
	Economic opportunities	Financial resources
Iquique	Market opportunities	Willingness
	Financial resources	Culture
Concepción	Human capital	Economic opportunities
	Culture	Public capital
Valdivia	Public capital	Market opportunities
	Feasibility	Economic opportunities
Puerto Montt	Market opportunities	Financial resources
	Economic opportunities	Human resources

immediately focuses attention on a point that the city should address if it wants to create new knowledge-based enterprises.

The data show that in the city of Iquique something very similar is happening. This location presents good market opportunities and important financial resources that can initiate commercial ventures, but these capacities are counterbalanced by problems in terms of cultural barriers and by the unfavorable disposition toward innovative projects and business. Valdivia is characterized by a relative weakness in public capital and by the capability of realizing new projects. At the same time, it seems that Valdivia's largest weaknesses relate mainly to the opportunities which the economic and market environments offer. In respect to Puerto Montt, it is quite clear that the city's main strengths are the opportunities offered by the economic environment. However, human and financial resources are its great weakness. These data confirm the central role of human capital that cities dispose for the creation of new enterprises. In this dimension, Concepción significantly exceeds the others, based on the quantity and quality of the centers of higher learning that it possesses.

Correlation with Other Data Sources

Our goal was to construct an index that would be highly correlated with the real patterns of knowledge-based enterprise creation in each city. We now compare our index results with data on the creation of enterprises in the year 2001. These data were taken from the database of Diario Oficial de Chile. Our criteria for selection of knowledge-based start-ups was based on the definition we described earlier, taken from Schumpeter (new firms based on product innovation, process innovation, new materials inputs, new markets, or industrial reorganization).

These data clearly show the index predicts the tendencies toward the number of new knowledge-based companies as well as the total number of start-ups in each city. Concepción was the city that created the largest number of enterprises in 2001, and, at the same time, was the city that generated the largest number of knowledge-based enterprises. At the other extreme, Arica is seen to be relegated to the last position, not only in terms of total creation of enterprises, but in those based on knowledge. The data are tabulated in Table 13.4. We must note, however, that our index attempts to portray the initial creation and subsequent development and early stage growth of knowledge-based enterprises, but the data available from the Official Gazette only allow us to measure start-ups.

Basically, the empirical data confirm the index ranking, except in the case of Valdivia, since this city shows a high index but not such a high real creation of companies. This led us to consider creating a new index to see

Table 13.4
Data on Start-up Firms in 2001

	Index	TCC	KBC	TCC/ 100,000 pop.	KBC/ TCC	KBC/ 100,000 pop.
Concepción	3.93	573	10	260.32	1.75%	4.51
Valdivia	3.87	88	6	64.26	6.82%	4.4
Iquique	3.80	249	7	131.14	2.81%	3.71
Puerto Montt	3.80	258	6	159.51	2.33%	3.71
Arica	3.46	66	0	33.7	0%	0
Total	–	1234	29	129.79	2.74%	3.27

Source: Base de Datos Diario Oficial and INE 2001
TCC: Total Companies Created
KBC: Knowledge-based Companies

we if we should control for the impact of population size. In making this calculation, Concepción keeps its leadership, since the number of new firms created for every 100,000 inhabitants is higher than all the other cities. This new indicator makes Puerto Montt better its own position.

We call this relative index (TCC/100,000) the Propensity to Create Companies, and in our judgment it is a better measure of the real potential for each city.[1] Although a city like Rio de Janeiro may create absolutely more firms than Santiago, this hides the fact that Santiago is likely to be significantly more involved, efficient, and productive, in this area. Since our goal is to extend this index across Latin America and involve not only the few capital cities, but all the provincial ones, it is important we have a means to effect cross-cutting analysis.

To focus more explicitly on the science and technology aspects of innovative entrepreneurial firms, we also propose a modified index to measure the relative weight that knowledge-based firms have in the total firm creation numbers. This new measure we have labeled the Propensity to Generate Knowledge-Based Enterprises. If we examine the column KBC/TCC, it is possible to see that even when Concepción generated a very high number of enterprises in 2001, the relative importance of knowledge-based enterprises is much less than in the case of Valdivia, where it appears that innovation and entrepreneurship play a much greater role (6.82% of the firms created are knowledge-based).

The final index in this table (KBC/100,000 inhabitants) seems to be the best in showing the creation of knowledge-based enterprises per capita. In fact, the ranking generated by the index is repeated exactly by the real creation rate per capita: Concepción, 4.51; Valdivia, 4.40; Iquique and Puerto Montt, 3.71 (note here that these data are once again tied, as we showed before in the index results); and Arica with no firms.

Conclusions

We have designed an index that measures the capability of Latin American cities to create and grow knowledge-based enterprises. Application of this index will help cities measure how they compare relative to other cities in the region in terms of innovative and entrepreneurial potential, and then diagnose strengths and weaknesses, with the goal of implementing changes to further strengthen their competitiveness in a global economy. Some of the data generated are new, and the new focus gives this index the potential to be a very useful tool in the development and application of public policies both at national and local levels, as well as aid the private sector in taking investment decisions and guiding firms to participate more in building local innovation clusters.

In the initial study undertaken in Chile, with five cities, the index showed Concepción as the leader. Its leading position seems to rest on the availability of infrastructure, the strong functioning of the financial system, and the powerful development of educational resources. The results obtained for the other cities point out key differences in their local systems, involving all of the factors making up the index. The advantages represent strengths that each city must take advantage of and the disadvantages are weaknesses that can and should be corrected by means of public as well as private actions.

Modeling such complex phenomena as this is to a significant extent an art, not a science. We are encouraged that the initial test of this model seems to correlate so closely to the data set available, but we remain aware of the limitations of the quantitative data and the qualitative methodology that compares subjective viewpoints in rather uncontrolled situations. We need more tests of different cities in different categories of development and in other countries to see how well the predictions relate to start-up realities and ensure there is appropriate spread of the index numbers from lows near 2 to highs near 5 or 6. For now, we consider this an interesting first step, not a mature tool for professional application.

References

Angelelli, P., and J. Llisterri. 2001. *Algunas consideraciones sobre la experiencia del Banco Interamericano de Desarrollo (BID) en la promoción de la empresarialidad.* Washington, DC: BID, Septiembre.

"Base de Datos." 2001. Diario Oficial de Chile.

Bhidé, Amar. 2000. *The Origin and Evolution of New Business*. Oxford: Oxford University Press.

Bortagaray, I., and S. Tiffin. 2000. "Innovation Clusters in Latin America." Presented at 4th International Conference on Technology Policy and Innovation, Curitiba, Brazil, August 28–31.

Comision Economica para America Latina (CEPAL). 1998. "Desarrollo productivo: indicadores de competitividad y productividad." Revisión analítica y propuesta sobre su utilización. Santiago, Chile: CEPAL.

Fairbanks, M., and S. Lindsay. 1997. *Plowing the Sea*. Cambridge, MA: Harvard Business School Press.

Gaynor, G. 1999. *Manual de Gestión en Tecnología*. New York: McGraw-Hill.

Hall, P. 1999. *Cities and Civilization*. London: Phoenix.

Heitor, M., D. Gibson, and M. Ibarra, eds. 2002. *Technology Policy and Innovation*, vol. 5. Westport, CT: Quorum Books.

Kim, L. 1992. "Entrepreneurship and Innovation in a Rapidly Developing Country." Working paper, International Labour Organization, Geneva.

Organization for Economic Cooperation and Development (OECD). 1997. *Sistemas Nacionales de Innovación*. Paris: OECD.

Porter, M. 2002. *Research Triangle: Clusters of Innovation Initiative*. Cambridge, MA: Harvard University Press.

Programa de las Naciones Unidas sobre el Desarrollo (PNUD). 2001. *Informe sobre el Desarrollo Humano*. New York: PNUD.

Reynolds, P. D., S. M. Camp, W. D. Bygrave, and E. Autio. 2001. *Global Entrepreneurship Monitor*. Executive report.

Sahlman, W., H. Stevenson, M. Roberts, and A. Bhidé. 1999. *The Entrepreneurial Venture*. Cambridge, MA: Harvard Business School Press.

Schumpeter, J. A. 1934. *The Theory of Economic Development: An Inquiry into Profits, Capital, Credit, Interest, and the Business Cycle*. Cambridge, MA: Harvard University Press.

Stevenson, H. 2000. *Intellectual Foundations of Entrepreneurship*. Cambridge, MA: Harvard University Press.

Zoltan, J. Acs. 2002. *Innovation and the Growth of Cities*. Cheltenham, UK: Edward Elgar.

Note

1. Note that the business journal AmericaEconomia (August 2002, no. 238) has a survey about which cities in Latin America are the best for doing business, and in their ranking they choose not to control for city size. Santiago, with a population of about 5 million, ranks fourth, but is competing against São Paolo and Mexico City, with far more people. In our index, Santiago would probably rank far higher than these two competitors.

CHAPTER 14

Entrepreneurship and Innovation in Brazilian Incubators[*]

José Dornelas

Scott Tiffin

In recent years many Brazilian experts have been discussing entrepreneurship as being one of the critical factors for economic development, generation of employment, and wealth. The discussion in Brazil parallels what is occurring internationally. Developed nations as well as developing ones have been looking both at local characteristics as well as comparing the situation in different countries. Examples of this can be found in recent studies undertaken by the Global Entrepreneurship Monitor (GEM)–led by Babson College and London Business School–that aim to understand the relationship between entrepreneurship and economic development (GEM 1999, 2000, 2001).

As early as 1934, Schumpeter opened the discussion of the role of new businesses as being the main source for economic development based on innovation. Such companies promote technological innovation (Tushman and Anderson 1986) and technology transfer (Dornelas, Nunes, and Oliveira 2000); they create new employment and generate wealth for society (Kao 1995). Many studies have been made in the last years in order to provide a framework of the entrepreneurial process

[*]This work was financed by the Institute for Latin American Business at Babson College.

and to understand the critical factors involved in it, from the generation of an idea, analysis of an opportunity, up to the conception and effective creation of a new company (Timmons 1994; Bygrave 1994; Hisrich and Peters 1998). Based on these results, models have been proposed to represent the entrepreneurial process. Several environmental and internal factors related to the companies in formation have been identified as vital for increasing the probability of an enterprising adventure to succeed. A group of best entrepreneurial practices have been obtained, which have been validated and analyzed by several international researchers, as well as used as a base for entrepreneurship teaching (Bechard and Gregoire 2002).

In the Brazilian case, entrepreneurship has been growing quickly in the last years; post-secondary as well as high school courses have been creating disciplines focused on entrepreneurship (Dornelas 2001). Business incubators are the major support programs for creation of new companies in the country, especially technological start-ups. However, there still lack studies that analyze the Brazilian entrepreneurial process and its particularities, and that compare Brazilian entrepreneurial practices to best international practices (Dornelas and Tiffin 2002).

The objective of this chapter is to provide a better understanding of entrepreneurial practices in Brazil and the innovation of technology-based companies starting up in Brazilian incubators by analyzing the results of a questionnaire sent to a sample of incubators in Brazil. When identifying the patterns in these businesses and comparing them to best international practices, this can provide both the entrepreneurs and the managers of incubators with information that will assist them in improving their management. In addition, our results will help define training programs that could be developed to fill-in current management deficiencies.

The Entrepreneurial Process

Bygrave (2002) presents entrepreneurship, joined with innovation, as a synonym of prosperity, based on the example of the United States. In his vision, which is shared by Timmons (1994), the entrepreneur is the person who identifies an opportunity and creates an organization to pursue it. According to Bygrave (2002), the entrepreneurial process includes all the functions, activities, and actions associated with the perception of this opportunity and the creation of a new company around the objective of capitalizing on it.

According to Hisrich and Peters (1998), the entrepreneurial process has four different phases: (1) identify and evaluate the opportunity, (2) develop the business plan, (3) determine and obtain the necessary resources, and (4) manage the company. When identifying a business opportunity, the entrepreneur should test it to evaluate its commercial viability through the elaboration of a business plan. The second phase of the entrepreneurial process–to develop the business plan–involves several concepts that should be understood and expressed, in a few pages, giving form to a document that synthesizes the essence of the company, its business strategy, and its market and competitors as it will generate revenues and grow. This will facilitate the determination of the necessary resources to run the company.

Critical Factors for Enterprise Success

Many internal and external factors influence the entrepreneurial process. Some of these factors can be measured and others just assessed qualitatively. Some studies have been developed in order to define the main characteristics that influence this process. Lee et al. (2001) make an extensive bibliographical study on the external and internal factors that influence the performance of technological start-ups, analyze their interactions, and define major groups of relevant parameters.

1. Internal factors
   * Entrepreneurial orientation
   * Technological capability
   * Financial resources invested during the period of development of the company
2. External factors
   * Networks
   * Unilateral relationships
   * Bilateral relationships

According to Miller (1983), it is possible to identify three dimensions for entrepreneurial orientation: innovation, propensity to take risk, and proactiveness. These dimensions have been used by other authors (Covin and Slevin 1989; Lumpkin and Dess 1996) and they are found to come into play most effectively when companies have a well-balanced managerial team (meaning a balance between technical and administrative abilities of the founders). The literature on entrepreneurship suggests that entrepreneurial orientation constitutes one of the most critical resources for the performance of a start-up company, bringing them competitive advantages (Covin and Miles 1999; Zahra, Nielson, Bogner 1999). The dimension of innovation reflects the propensity of the company to engage in the generation of new ideas, to make new discoveries, and activities of research and development (R&D) that result in new products and processes (Lumpkin and Dess 1996). The propensity to take risk can be exemplified through the commitment of a large amount of resources of the company in activities of great uncertainty that present probability of high profits. Proactiveness refers to the approach of the company in relation to the market opportunities, through constant market research, pioneering actions and anticipation of competition, and the introduction of new products or services in the market.

Technological capability defines the roots of the competitive advantages of the company, through patents that are protected by law, and by joining technological knowledge and different abilities of the founders to the business, which are difficult to imitate by competitors. Certifications and other types of intellectual property are also applied.

Lee et al. (2001) argue that the literature does not consider financial resources as being capable of providing and sustaining a competitive advantage for the company, since such resources are not necessarily rare, capable of imitation, or tradable. However, if the company does not know how to manage its financial resources appropriately in its early stage, this may limit its growth and the ability of investors to harvest.

Networks, in spite of being intangible in many cases, are vital to discover new opportunities, to test new ideas, and to obtain resources for the formation of a new company (Aldrich and Zimmer 1986). They provide information and social capital to the company, a group of resources, tangible or intangible, that revert to the company through its relationships, facilitating the attainment of objectives (Gabbay and Leenders 1999).

The partnerships that a company establishes with the external actors of its business can be constituted through unilateral and bilateral relationships. Strategic alliances with other companies, vendors, key customers, and so forth are examples of these relationships. Lee et al. (2001) present four types of bilateral relationships as being crucial for good performance of a technology start-up company: (1) with other companies, (2) with investors, (3) with universities and research centers, and (4) with business associations. The unilateral relationships happen when only one of the parties gets benefits, and the other party doesn't demand anything in exchange. Examples of this relationship are the resources offered by governments (federal, state, and municipal) and support agencies to the nascent companies, such as the support at a low cost given by incubators.

Objectives

We have gathered data on companies being incubated in Brazil that displays how they behave relative to these best-practice factors. This will help us not only understand how technology-based start-ups are evolving, but how the Brazilian incubator program is faring, and allow us to suggest some ways to overcome any weaknesses we might diagnose. This chapter reports on a part of the larger research project we undertook, focusing on the following limited set of objectives.

• What is the pattern of management in the Brazilian incubated companies in light of the critical factors for the success of an enterprise mentioned above, being considered the best international practices?

• What innovation patterns can be observed in these companies?

• What suggestions can be made for incubators to help overcome any management weaknesses evident in the start-ups?

Methodology

Based upon the literature review of best practice, a questionnaire was developed with 26 questions. Questions were multiple choice and, in some cases, the entrepreneur had the opportunity to provide specific information about his or her company. Twelve technological business incubators located in the states of Sao Paulo, Rio de Janeiro, Santa Catarina, Minas Gerais, and Parana were selected, based on their previous success, which was measured by the number of graduated companies, experience and quality of the incubated companies, positive references in the media, and so forth. The questionnaires were delivered by e-mail to the managers of the participant incubators, who distributed the same ones to the incubated companies, a total of 150. Ninety-six incubated companies answered the questionnaire, a very high return rate (64%). The managers of the incubators collected the answered questionnaires and sent them back. Overall, the resulting data can be considered of high quality, with a few exceptions. Some questions will have to be reviewed in an eventual follow-up stage of the research (with more incubators or with the same ones in the future), since they were not answered appropriately or were not well interpreted by the entrepreneurs.

Results[**]

The most striking fact about the start-ups is the very high percentage of software firms, as shown by Figure 14.1. Perhaps the most important reason for this is the strong presence of the Softex (Society for the Promotion of Excellence in Brazilian Software) project around the country, as a partner of several incubators. Another possible explanation is the

---

[**]In Figures 14.1, 14.5, 14.9, and 14.10 multiple answers were allowed.

Figure 14.1
Industrial Sectors the Start-ups Are Working In

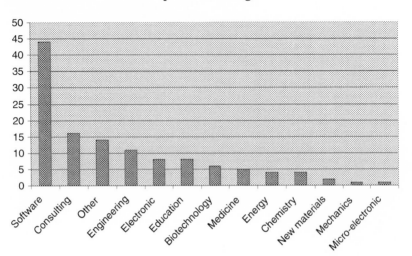

fact that the universities with computer science courses have the oldest courses on entrepreneurship in the country. Also, to create a software company, the investments in infrastructure are usually less significant compared with other industry sectors.

Other industrial sectors are present, with less emphasis than the software sector. Many companies are in the consulting and engineering services area. Sectors with heavy requirements in laboratory equipment, deep R&D investments, and large-scale manufacturing links do not seem to be involved with these technology incubators. We do not know yet, of course, how this pattern relates to what is found in incubators in other developed countries.

The majority of businesses are financed by the entrepreneurs themselves, through their personal savings (see Figure 14.2). Many people answered that the cash flow of the company was also used for re-investment. The venture capital and angel investments are still extremely small if compared with other financing sources: added up, they represent just 6% of the total investments in the 96 companies. Research grants from governmental sources are relatively important, (but their importance stands to be significantly increased as the grants are increased); they correspond only to 8% of the investments. Unlike the United States, for example, where family and friends in many cases participate in the initial financing of the business, in this study their participation was much less, only 3%. Finally, the difficulty in getting financing for start-ups from commercial banks is notorious in Brazil; the results here show only 2% of the investments coming from banks.

Figure 14.2
The Origin of the Financial Resources Used to Finance the Operation of the Business Since Its Creation

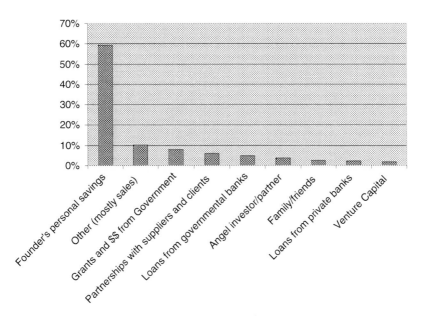

Figure 14.3 presents the total of the investments made by the companies until the date of the research (April 2002). There is a very wide distribution, with investments from $4,000 up to $200,000. This means that technology incubators in Brazil select a variety of companies in different areas of knowledge to be incubated, which require more or less investment. On the other hand, only 13% of the total of investment in the companies is more than $200,000. Since the entrepreneurs themselves finance the larger part of the companies, such a range of investments would be expected, as it is compatible with the entrepreneur's savings.

Figure 14.4 shows how much the companies are committing from their budgets for R&D. Forty-five percent of the companies answered that they commit more than 20% of their budget to R&D. This is a very interesting finding, and the survey will need to be modified in future research in order to capture the values above 20% to give a better understanding of what is happening here. Although we commented earlier that most of the innovation is occurring in software, and we suspect the products are largely customizations to geographic markets, the investments in R&D are still very large, exactly what one would expect from technology-based start-ups anywhere. We will also need to analyze these data more finely to see how the R&D investments relate to the industrial sectors.

Figure 14.3
Total Investments to Date in the Companies

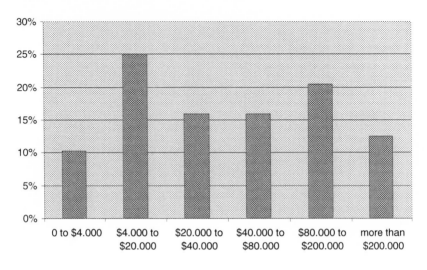

Figure 14.4
R&D Investment (as Percent of Budget)

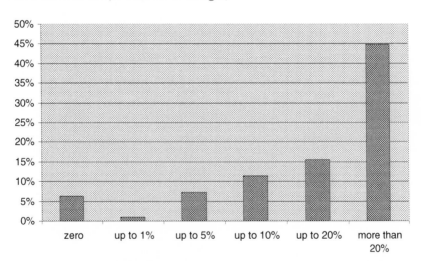

The data shown in Figure 14.5 are equally intriguing, perhaps raising more questions than they answer. It can be seen that many companies (60%) use their own laboratories for developing research, and only 34% of the companies use the incubators' laboratories. This seems a small percentage, since the technological incubators have good infrastructure

Figure 14.5
Where the R&D Is Done

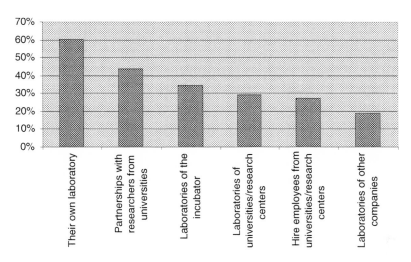

and good laboratories (mainly for computer science). Despite the quality of the incubator's infrastructure, incubated companies don't seem to be using them; perhaps the incubators laboratories are not adapted to their customers' requirements. On the other hand, it can be observed that a good relationship exists between the incubated companies and the universities and research centers, showing that incubators are an effective instrument for technology transfer.

Regarding intellectual property (Figure 14.6), we see a considerable number of patents owned by these incubated companies (28 companies have at least one patent). There was no distinction between national patents and international; even so, it is believed that most of these patents are national. Other types of intellectual property also appear frequently. Brazil has made a tremendous effort to increase its number of patents internationally. Incubators can play an important role in this, but it seems they are still focused on the local market.

Figure 14.7 summarizes the sources for the ideas of innovation, that is to say, where the business opportunity comes from. Once again, the important role of universities and centers of research as places of innovation sources stands out, as well as the role of the incubator as an instrument of technology transfer. The opportunities identified inside private companies are also extremely important. This is entirely consistent with the literature, which stresses the prior industrial or business experience of the founding team as the source of the underlying idea for innovation.

Figure 14.6
Use of Intellectual Property and Certification

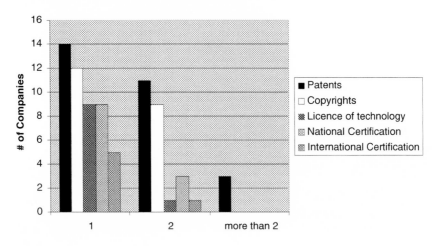

Figure 14.7
Where the Business Opportunity Comes from

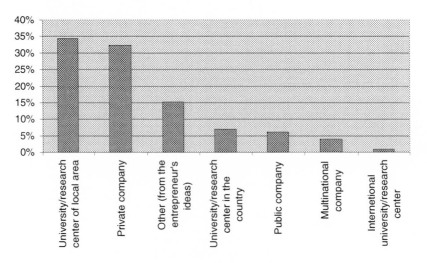

One of the critical factors for business success mentioned in the literature is the necessity of having a well-balanced team. A company has to have people (generally the founders) with complementary abilities and managerial knowledge. In a high-tech business, there should be people with knowledge of the key technology, the internal processes, and, not less important, people with knowledge and experience in administration of business, who know how to negotiate, sell technological products, manage a growing company, and define and implement

Figure 14.8
Entrepreneurs' Education

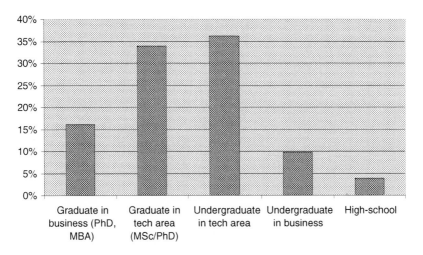

strategies. Figure 14.8 shows that many entrepreneurs have a formal education, with a master's degree and even higher, but just a few have formal education in business (26%).

How this lack of business education has manifested itself in the performance of these start-ups is impossible to tell from our data, but it is in such contrast to international best practice that remedying it through training or adding to the founding team would seem of very high importance.

Training programs are a resourceful way to bridge the gap of managerial knowledge. The incubators we studied and their partners offer several programs to entrepreneurs (Figure 14.9). However, it is known that these are short-term training courses. Perhaps longer-term training activities should be offered by these programs as well. These should still have a practical approach in order for entrepreneurs apply them in their businesses. A few entrepreneurs have had training in the export area (8%). That again gives an indication that these businesses are more focused on the local market, rather than international.

Finally, Figure 14.10 shows us where advisory services come from. Our data indicate that most entrepreneurs look for advice inside the incubator. From conversations we had with survey respondents during the development of the questionnaire, we understand this to mean mainly the incubator manager, who works closely with the entrepreneur (70%). Sebrae (Brazilian service for helping micro and small companies) and universities, as well as other entrepreneurs who are already successful, are also mentioned as major advisors. Even though a few entrepreneurs work their network formally, through clubs and business

Figure 14.9
Training Courses That Entrepreneurs Have Attended

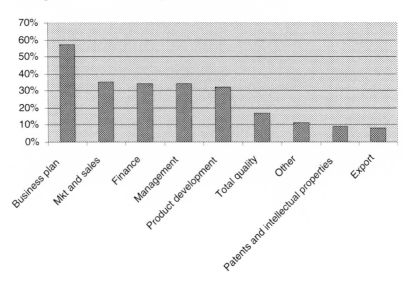

Figure 14.10
Where They Get Advice

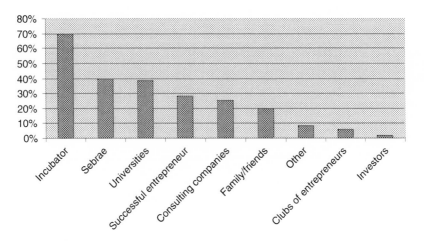

associations (6%), it happens differently than it happens, for example, in the United States. Future research will need to discover if the incubator managers are adequately prepared to give this critical business advice that the companies seem to be requesting.

Final Considerations

It seems as though many start-ups located in incubators in Brazil are active in creating important new, market-oriented products, and are investing heavily in R&D to undertake the innovation. The founders seem to be coming out of the universities where the incubators are located, to a significant degree. If better links to the incubator and university labs could be arranged during the innovation process, and more risk financing made available, these companies would likely deepen the innovativeness of their products and manage the innovation process more effectively. Training in entrepreneurship seems to be a high priority for the founders, who typically lack business management and start-up skills. They depend heavily on the incubator managers for market and management information; to ensure they are getting the best advice, it would perhaps be a good idea to develop training programs and information products for the incubator managers as well.

More detailed follow-up of this initial research project will be required to get finer data on some key points of innovation management and technology sector involvement, as well as make more accurate comparisons with international best practice. Possible extensions of this work could be the comparison of the results here obtained with companies in the same stage of development and industrial sector, but located outside the incubators. This research can still be developed periodically (annually for example) in order to compare the evolution of the results in each period.

References

Aldrich, H. E., and E. R. Zimmer. 1986. "Entrepreneurship Through Social Network." In *The Art and Science of Entrepreneurship,* D. L. Sexton and R. W. Smilor, eds. Cambridge, MA: Ballinger, 3–24.

Bechard, J. P., and D. Gregoire. 2002. "Entrepreneurship Education Revisited: The Case of Higher Education." Babson-Kauffman Entrepreneurship Research Conference, Boulder, CO, USA, June.

Bygrave, W. 1994. *The Portable MBA in Entrepreneurship.* New York: John Wiley and Sons.

Bygrave, W. 2002. *The Entrepreneurial Process.* Aula de empreendedorismo ministrada no. Babson College, Babson Park, MA.

Covin, J.G., and D. P. Slevin. 1989. "Strategic Management of Small Firms in Hostile and Benign Environments." *Strategic Management Journal* 10, no.1: 75–87.

Covin, J.G., and M. P. Miles. 1999. "Corporate Entrepreneurship and the Pursuit of Competitive Advantage." *Entrepreneurship: Theory and Practice* 23, no.3: 47–63.

Dornelas, J. C. A. 2001. *Empreendedorismo: transformando idéias em negócios.* Rio de Janeiro: Campus.

Dornelas, J. C. A., and S. Tiffin. 2002. "Patterns of Entrepreneurship and Innovation in Brazilian Incubated Companies." Research Forum on Entrepreneurship in Latin America. Babson College, Babson Park, MA, USA, June.

Dornelas, J. C. A, M. G. V. Nunes, and O. N. Oliveira, Jr. 2000. "Bridging the Gap Between Technological Innovation and Effective Transfer of Technology." 4th International Conference on Technology Policy and Innovation, Curitiba, Brazil, August.

Gabbay, S. M., and R. T. A. Leenders. 1999. *The Structure of Advantage and Disadvantage.* In *Corporate Social Capital and Liability*, R. T. A. Leenders and S. M. Gabbay, eds. New York: Kluwer, 1–16.

Global Entrepreneurship Monitor (GEM). 1999. Executive report. www.ncoe.org. Boston, July.

Global Entrepreneurship Monitor (GEM). 2000. Executive report. www.ncoe.org. Boston, November.

Global Entrepreneurship Monitor (GEM). 2001. Executive report. www.gemconsortium.org. Boston, November.

Hisrich, R. D., and M. P. Peters. 1998. *Entrepreneurship.* 4th ed. Boston: Irwin McGraw-Hill.

Hisrich, R. D. and M. P. Peters. 2001. *Entrepreneurship.* 4th ed. Boston: Irwin McGraw-Hill, 1998. In *Empreendedorismo: transformando idéias em negócios*, J. C. A. Dornelas, ed. Rio de Janeiro: Campus, 304.

Kao, J. J. 1995. *Entrepreneur: A Wealth-Creation and Value-Adding Process.* New York: Prentice-Hall.

Lee, C., K. Lee, and J. M. Pennings. 2001. "Internal Capabilities, External Networks, and Performance: A Study on Technology-Based Ventures." *Strategic Management Journal* 22: 615–640.

Lumpkin G. T., and G. G. Dess. 1996. "Clarifying the Entrepreneurial Orientation Construct and Linking It to Performance." *Academy of Management Review* 21: 135–173.

Miller, D. 1983. "The Correlates of Entrepreneurship in Three Types of Firms." *Management Science* 29: 770–791.

Schumpeter, J. A. 1934. *The Theory of Economic Development.* Cambridge, MA: Harvard University Press.

Timmons, J. A. 1994. *New Venture Creation.* 4th ed. Boston: Irwin McGraw-Hill.

Tushman, M., and P. Anderson. 1986. "Technological Discontinuities and Organizational Environments." *Administrative Science Quarterly* 31: 439–465.

Zahra, S. A., A. P. Nielson, and W. C. Bogner. 1999. "Corporate Entrepreneurship, Knowledge and Competence Development." *Entrepreneurship: Theory and Practice* 23, no. 3: 169–189.

CHAPTER 15

The Family Business in Chile and Mexico: Organizational Climate as Antecedent of Entrepreneurial Orientation[*]

Imanol Belausteguigoitia

Soledad Portilla

There is an increasing interest worldwide in understanding family business, because of its importance to the economy and social relations. Family business (FB) has been defined in many different ways, and until now there is no unified definition. For the purpose of this study, Rosenblatt's (1990) definition is used: "[F]amily business is any business in which majority ownership or control lies within a single family and in which two or more family members are or at some time were directly involved in the business."

Most family firms are intergenerational, where the older generation (usually father and/or mother) are actively involved in the operation or management of the business with their adult children (Weigel 1992).

---

[*]Special acknowledgment to Julio Alvear and Jorge Israel (Chile), who helped to design this research.

Figure 15.1
The Intergenerational Family Firm

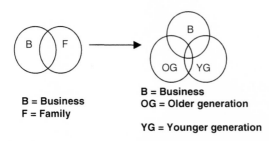

B = Business
F = Family

B = Business
OG = Older generation

YG = Younger generation

   The intergenerational family business (IFB) is a peculiar system that can be represented by three overlapped circles, as shown in Figure 15.1. Compared to a traditional family business model, the family is divided into old and young generation subsystems. The model suggests analyzing each of these three subsystems (old and young generations, and business) and their four overlapping areas (interactions) (Weigel 1992).

   The lack of commitment of younger generations toward their families' organizations is frequently a great concern of the old generations, and perhaps also the cause of failure of many family firms. Frequently, the founders of these companies do not know if they could take some actions to enhance the involvement of their offspring in their businesses. On the other hand, young generations believe that it is not enough to devote their lives to companies that cannot provide satisfaction (not only material) to their needs, even if the firms belong to their own family (Belausteguigoitia 2001). They frequently complain about their lack of independence and power to make important managerial decisions. In this sense there is concordance with the norm of reciprocity of Gouldner (1960), which states that one who receives some benefit acquires the moral duty to give back to the one who gave. On the other hand, one's negative perception of the organization will affect his or her job involvement. The loss of entrepreneurial activity in FBs might have its origin in the inability to create an adequate climate that enhances the entrepreneurial spirit of all members, especially those of younger generations.

   According to empirical evidence, there is some truth to the common observation that the first generation builds the company, the second preserves it, and the third squanders it. Fewer than 15% of family-owned businesses survive under family control beyond the third generation. IFBs need stronger governance structures to survive and thrive in an era of globalization. Through this structure, the firms are more likely to design appropriate strategies and labor conditions, as the organizational climate variables studied in this chapter indicate.

Latin American Family Businesses

In the case of Latin America, approximately 90% of all businesses are family owned (Belausteguigoitia 2004; Ginebra 1997), from the small mom-and-pop hardware store to the large corporations like Televisa in Mexico and Grupo Luksic in Chile. Family business dynamics in Latin America are unique due to the great influence of the family over the business (Ferkany 1992). Latin American families are numerous and traditional compared to other regions. As a consequence of family pressure over the business in order to satisfy the family needs, members of the nuclear and extended families, in-laws, and close friends usually have a place in these organizations. According to De la Cerda and Nuñez (1993), the inclusion of family members who are not accountable leads to the *familism* phenomenon (*familismo*), and in relation to the transnational point of view, is a salient characteristic of Latin American organizations.

Latin American culture was determined mainly by the fusion of the Hispanic (and Portuguese, in the case of Brazil) and the Indian civilizations. This common background explains the similarities between the countries of this region (Calderón 1988). Family members are physically and emotionally close to each other. In relation to Mexico, Kras (1991) suggests that Mexican workers are emotionally sensible compared to other cultures, personal relations are extremely important, and workers are highly motivated when they feel recognized and respected.

Family businesses in Latin America are experiencing hard times competing against aggressive and well-prepared multinationals. In the ranks of the top 100 family businesses, they have fallen dramatically in the proportion of total sales compared to multinationals, from 70.8% in 1994 to 57.1% in 1999 in Mexico (−19.4%), and from 24% to 18.8% in Argentina (−21.7%). According to Andrade, Barra, and Elstrodt (2001) they cannot match the multinationals' scale, strategic focus, cutting-edge management techniques, and deep pockets.

Lumpkin and Sloat (2001) suggest that an entrepreneurial orientation (EO) may be useful for enhancing the performance of family firms. They might improve their odds at succeed by making them more competitive.

The Process of Stagnation in Family Firms

One model that explains the lack of ability to grow and the process of stagnation experienced by family firms is the plateau effect (Malone and Jenster 1992) (see Figure 15.2). Although this effect can be seen in different companies and workers, it seems to appear more frequently in members of family firms. This term refers to a loss of entrepreneurial orientation, and a comfort zone for high-level executives who work less

Figure 15.2
The Plateau Syndrome

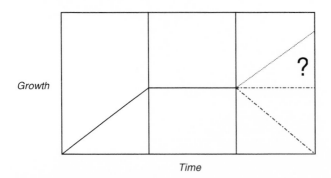

than in the past and tend to be involved in activities that provide them more satisfaction than those that are relevant for their business.

Some studies suggest that commitment of family members toward their organizations and the effort that they are willing to invest are affected by organizational climate factors (Belausteguigoitia 2000). This leads to the conclusion that leaders can enhance the commitment and entrepreneurial activity of workers, managing the business environment appropriately.

Due to the high importance of family business in the Latin American economy, it is worth trying to understand its nature and the motivations of its members and the way the entrepreneurial orientation can be enhanced.

Entrepreneurial Activity in Latin America

According to the Global Entrepreneurship Monitor Report (GEM) (2002), Latin America (represented by Argentina, Brazil, Chile, and Mexico) is a highly entrepreneurial region, where close to 15% of adults (18 to 64 years old) are involved in entrepreneurial activities. Chile was considered the third most entrepreneurial country out of 37, while the previous year Mexico showed the maximum entrepreneurship level of 29 nations.

According to the GEM, the number of adults engaged in some form of entrepreneurial activity in Latin America is almost twice the average of all countries involved in the study. The strong and wide family network, the high cost of capital, and the near absence of financial banking support are variables that explains a high level of business angel rate (4.3% in the case of Mexico), compared with the GEM 2001 average (3.1%).

To survive, big family businesses in Latin America must change their strategies to compete more successfully. To execute any high-performance strategy, they first need stronger governance models that can prevent family conflicts from affecting the business. Additionally, an adequate governance system would help to more easily obtain qualified professionals, and provide a smooth succession of power across generations.

Entrepreneurial Orientation Construct

An entrepreneurial orientation (Lumpkin and Dess 1996) refers to the process, practices, and decision-making activities that lead to a new entry and includes the intentions and actions of people involved in a new venture creation. Different multidimensional models describe the entrepreneurial orientation of organizations. According to Lumpkin and Dess (1996), this entrepreneurial orientation (EO) construct should include a propensity to act autonomously, a willingness to innovate and take risks, and a tendency to be aggressive toward competitors and proactive relative to marketplace opportunities (see Table 15.1); nevertheless these characteristics may vary independently of each other in a given context. EO is linked to environmental factors and performance, as shown in Figure 15.3.

Organizational Climate

Due to its influence on performance, organizational climate (OC), or the workers' interpretation of the surrounding environment, cannot be overlooked. Brown and Leigh (1996), based on Kahn's (1990) writings,

Table 15.1
Entrepreneurial Orientation Factors and Definitions

Innovativeness (IN)	Willingness to depart from familiar capabilities or practices and venture beyond the current state of the art (Lumpkin and Sloat 2001)
Risk Taking (R)	Willingness to pursue or avoid risks; likelihood that someone will forego a safe alternative with a known outcome in favor of a more attractive choice with a less-certain reward. (Brockhaus 1980)
Proactiveness (PR)	Acting in advance to deal with an expected difficulty (Dictionary.com)
Competitive Aggressiveness (C)	Adopting a strong-offense posture or a combative response (Lumpin and Sloan 2001)
Autonomy (AU)	Independent action of an individual or a team in bringing forth an idea or a vision and carrying it through to completion (Lumpkin and Dess 1996)

(Lumpkin and Dess 1996)

Figure 15.3
Conceptual Framework of Entrepreneurial Orientation

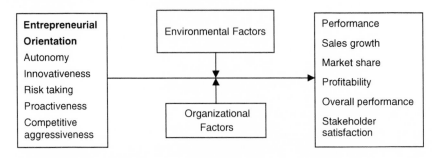

proposed six components of OC divided into two groups, psychological safety and psychological meaningfulness (see Table 15.2). Kahn (1990) defined psychological safety as the employee's sense of being able to show one's self without fear of negative consequences to self-image, status, or career. The dimensions considered by Brown and Leigh in this group are supportive management, clarity, and self-expression.

Psychological meaningfulness, in turn, is defined as a feeling that one is receiving a return on investment of one's self in a currency of physical, cognitive, or emotional energy. People experience their work as meaningful when they perceive it to be challenging, worthwhile, and rewarding. Thus, the three factors associated with psychological meaningfulness are contribution, recognition, and work as a challenge.

According to Brown and Leigh (1996), an OC that is perceived as safe and meaningful will be connected with a higher level of job involvement, effort, and performance. Toro Alvarez (1998), in a study of 2,426 employers in different regions of Colombia, has found that commitment to work and to the organization is influenced by the psychological climate. Eisenberger, Huntington, Hutchison, and Sowa (1996) demonstrated that as a result of supportive leadership behaviors and a generally facilitative organizational climate, individuals feel the need to reciprocate favorable organizational treatment with positive attitudes and behaviors.

Hypotheses

1. Organizational climate factors (supportive management, clarity, self-expression, contribution, recognition, challenge) and EO factors (autonomy, proactiveness, risk taking, innovation, aggressive compe-

Table 15.2
Psychological Safety and Psychological Meaningfulness Factors

	Factors and Concepts
Psychological Safety	*Supportive Management (SU)*: A supportive management style that allows workers to try, and to fail, without fear of reprisals. It gives them control over their work and the methods they used to accomplish it.
	Clarity Role (CL): Expectations and work situations that are clear, consistent, and predictable. It is expected that clear, consistent, and predictable work norms create a psychologically safe environment and increase job involvement.
	Self-expression (EX): When employees feel psychologically safe, they are more likely to infuse their personalities, creativity, feelings, and self-concepts into their work role.
Psychological Meaningfulness	*Contribution (CO):* The perception that one's work significantly affects organizational processes and outcomes is likely to contribute to the perceivers' meaningfulness of work and enhance employees' identification with their work roles.
	Recognition (RE): The belief that the organization appreciates and recognizes one's effort and contributions is likely to increase job involvement and identification.
	Work as a Challenge (CH): Personal growth in the work role can only occur when work is challenging and requires the use of creativity and a variety of skills. Challenging work induces employees to invest greater amounts of effort.

tition) are positively correlated in Chilean and Mexican family and nonfamily firms.

2. A causal association exists between organizational climate and EO factors in Chilean and Mexican family and nonfamily firms (see Figure 15.4).

Figure 15.4
Causal Association Between Psychological Climate, Entrepreneurial Orientation, and Performance

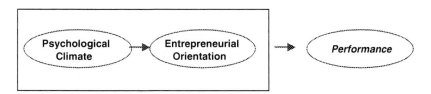

Table 15.3
Chilean and Mexican Samples

	Chile	Mexico
Sample	200 executives and entrepreneurs of Chile (Concepción and Santiago)	317 executives and entrepreneurs of Mexico City
Gender	Men (79%) Women (21%)	Men (64%) Women (36%)
Age	20–29 (32%) 30–39 (25%). 40–49 (21%) 50–59 (17%) +59 (5%) **X = 39**	20–29 (46%) 30–39 (44%) 40–49 (8%) 50+ (2%) **X = 32**
Position	Directors (1st level): 7% Managers (2nd level): 52% Supervisors (3rd level): 24% Other: 18%	Directors (1st level): 9% Managers (2nd level): 50% Supervisors (3rd level): 33% Other: 9%
Business Type	Small: 16% Medium: 50% Large: 34% Family firms: 40% Nonfamily firms: 60%	Small: 24% Medium: 20% Large: 56% Family firms 28% Nonfamily firms: 78%

Methods and Measures

This empirical study surveyed directors, managers, and supervisors of
family firms and nonfamily firms, which included a total of 200 workers
from Chile and 317 from Mexico (see Table 15.3). Questionnaires were
applied during March and April 2002. Pearson's correlation was used to
identify the association between OC and EO variables of Chilean and
Mexican family and nonfamily firms (jointly). Structural equations modeling (SEM, AMOS 3.6) was used; a model explains the causal relationship between six OC factors (antecedents) and five dimensions of EO
(consequences, see Table 15.4. The model shows every causal relation
(OC factors$\rightarrow$ EO factors) which is greater than 0.10 (r > 0.10). The
value of the standardized regression coefficient r, was shown (values of
p, x2, and r2 were not estimated).

Table 15.4
Instruments, Authors, and Number of Items

Instrument	Authors	Number of Items
Entrepreneurial Orientation	Lumpkin and Dess	12
Psychological Climate	Brown and Leigh	18

Results and Implications

It was decided not to present Pearson's correlation results of family and nonfamily firms separately, because it requires exhibiting four more correlation tables, and essentially the results of family and nonfamily firms were similar. The SEM presented family and nonfamily firms jointly, because the size of the sample does not allow for modeling separately.

The results for Chile and Mexico differ essentially in the following aspects:

1. More significant associations between OC and EO factors were found in the case of Mexico than in the case of Chile (Pearson's correlation);
2. Three negative causal association were found in the case of Chile, and none in the case of Mexico (SEM);
3. For Chile, the psychological meaningfulness factors (OC) had more significant causal relations with EO factors (10 of 17); for Mexico the psychological safety factors had more causal connections with EO factors (10 of 14).

Chile

As was mentioned before, the Pearson's correlation of family and nonfamily firms are presented jointly. Eighteen out of thirty associations between OC and EO factors were significant at the 0.01 level (nineteen at the level 0.05). In the case of innovation and competitive aggressiveness (EO factors), less-significant correlations with OC factors were found, in comparison with the other four dimensions of EO. In relation to the OC factors, supportive management was the least significantly correlated with EO factors (one of five), and contribution was the most significantly correlated (five of five). Table 15.5 shows the Pearson's correlation analysis in the case of Chile (family and nonfamily firms). EO dimensions were more significantly correlated with psychological meaningfulness factors than with the psychological safety factors.

It is interesting to note that all factors of OC are significantly correlated at a 0.01 level with each other (OC-OC). In the case of EO factors, there is a high correlation too, except the association between autonomy and competitive aggressiveness (see Table 15.4).

The highest correlation in Table 15.5 was between autonomy (EO) and self-expression (0.607), two variables belonging to different constructs, but intimately linked.

Table 15.5 Association of Entrepreneurial Orientation and Organizational Climate Factors in Chile (Family and Nonfamily Firms)

Correlations

		AU	PR	IN	RI	C	CH	CO	RE	EX	CL	SU
AU	Pearson Correlation	1.000	.301**	.139*	.168*	.064	.137	.338**	.468**	.607**	.513**	.485**
	Sig. (2-tailed)		.000	.049	.018	.365	.053	.000	.000	.000	.000	.000
	N	200	200	200	200	200	200	200	200	200	200	200
PR	Pearson Correlation	.301**	1.000	.434**	.418**	.382**	.278**	.240**	.283**	.240**	.198**	.086
	Sig. (2-tailed)	.000		.000	.000	.000	.000	.001	.000	.001	.005	.224
	N	200	200	200	200	200	200	200	200	200	200	200
IN	Pearson Correlation	.139*	.434**	1.000	.250**	.436**	.281**	.286**	.081	.070	.115	.107
	Sig. (2-tailed)	.049	.000		.000	.000	.000	.000	.254	.324	.105	.130
	N	200	200	200	200	200	200	200	200	200	200	200
RI	Pearson Correlation	.168*	.418**	.250**	1.000	.473**	.247**	.318**	.212**	.045	.263**	.150*
	Sig. (2-tailed)	.018	.000	.000		.000	.000	.000	.003	.529	.000	.034
	N	200	200	200	200	200	200	200	200	200	200	200
C	Pearson Correlation	.064	.382**	.436**	.473**	1.000	.312**	.286**	-.016	.002	.059	.062
	Sig. (2-tailed)	.365	.000	.000	.000		.000	.000	.827	.975	.407	.381
	N	200	200	200	200	200	200	200	200	200	200	200
CH	Pearson Correlation	.137	.278**	.281**	.247**	.312**	1.000	.570**	.186**	.222**	.201**	.209**
	Sig. (2-tailed)	.053	.000	.000	.000	.000		.000	.008	.002	.004	.003
	N	200	200	200	200	200	200	200	200	200	200	200
CO	Pearson Correlation	.338**	.240**	.286**	.318**	.286**	.570**	1.000	.360**	.340**	.552**	.310**
	Sig. (2-tailed)	.000	.001	.000	.000	.000	.000		.000	.000	.000	.000
	N	200	200	200	200	200	200	200	200	200	200	200
RE	Pearson Correlation	.468**	.283**	.081	.212**	-.016	.186**	.360**	1.000	.518**	.420**	.451**
	Sig. (2-tailed)	.000	.000	.254	.003	.827	.008	.000		.000	.000	.000
	N	200	200	200	200	200	200	200	200	200	200	200
EX	Pearson Correlation	.607**	.240**	.070	.045	.002	.222**	.340**	.518**	1.000	.378**	.398**
	Sig. (2-tailed)	.000	.001	.324	.529	.975	.002	.000	.000		.000	.000
	N	200	200	200	200	200	200	200	200	200	200	200
CL	Pearson Correlation	.513**	.198**	.115	.263**	.059	.201**	.552**	.420**	.378**	1.000	.371**
	Sig. (2-tailed)	.000	.005	.105	.000	.407	.004	.000	.000	.000		.000
	N	200	200	200	200	200	200	200	200	200	200	200
SU	Pearson Correlation	.485**	.086	.107	.150*	.062	.209**	.310**	.451**	.398**	.371**	1.000
	Sig. (2-tailed)	.000	.224	.130	.034	.381	.003	.000	.000	.000	.000	
	N	200	200	200	200	200	200	200	200	200	200	200

**. Correlation is significant at the 0.01 level (2-tailed).

*. Correlation is significant at the 0.05 level (2-tailed).

Figure 15.5
**Causal Association Between Organizational Climate and Entrepreneurial
Orientation Factors in Chilean Family and Nonfamily Firms**

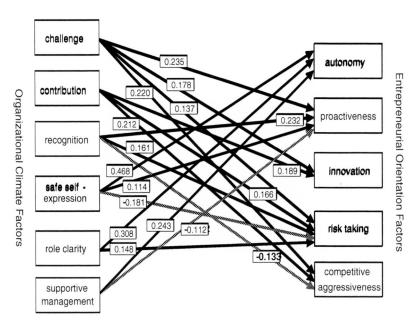

Three causal associations between variables were negative (recognition to competitive aggressiveness, safe self-expression to risk taking and supportive management to proactiveness). According to the SEM results, challenge (OC) is the most significant antecedent in Chilean firms (see Figure 15.5)

Mexico

As expected, according to Pearson's correlations, the six OC factors (1) supportive management, (2) clear role expectations, (3) safe self-expression, (4) perception that one's work significantly affects organizational processes and outcomes, (5) belief that the organization appreciates and recognizes one's effort and contribution, and (6) challenging work that requires the use of creativity and a variety of skills, are positively associated to EO factors (autonomy, proactiveness, risk taking, innovation, and competitive aggressiveness). Results are shown in Table 15.6.

All associations shown in Table 15.6 are significantly correlated. (EO-EO, EO-OC, OC-OC correlations). It is interesting to see that, as in the Chile case, the data for Mexico show the highest correlation (0.643) between autonomy (EO) and self-expression (OC). According to the

Table 15.6 Association of Entrepreneurial Orientation and Organizational Climate Factors in Mexican Family and Nonfamily Firms

Correlations

		AU	PR	IN	RI	C	CH	CO	RE	EX	CL	SU
AU	Pearson Correlation	1.000	.301**	.139*	.168*	.064	.137	.338**	.468**	.607**	.513**	.485**
	Sig. (2-tailed)		.000	.049	.018	.365	.053	.000	.000	.000	.000	.000
	N	200	200	200	200	200	200	200	200	200	200	200
PR	Pearson Correlation	.301**	1.000	.434**	.418**	.382**	.278**	.240**	.283**	.240**	.198**	.086
	Sig. (2-tailed)	.000		.000	.000	.000	.000	.001	.000	.001	.005	.224
	N	200	200	200	200	200	200	200	200	200	200	200
IN	Pearson Correlation	.139*	.434**	1.000	.250**	.436**	.281**	.286**	.081	.070	.115	.107
	Sig. (2-tailed)	.049	.000		.000	.000	.000	.000	.254	.324	.105	.130
	N	200	200	200	200	200	200	200	200	200	200	200
RI	Pearson Correlation	.168*	.418**	.250**	1.000	.473**	.247**	.318**	.212**	.045	.263**	.150*
	Sig. (2-tailed)	.018	.000	.000		.000	.000	.000	.003	.529	.000	.034
	N	200	200	200	200	200	200	200	200	200	200	200
C	Pearson Correlation	.064	.382**	.436**	.473**	1.000	.312**	.286**	-.016	.002	.059	.062
	Sig. (2-tailed)	.365	.000	.000	.000		.000	.000	.827	.975	.407	.381
	N	200	200	200	200	200	200	200	200	200	200	200
CH	Pearson Correlation	.137	.278**	.281**	.247**	.312**	1.000	.570**	.186**	.222**	.201**	.209**
	Sig. (2-tailed)	.053	.000	.000	.000	.000		.000	.008	.002	.004	.003
	N	200	200	200	200	200	200	200	200	200	200	200
CO	Pearson Correlation	.338**	.240**	.286**	.318**	.286**	.570**	1.000	.360**	.340**	.552**	.310**
	Sig. (2-tailed)	.000	.001	.000	.000	.000	.000		.000	.000	.000	.000
	N	200	200	200	200	200	200	200	200	200	200	200
RE	Pearson Correlation	.468**	.283**	.081	.212**	-.016	.186**	.360**	1.000	.518**	.420**	.451**
	Sig. (2-tailed)	.000	.000	.254	.003	.827	.008	.000		.000	.000	.000
	N	200	200	200	200	200	200	200	200	200	200	200
EX	Pearson Correlation	.607**	.240**	.070	.045	.002	.222**	.340**	.518**	1.000	.378**	.398**
	Sig. (2-tailed)	.000	.001	.324	.529	.975	.002	.000	.000		.000	.000
	N	200	200	200	200	200	200	200	200	200	200	200
CL	Pearson Correlation	.513**	.198**	.115	.263**	.059	.201**	.552**	.420**	.378**	1.000	.371**
	Sig. (2-tailed)	.000	.005	.105	.000	.407	.004	.000	.000	.000		.000
	N	200	200	200	200	200	200	200	200	200	200	200
SU	Pearson Correlation	.485**	.086	.107	.150*	.062	.209**	.310**	.451**	.398**	.371**	1.000
	Sig. (2-tailed)	.000	.224	.130	.034	.381	.003	.000	.000	.000	.000	
	N	200	200	200	200	200	200	200	200	200	200	200

**. Correlation is significant at the 0.01 level (2-tailed).

*. Correlation is significant at the 0.05 level (2-tailed).

Figure 15.6
Causal Association Between Organizational Climate and Entrepreneurial Orientation Factors in Mexican Family and Nonfamily Firms

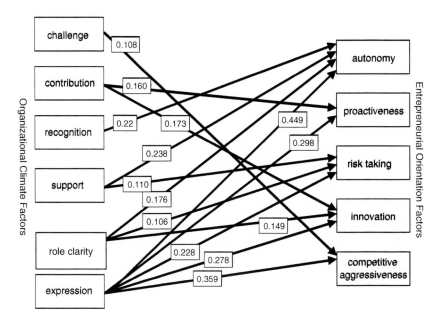

SEM results, all factors (six) of OC significantly affect at least two of five EO factors in Mexican firms. Safe self-expression was the only dimension that was linked to all EO factors, and its regression weights were the highest of all. According to the results of this study, the safe self-expression dimension is the most significant variable that explains EO in Mexican firms. In the case of family firms, to enhance the EO of younger generations, the firms should provide a safe self-expression environment for them (see Figure 15.6).

Discussion

There is an increasing interest in understanding the family business because of its importance to the economy and to social relationships. It is recognized that special forces drive these unique types of organizations, a fact that makes the study of them worthy.

Family businesses in Latin America are experiencing hard times competing against aggressive and well-prepared multinationals, and a way to improve their odds of success might be to turn more entrepreneurial. Recently, researchers have shown a strong interest in understanding the

EO and the antecedents and consequences of it. Factors that enhance EO of family members have not been fully identified; some studies have shown that climate factors influence entrepreneurial orientation.

The Pearson's correlation analysis and the SEM showed that the Mexican and Chilean samples differ in the way OC factors affect EO factors. Each of the six OC dimensions were relevant antecedents for Chile and Mexico, with some important differences. It is interesting to see that in the case of Chile, psychological meaningfulness factors (challenge, contribution, and recognition) had more causal connections (antecedents) with EO factors (autonomy, proactiveness, risk taking, innovation, and competitive aggressiveness) than with psychological safety factors (managerial support, role clarity, and safe self-expression). In the case of Mexico, the psychological safety factors were more relevant to explain EO. According to these findings, younger generations in Chilean family firms will be more likely to be entrepreneurial if they feel that their effort is decisive in achieving their business goals (contribution), if their work is recognized (recognition), and especially if they have interesting and challenging work (challenge). Older Chilean generations should take care of these three climate factors to enhance the EO of the next generation. Psychological safety factors also are important in Chilean firms, especially role clarity and self-expression factors.

According to the results of Mexican firms, the safe self-expression dimension is the most significant variable explaining EO. In the case of family firms, to enhance the EO of younger generations, the firms should provide a safe self-expression environment for them. An organizational culture that allows diversity thinking and feeling, and also provides a safe environment to express ideas and emotions will enhance the EO. Traditional family businesses tend to be autocratic, and frequently there is no space for different ideas from the founder's point of view. Younger generations that feel unsafe expressing their own feelings and thoughts will be less likely to get involved in these companies. On the other hand, they will be more committed if they feel that there is space in the firm for their own ideas and sentiments. This finding is relevant, especially for family businesses, which tend to underestimate the younger generation's ideas.

In family businesses, members of younger generations could feel frustrated because even if they are in important organizational positions, they cannot make important decisions by themselves. The lack of autonomy seems to be a great problem in many of these organizations. Firms that are capable of assigning interesting and challenging work to their employees may find that their employees perceive that they are not doing challenging and interesting work. It could happen, in the case of a family business, that the founder makes many of the decisions that should be left to younger family members, making their work more exciting.

This exploratory research has some limitations that make it difficult to generalize results. Samples of Mexico and Chile are not totally comparable, because the nature of them is different, as we saw in Table 15.3. On the other hand, unfortunately, the number of family firms was not large enough to pursue a SEM analysis independently for these organizations, and instead the analysis had to include both family and nonfamily firms.

It is important to exert caution when generalizing. Before attempting to think of these results as broad and all-inclusive, further research is needed.

References

Andrade, L. F., J. M. Barra, and H. Elstrodt. 2001. "All in the Familia", *McKinsey Quarterly* 4.

Belausteguigoitia, I. 2000. "La influencia del clima organizacional en el compromiso hacia la organización y el esfuerzo en miembros de empresas familiares mexicanas." Doctoral thesis, Universidad Nacional Autónoma de México.

Belausteguigoitia, I. 2004. *Empresas Familiares: Su Dinámica, Equilibrio y Consolidación.* México: McGraw Hill.

Belausteguigoitia, I., and Galicia F. Arias. 2001. "Influence of Organizational Climate on Commitment and Effort in Mexican Family Firms." In *Frontiers of Entrepreneurship Research.* Babson Park, MA: Arthur M. Blank Center for Entrepreneurship.

Brockhaus, R. H. 1980. "Risk Taking Propensity of Entrepreneurs." *Academy of Management Journal* 23: 509–520.

Brown, S. P., and T. W. Leigh. 1996. "A New Look at Psychological Climate and Its Relationship to Job Involvement, Effort, and Performance." *Journal of Applied Psychology* 81: 358–368.

Calderón, R. F. 1988. "Historia Económica de la Nueva España en Tiempo de los Austrias." *Fondo de cultura económica*, México.

De la Cerda, J. and F. 1993. Nuñez de la Peña. *La Administración en Desarrollo: Problemas y Avances de la Administración en México.* Instituto Internacional de Capacitación y Estudios Empresariales. México.

Dictionary.com. 2000. *The American Heritage Dictionary of the English Language. 4th ed.*

Eisenberger, R., R. Hungtington, S. Hutchinson, and D. Sowa. 1996. "Perceived Organizational Support." *Journal of Applied Psychology* 71: 500–507.

Ferkany, S. T. 1992. *For the Family: Building Business in Monterrey.* Wayne State University. Dissertation Abstracts International.

Ginebra, J. 1997. *Las empresas familiares: su dirección y continuidad.* Editorial panorama. México.

Gouldner, A. W. 1960. "The Norm of Reciprocity: A Preliminary State-ment." *American Sociological Review* 25: 161–178.

Kahn, W. 1990. "Psychological Conditions of Personal Engagement and Dis-engagement at Work." *Academy of Management Journal* 33: 692–724.

Kras, E. 1991. *La Administración Mexicana en Transición.* Grupo Editorial Iberoamericana, México.

Lumpkin, G. T., and Cheri B. Sloat. 2001. "Do Family Firms Have an Entre-preneurial Orientation?" In *Frontiers of Entrepreneurship Research.* Babson Park, MA: Arthur M. Blank Center for Entrepreneurship.

Lumpkin, G. T., and G. Dess. 1996. "Clarifying the Entrepreneurial Orienta-tion Construct and Linking It to Performance." *The Academy of Management Review* 21: 135–172.

Malone, S. C., and P. J. Jenster. 1992. "The Problem of the Plateaued Owner-Manager." *Journal of the Family Firm Institute* 1: 25–42.

Meyer, J. P., and N. J. Allen. 1991. "A Three-Component Conceptualization of Organizational Commitment." *Human Resource Management Review,* 61–98.

Reynolds, D. P., et al. 2001. "Global Entrepreneurship Monitor: 2001 Exec-utive Report," *Kauffman Center for Entrepreneurial Leadership at the Ewing Marion Kauffman Foundation.* Wellesley, MA: Babson College.

Reynolds, D. P., et al. 2002. "Global Entrepreneurship Monitor." *Kauffman Center for Entrepreneurial Leadership at the Ewing Marion Kauffman Founda-tion.* Wellesley, MA: Babson College.

Rosenblatt, P. C., et al. 1990. *The Family in Business.* San Francisco: Jossey Bass Publishers.

Toro, F. 1998. Predicción del compromiso del personal a partir del análisis del clima organizacional. *Revista Latinoamericana de Psicología Ocupacional* 14, no. 3.

Weigel, D. J. 1992. "A Model of Interaction in the Intergenerational Family Business." Master's thesis, University of Nevada. UMI Dissertation Ser-vices, Michigan.

CHAPTER 16

Venture Capital in Chile: Flying Angels . . . Lingering Funds

Alicia Castillo Holley

Writing about venture capital in Chile, and probably in all Latin American countries, is important but challenging. Information is limited, sources are scarce, and follow-up is almost impossible. As a Venezuelan living in Chile for the past 6 years, I have been a spectator and participant in the changes in the Chilean entrepreneurial world. I see with joy that entrepreneurship is no longer considered by its impact on employment, but more as a means of wealth creation.

Throughout my stay in Chile, I have been an entrepreneur, a professor, a researcher, and an investor. This chapter is related mostly to the last category. I have been fortunate to experience the changes in a nation that is very motivated to succeed and very different than many other Latin American countries. Chile stands out for its free market approach, public safety, clear regulations, and stability, and I consider it a great country to invest in.

I have heard and read so many variations on the concepts associated with venture capital that I consider it wise to first describe some basic concepts that will be used throughout the chapter.

Let us begin with *venture capital.* I consider venture capital as a type of investment, where cash is exchanged for less than 50% of equity in a firm, with the purpose of selling that equity at a profit in less than 10 years. The

50% hurdle identifies that the investor does not want to take control over the business at the time of investing. The intent to sell differentiates what we call a *socio capitalista*, who usually stays in the firm, and seeks to profit by the payment of dividends instead of the sale of his or her stock. The time frame of 10 years is my own definition, since some individuals or funds will stay longer, but they do evaluate at that time span or earlier to exercise an exit.

Let us now consider *formal venture capital.* I consider that venture capital is performed formally when there is a structure and business model to support it; the structure includes a *fund* and a *management company.* The purpose of the fund is to provide the necessary funds to make investments. The fund contracts a management company on an exclusive basis to promote, evaluate, propose, follow-up, and exit its investments. The fund per se is just a money source that executes no other action. The management company has professionals with experience to carry out the tasks involved and should also contract to lawyers, accountants, board members, external evaluators, and so forth to work on specific deals.

Informal venture capital is carried out without the structure described above. It is commonly accepted that the informal sector of venture capital is performed by angel investors, who evaluate, invest, and follow-up their personal investments. I consider the main difference between informal and formal venture capital is not the structure but the ownership of the funds. A manager will have a different approach to investment than the owner of the funds, particularly when considering how opportunities are evaluated, what degree of involvement is needed, and how the risk is assessed. Fund managers usually structure better exits than capital owners.

Small and medium enterprises (SMEs), or its Spanish equivalent *pequeña y mediana empresa* (PYME), are companies that have annual sales of fewer than a million dollars and usually have fewer than 100 employees. An SME in Chile is much smaller than in the United States because cost of living, labor-related expenses, and market size are much smaller. In order to grow, a company in Chile is forced to export at an earlier stage or at a smaller size than in the United States.

The next concept to discuss is *business format.* Among the various legal formats for businesses in Chile, there are two that are the most commonly used by new companies or by SMEs: *Sociedad de Responsabilidad Limitada* and *Sociedad Anónima.* The Sociedad de Responsabilidad Limitada (commonly referred to as Limitada) is similar to a limited partnership: it is a people-based company, where owners' salaries are limited, but they can take money out of their firm as withdrawals. Any change in ownership is heavily regulated. Typical big Limitadas are law firms. The

Sociedad Anónima is a capital-based company, where owners are established based on the capital invested, unless different types of stock are issued.[1] Change in ownership is very easy, but all paperwork must be reported for tax purposes. A privately held company is referred to as a *Sociedad Anónima Cerrada* (closed); a public company is referred to as *Sociedad Anónima Abierta* (open). *Público* and *privado* refer to state-owned or privately owned businesses or institutions.

Investment companies are companies that perform investment services for their stockowners. Since Chilean law does not contemplate limited liability corporations, many individuals opt to create Sociedades Anónimas or Limitadas to invest through them and deduct investment-related costs. Many angel investors will use this format, and many family groups have established this format. Investment companies do not necessarily have a management team and do not necessarily carry out venture capital–style investments but usually receive deals to invest in.

Exit is the liquidity event that allows a venture capitalist to divest his equity in a firm. After an exit, the venture capitalist is no longer in possession of part of the company and can evaluate the impact of a particular deal on its revenues and return. Exit includes an initial public offering (IPO) through the stock market, a sale, or a write-off due to a company closing.

Now that we have covered some basic concepts, let's get into some history. I like talking about the informal sector because I believe it has existed throughout Chilean history. The southern part of the country is filled with stories of entrepreneurs who sailed from remote places to establish fishing, wood, shipping, or sheep farming businesses. Those were the days before the Panama Canal was built, when ships had to go around Cape Horn to cross from the Atlantic to the Pacific.

I have met descendants of those entrepreneurs and, yes, their grandparents and great-grandparents received funding from families and friends, but most likely from wealthier individuals in their homelands in northern Europe. Some of these experiences can be found in local schools, where elementary professors have taken the time to write about their town's history or where people take the time to reflect on their roots. Thus, in Chile, as in other parts of the world, the words *entrepreneur, venture capital,* and *angel investors* are of recent conception, but have existed previously in various forms.

Informal Venture Capital

Unveiling Angels

In 1996, when I first went to Chile, venture capital concepts were still unknown to many, even in business schools. Even today, no college or university offers a course on venture capital. There is very limited research in this area. In my experience an angel investor will typically act as a *socio capitalista* or as a gift investor for a family or friend. The gift approach is common in family settings, not only at the higher end of society, but at all levels. I prefer to refer to this kind of person as potential angel investor.

I have met a wide range of angel investors, from taxi drivers to top executives. Because the market is informal, it is extremely hard to find information about them. Most of my students were reluctant to accept that they too could find potential angel investors. Therefore, since 1998, I have asked them to interview potential angel investors. During these years, over 300 students have found such individuals. In all of those cases, the students have been able to identify and survey a wealthy individual who could have capital to invest in emerging businesses. These surveys are not limited to Chile, but include several other countries of Latin America. During the last 5 years, around 30% of those individuals have personally invested in businesses not controlled by them or their relatives, and all of them have received proposals for investing. Thus, I think that the general perception that angel investment does not exist could be due to the lack of understanding of the concept or our reluctance to accept that a person who declines a specific proposal can still be an angel investor.

Flying Angels

I wish I could say that angels are flying around deals in Chile, but, sadly, angel capital is flying out of the region instead. Currently, investors are suffering from a shortage in cash, and most will seek to shelter the effect of devaluation in the dollar. Surprisingly enough, the fund we initiated in late 2000[2] has suffered from a devaluation of over 25% of the Chilean peso, not to mention the outrageous 360% devaluation suffered by the Argentinean peso. Most Latin American currencies have weakened because of the slowing of the economy worldwide, and some due to political instability. Most emerging companies have experienced a decline in the expected growth for the same reasons. Thus the much-needed capital to fund wealth creation is fleeing the region, and Chile cannot escape from that effect.

In 2000, push and pull entrepreneurs[3] faced the best market for rising capital. The Internet explosion introduced venture capital to many individuals who sought better alternatives to invest in. I will try to summarize what private individuals dealt with during the past 6 years in Chile. This recollection has no substantial research to back it up, but I hope to give a sense of the mindset of individuals who could act as angel investors, investing up to $500,000 from their private assets in various alternatives. Bigger investors usually do have a professionally managed company that deals with several investment alternatives.

In 1996, Chilean individuals primarily used real estate investments, the stock market being too unpredictable to make them feel comfortable. An increasing number of funds targeted this segment, promising to take advantage of the local and international stock markets. Heavily regulated, the IPO[4] market in Chile was limited, and, in general, the impact of the few main pension funds decisions on the market limited individuals from actively participating in the stock game, much the less understanding it.[5] Investing through funds gave individuals the feeling of diversifying a portfolio and the ability to invest overseas.

The 1998 Asian crisis heavily affected the Chilean economy, nearly collapsing the real estate market. Prices–and real estate value–plummeted 20 to 45%. Construction was virtually paralyzed, forcing the government to issue a tax benefit for first purchases of houses (not first buyers, but buyers of newly constructed houses), with diminishing benefits until the year 2001. Even thought the measure did help deal flow, real estate investment was no longer attractive to investors.

During 1999, individual investor's capital went to mutual funds, especially those investing in emerging technologies or specific funds: Asian markets, Eastern European markets, Latin American markets, high-tech, and so forth. At the end of that year, several initiatives that promoted venture capital took place. The most publicized was Endeavor, the nonprofit organization based in New York City. Other highly visible initiatives were Internet holdings, e-latin ventures, and First Tuesday (the Chilean First Tuesday's branch organized meetings with investors for 10 consecutive months). Capital gushed for 18 months, although there are no records of the amounts invested. Less enthusiastic about risk, Chile was far from the frenzy in neighboring countries like Argentina, Uruguay, and Brazil.

By the end of the year 2000, we organized a group of angels and formed a seed capital fund. In the 6 months that it took to create the business model and business plan, three other private funds were created to invest in the Internet, each one accounting for 10 to 20 million dollars. Neither of these funds received or wanted capital from the pension funds. Entrepreneurs were raising up to a million dollar in seed capital from wealthy individuals with limited or no experience in venture capital. The legal structure made it extremely complicated to do rounds of stocks, and those businesses which received over half a million dollars were usually set up overseas. Delaware, the British Virgin Islands, and the Cayman Islands were favorite places. Thus, most of the higher investments are not recorded in the Chilean capital market.

Chilean Internet companies followed the same path as elsewhere. Those without a coherent revenue stream closed, second rounds became harder, and most of the investments were lost. Currently, in mid-2002, angels are now more experienced and risk averse. Their capital is safer outside of the region, and some have found and pursued amazing deals from the deep devaluation Argentina faced. Today, Chilean entrepreneurs face fierce competition in the capital market. It is hard to convince an individual to invest in a risk venue in local currency when he or she can purchase an asset in Argentina for a third of its value or be shielded from exchange risks in a dollar account. Real estate, art, and antiques auctions have created an interesting alternative for investors.

I perceive that many Chilean angel investors wish to remain private, but entrepreneurs with a sound business plan and an interest in win-win situations will find the resources needed. Many entrepreneurs-to-be lack the knowledge to prepare and present sound business plans and are instead looking for self employment. Others forget that investors want a return on their investments, not to have stock in several businesses. Most importantly, most business plans forget the need for a credible exit strategy. If magic needs to happen for the investor to recuperate his or her capital, magic is needed for him or her to make the decision to enter in the first place.

Where Are Angels Now?

During 2000 and 2001, Ventures Latinas performed a detailed study of potential angel investors. This information was gathered between March and July 2001. A similar research study was carried out in Brazil, Argentina, and Uruguay as part of a bigger effort throughout the southern cone.[6] This is probably the most detailed study to date that includes potential or real angel investors directly.[7] The results show that the angel investor market is active, hidden, and challenging. The study considered individuals who could have the capital to invest. Seventy-nine responded from a pool of 1300. Most of them were men (88%), had some sort of college education (70%), and were older than 30 years old (70%). The study shows that individuals prefer to invest in the stock market, mutual funds, real state, and bank deposits (see Figure 16.1). Almost 80% would consider investing as angel investors, while 20% would not be willing to accept the risk of venture capital personally.

The capital to make investments came from their own efforts, by means of their own firms (63%), or salaries (44%), and less commonly from gains in the stock market (28%), inheritance (22%), or other angel investments (16%) (see Figure 16.2).

Figure 16.1
Prefered Individual Investment Alternatives

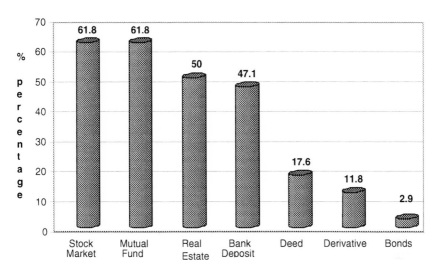

Figure 16.2
Percentage Using This Source of Funds

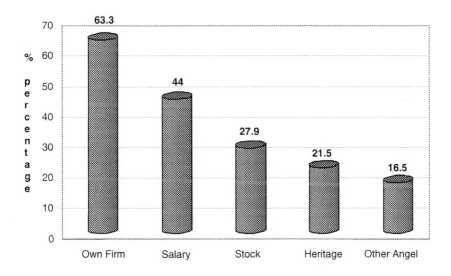

Most angels limited their investments to $250,000. After the initial riskier stages, firms must seek bigger and more organized investments. Sometimes they do not receive angel financing and are too big to be considered interesting to angels. Bigger investments are less attractive to investors since the risk inherent to the firm is allocated to fewer deals, the return per dollar invested is less, and the skills needed are different. Figure 16.3 shows the funds available and invested in new businesses.

Some key points will be interesting to deal flow from the capital supply side: potential angel investors described as the main limiting factor the lack of commercially attractive proposals (83%). The rate of rejection for such projects is high, but individuals do not have the time to evaluate each opportunity; hence, the second limiting factor was lack of time (72%). Other factors considered were lack of proposals with trustworthy information, and lack of capital (57% each). Less important were trust of the entrepreneur's work ethic, commitment, or capabilities (37%, 13%, and 9% respectively). We recurrently find bland business plans, without an innovative edge, and with high self-referral. It has been common for us at the Fondo Emprendedores to run into business plans that promise to be the first in the market, but without having analyzing existing players. Although an entrepreneur's work ethic is important, we do not follow-up a deal unless the proposal is attractive by means of return. Most entrepreneurs fail to consider that they are competing in a capital market, where their business idea has to provide the best return for investment and not the best product or service to a particular niche. Thus, for the sample, the expected return on investment (68% to make the first investment and 42% to continue investing) is the main motivation to start investing as an angel; much less important are personal gratification and curiosity (20% each). The effect of tax benefits is nil, as well as the feeling of social responsibility (over 2% each). Some experts have argued that the 45% capital gain tax is adverse to the development of venture capital.[8] I personally find that it is extremely difficult to account for losses both at the personal and at the business level, thus increasing the risk of venture capital investments.

Another important consideration is the cost of follow-up. Help from the angel is not accounted for, but proves to be more important than the cash invested in the firm. Active participation is important to potential angels. Most would request to be a board member (63%); 12% would like to participate as fund provider and in some operational activity; 29% would also like to participate as a partner, in the operations and in the board; and only 8% would provide just capital. Most individuals perceive that contracts will not prevent mismanagement and prefer to take preventive measures and have a hands-on approach to at least their first investment. I have found that high-end executives tend to enjoy more board participation and business people tend to enjoy a more active role

Figure 16.3
Funds Available and Invested in New Ventures (Data in US $)

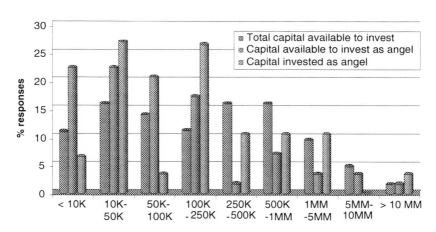

in the day-to-day operations. As with any deal, the best help from investors depends on the quality of the founder's team. Entrepreneurs in Chile do not accept investor's active role easily.

Finding angels and getting information to them is not an easy task, but in my experience capital is not a scarce resource and good business plans and teams do get funded. The general perception is that individuals will not be able to get to an angel unless they are in their inner circle, but we found otherwise. *Pituto* is a common word in Chilean business life. It refers to personal networking that goes back to school and neighborhood and is used to opens doors. A referral will certainly help, and indeed the individuals surveyed indicated that 63% received proposals through professional referrals, and 60% through personal referrals. However, contrary to the general belief, entrepreneurs do seek investors: 40% of proposals received came directly from founders without referrals and fewer than 10% via consultants. Almost 70% of the investors stated that they would use a professional referral service.

It is crucial that the initial information sent to a potential investor be short and concrete (see Figure 16.4). They prefer to receive a mini-business plan of 10 to 14 pages, rather than a full plan with all the details. I also recommend the former to the latter, since details of a new business should be distributed only to pre- or self-selected outsiders who are seriously considering the proposal.

Most individuals (75% of the sample) received proposals from entrepreneurs during the last 12 months. Almost half of them (42%) considered these proposals attractive, and 96% of the attractive proposals were evaluated, including an interview with the entrepreneur. A due diligence

Figure 16.4
Preferred Initial Information

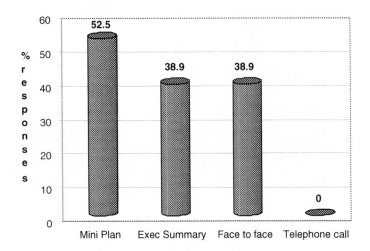

was carried out in 79% of the cases, and in all of these they closed the deal! We also found that angel investors are not familiar with some concepts, such as the definition of angel investment per se, start-up phase, seed capital, and first round. However, once the concepts are explained, we found out that they do fund initial stages (53.2% seed and 27.7% first round). Of the sample, almost 40% have invested in the previous 12 months, in one to three new ventures.

The results of this survey show that angel investing exists in Chile, but much more research should be carried out. I think longitudinal surveys are needed in order to understand how the choices of entrepreneurs and investors affect success or failure throughout time.

Once a business is established or if the amount of capital needed is bigger, formal venture capital is needed. In lack of a strong angel presence, many entrepreneurs used their own resources, gifts from relatives or friends, or a *socio capitalista* scheme to set up their firms. If the capital sought was over 1 million dollars, chances were that no single individual would be able to invest as an angel. Big family groups do provide for such capital but usually take control of the company or the idea. Another alternative is to seek formal venture capital. It is unlikely than a formal venture capital fund in Chile invests less than 1 million dollars, due to administrative costs. We will now refer to the formal side of the market.

Formal Venture Capital

The Dormant Giants

Probably the closest thing to formal venture capital can be tracked back to 1989, with the 18.815 law[9] that allowed pension funds to invest a small portion of their portfolio in emerging ventures. Another important law (19.705, in December 2000) regulates IPOs. Venture capital was therefore born as a capital-driven instrument to allow pension funds to benefit from high-risk high-return opportunities. It served more as an investment opportunity for pension funds than as a demand-driven wealth creation tool based on capital needs from entrepreneurs and emerging businesses. I would like to mention that high-risk investments can and usually do need to consider a loss; however investors and less likely venture capital managers will present a high-risk low-probability of success opportunity, and entrepreneurs seldom realize that offering a hypothetical high-return is not attractive enough.

Information on the formal market is abundant and in the public domain, but it is centralized by the Superintendencia de Valores in Santiago. Unless otherwise noted, the information provided here came from analyzing these data. Usually called Fondos de Inversion para el Desarrollo de Empresas (FIDE),[10] the formal venture capital funds invest in later stages of business development, seeking to enhance attractive firms, and take them to the stock market in around 5 years. Figure 16.5 shows a breakdown of FIDE's sources of funds.

The equity managed by all the regulated funds has remained stable in pesos since 1995, with current prices at Ch $116,510 billion or around US $20 billion (see Figure 16.6). These funds are facing high pressure to

Figure 16.5
FIDE's Sources of Funds

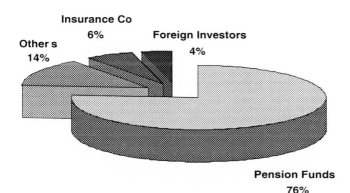

Insurance Co 6%

Others 14%

Foreign Investors 4%

Pension Funds 76%

Figure 16.6
FIDE Assets

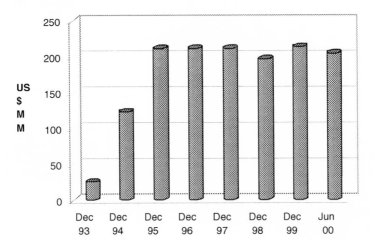

perform under extremely complicated circumstances. Currency exchanges have slashed fund values in terms of dollars in the last 2 years. Exit strategies have been complicated, the stock market in Chile not being liquid enough to provide for a sustainable IPO market. Hence, funds have to rely on dividend payments to support the administrative costs, and wait for a reasonable exit. The early FIDEs needed to liquidate assets in 2002, when the impact of the global economy made it quite unsuitable to sell stock in almost any method. Thus, there are no success stories with FIDEs. There have been success stories inside the FIDEs, but overall their performance fell short of expectations. FIDE managers must face a highly competitive pension fund market, a highly regulated stock market, legal constraints, business practices that are not aligned with public offerings, and a limited deal flow.

Many wealthy individuals (or families) do have investment firms, which receive, evaluate, and fund emerging business. These deals, however, go unnoticed to those not directly involved and are not accounted as venture capital, although they are. There are other smaller investors scattered throughout the country. They do not seem to get together with other investors to network and they evaluate businesses opportunities personally. The new law allows for private funds to act as venture capital funds with fewer limitations. Up to the 2002 legal reform and subject to the 18.815 law, only funds registered by the Superintendencia de Valores (Super) in Santiago were allowed to hold funds from the pension funds.[11] By the end of the year 2001, there were 11 registered funds.

- ChileTech Fondo de Inversión de Desarrollo de Empresas[12]
- Fondo de Inversión de Desarrollo de Empresas Las Américas Emergentes
- Fondo de Inversión de Desarrollo de Empresas Santander Crucero
- Fondo de Inversión de Desarrollo de Empresas Monitor
- Toronto Capital Group Fondo de Inversión de Desarrollo de Empresas
- Fondo de Inversión de Desarrollo de Empresas CMB-PRIME
- Fondo de Inversión de Desarrollo de Empresas Emergentes EME-CHILE
- Fondo de Inversión H&Q[13] S.A. Administradora de Fondos de Inversión
- Fondo de Inversión de Desarrollo de Empresas Sabco
- Fundador Fondo de Inversión de Desarrollo de Empresas
- Sur Fondo de Inversión de Desarrollo de Empresas

Changes within funds are common, so personnel, addresses, and telephones can vary. Some funds have Web sites, but not all of them. Updated information can be obtained in person at the Super's office.

A glimpse at the FIDE portfolio at the end of 1999 (see Figure 16.7) showed that the earlier funds have the higher percentage of venture capital investments.

Figure 16.7
Fide 1999 Portfolio

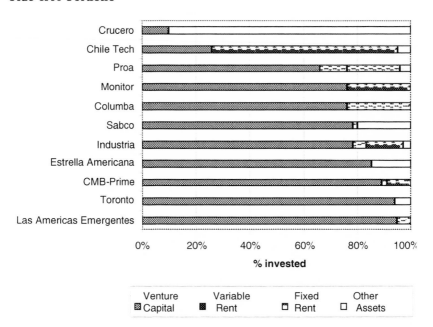

Most funds rely on liquid assets while looking for investment opportunities. By the end of each year, the funds must valuate their portfolio and submit audited financials for all investees by the end of March. This information, as well as the constitution of each fund, is available to the public. An estimated value is set for each investment on a yearly basis. A fund might chose to issue new shares, but it is more likely that the managing company sets up a new fund and invites equity holders in its previous funds to participate. The law requires shared partial ownership between of the fund and the management firm.

Exit Strategy: Stuck Stock

As previously stated, FIDE's investments sought to take attractive firms to the stock market, thus investments were made at later stages. The stock market, however, has not been liquid enough to be attractive to IPOs. It is expected that the new law on IPOs would allow emerging businesses to participate in the public sale of stock. In my view, the stock faces a demand dilemma, not a supply challenge. Efforts to promote a more active demand for stocks will have a greater impact than the supply of new stock.

The Bolsa de Santiago has established an annual contest amongst business administration seniors to promote stock investment. Recently that contest was opened to the general public, and the weekly results are heavily publicized in the media. It does create a general frenzy among students and other participants (even high schools). Winners, however, have not used the prize to purchase stock.

There are other quasi-capital alternatives that affect the venture capital market. Grants in various forms are available to individuals and firms, providing some needed cash to survive or implement a firm. I think it is important to outline these alternatives and their effect in the market.

Quasi-Capital Efforts

Three main public-sector programs foster the development of venture capital in Chile. All are managed by the Corporacion para el Desarrollo del Fomento Productivo (Corfo). These programs include FONTEC (Fondo para el Desarrollo de Innovación Tecnológica), Capital Semilla (seed capital) at the Fondo para el Desarrollo de Innovaciones (FDI), and a line of credit at the División de Intermediación Financiera.[14]

FONTEC promotes innovation, and grants 30 to 50% of research and development costs of innovations, up to $100,000 or $400,000 depending on the program. Usually it provides support to small businesses for new product development, but eventually can also co-fund individual efforts. FONTEC has five kinds of programs, but the most important and common is the first one, called Linea Uno. More information is available at www.corfo.cl.

Capital Semilla, at FDI, is a program that was launched at the end of 2001. It funds seed capital up to Ch$ 35 million (around US $50.000). Applicants can be individuals or newly formed companies (less than 1 year old) that provide an innovative product or service. Sponsorship is required and requirements vary. This is a new program and has radically changed the seed capital investment. The program can cover 100% of costs. Individuals might apply, but the grant requests that a company is created before completion of the grant.

Línea de Crédito is a line of credit for funds. It provides a risk-sharing grant of up to 50% of invested funds, with a very low interest rate (3 to 9%). With the 18815 law modification, private funds can apply. Funds must have a life of up to 15 years.

All these programs help entrepreneurs and business owners, but only the last one targets investors. Corfo has some strong programs for SMEs, and well as Prochile. Using those funds wisely can help an entrepreneur by means of capital, but it also requires substantial data filing. Some consultants provide writing services, but in my experience that is not necessary. I have found that entrepreneurs who understand how to best use these programs are less likely to understand or accept that investors will expect a high return for their high-risk investment. The Capital Semilla program at the FDI could provide entrepreneurs with enough funds to start and prove a concept and be better prepared to present their new firms to investors.

Other Sources of Funds

Venture capital is not the only or even the main capital source in Chile. Several state-funded grants are awarded yearly to researchers, entrepreneurs, and inventors. A preliminary study carried out by Ventures Latinas in August 2001, indicated that six programs are available to innovators as subsidies. In my views, these programs create a negative circle around funding. Among people who have received funds, I have found little understanding of venture capital. For over 2 years, we tried to find interesting deals to invest in. Some entrepreneurs have successfully launched their businesses and would not accept an outside investor. Most commonly, researchers and institutions face investors as public funds providers, overseeing the need for a return that considers the high risk, and the need of good management team. It is my understanding that those difficulties are faced around the world by researchers who wish to commercialize their innovations.

Specific regions benefit from local grants. Corfo is again the main reference at the local level.

A World of Opportunities

This has been a personal reflection of the years I have spent promoting entrepreneurship and venture capital in Chile. There are enormous opportunities to be discovered. Innovation is present throughout the country and despite some adverse circumstances, entrepreneurs do form businesses, and capital is needed to create more wealth.

Notes

1. Stock options were not legal until recently.

2. Fondo Emprendedores S.A. (Managing company's Web site: www.capitalsemilla.cl).

3. Push entrepreneurs are "forced" into entrepreneurship for lack of employment alternatives; pull entrepreneurs are following an opportunity, not out of necessity.

4. IPO stands for initial public offering; in Spanish, OPA (oferta inicial de acciones).

5. The Bolsa de Santiago and the Diario Financiero have an annual contest to promote stock investments.

6. IDRC, the Canadian International Development Research Centre, co-funded this study. Other participants were PUC-Rio, Brazil; Universidad de Quilmes, Argentina; and Market Plaza, Uruguay.

7. A Spanish version of the document can be found at www.ventureslatinas.com; link to "investigación."

8. Patricio Arrau, Gerens, personal communication. Most of their work can be found at www.Kybalion.cl. I have found the same perception at meetings at the Ministerio de Economia, Corfo, and Superintendencia de Valores, both from local and international experts.

9. The 18.815 law was published on July 29, 1989, at the Diario Oficial and modified on December 20, 2000, under law number 19.705.

10. The term FIDE was based on a legal requirement to have access to pension funds capital. Such requirement is no longer needed, so the term is no longer used formally but it is accepted.

11. Most of the information about FIDEs or formal venture capital funds in this section was gathered, processed, and analyzed by Ventures Latinas. I am grateful to Alberto Libedinsky, whom I consider one of the founders of venture capital in Chile, for his insight on the venture capital market.

12. Related to Ventana Group.

13. Related to Hambrech and Quest.

14. In my experience, Corfo is an outstanding institution in Latin America: transparent, focused on its mission, and innovative.

CHAPTER 17

A Note on Venture Capital in Brazil[*]

Antonio José J. Botelho, Gustavo Harckbart, Julian E. Lange, and José Antonio Pimenta Bueno

As Brazilians themselves say, Brazil is a country full of contrasts. It is certainly a challenge to provide a broad view of any subject in such an environment. The attempt to cover the Brazilian venture capital industry outlined in this chapter is the result of our brief experience selecting venture capital funds during Project Inovar's first round, and of a number of interviews with different members of the venture capital industry, such as fund managers, investment bankers, investors, and entrepreneurs. Due to the similarities between the Brazilian and European venture capital (VC) and private equity (PE) industries, much of this chapter compares the two environments. Given the blurred definition of VC and PE in both regions, these comparisons should be viewed with caution and should be taken as indications or trends, not as facts.

---

[*] The authors would like to emphasize that the opinions expressed in this chapter are their own views of the situation, not necessarily reflecting positions from any of the institutions herein mentioned. The chapter was written in 2001–2002 and some minor efforts were made to update it afterwards. The authors, however, believe that the general assessment made still holds true in early 2004.

We would like to thank the several institutions and VC firms that provided data and insight, making this article possible. Particularly, we would like to thank the Brazilian Venture Capital Association (ABRC), Investidor Profissional, Stratus Investimentos, and Finep for their involvement, countless suggestions, and data provided.

The Brazilian Economy in a Few Words*

With 170 million inhabitants, Brazil is known for its racial and social diversity. About 80% of its population lives in urban areas. The country has one of the most unequal societies in the world, and 22% of the population lives below the poverty limit. Another source of concern among Brazilians is the fact that 15% of the population over 15 years old is still illiterate.

On the other hand, Brazil is the eightieth largest economy in the world, with a GDP of US$ 595 billion in 2000. GDP per capita is relatively low, at US$ 2,300 in 2000. The Brazilian economy is a relatively closed one, with exports accounting for only 11% of the GDP, something that the current government is trying to change. The economy grew at a 2.9% annual rate during the 1990s and is expected to grow at a 3.6% pace from 2000 to 2004. Annualized short-term interest rates, although in a downward trend over the long run, are still at the 18 to 19% level. The service sector has been growing faster than other sectors and now accounts for more than 65% of GDP compared to 45% 20 years ago. Inflation is being kept under control; the Brazilian Central Bank's inflation target model forecasts a maximum 5.5% annual rate for 2002.

The country has one of the most developed telecommunications networks in the world, with a digitalization rate above 93% and a penetration ratio around 18.5 fixed lines per 100 habitants. According to Ibope, a research institution in Brazil, Internet usage is estimated to be around 32 million people, or 19% of the population. The IT industry accounted for around 2.3% of GDP in 2000, with the hardware sector responsible for more than two-thirds of it. The devaluation of the real, the local currency, in 1999 made Brazil one of the world's lowest-cost producers of steel, pulp and paper, iron ore, textiles, and other products. Exports are expected to increase, providing relief to the current account deficit of recent years. At the beginning of April 2002, the Brazilian Stock Market, BOVESPA, was composed by 412 listed companies with a total market capitalization around US$ 185 billion, approximately 30% of the GDP, well below the

---

* Most of the data in this section were obtained from the World Bank Web site. The telecom-related data were obtained from the Anatel (the Brazilian telecommunications agency) Web site.

United States level in 1998, which was around two times the GDP. The average daily volume traded from 2001 to April 2002 was US$ 200 to 300 million. The increased popularity of American Depositary Receipts (ADR), the devaluation of the real, and the high transaction costs[1] are attributed to the reduction of the US$ 1 billion daily trading volumes observed in 1998. A number of initiatives are being put in place in order to spur the development of the local stock market. Improvements have taken a long time from discussion to implementation and, in some cases, have not been up to the initially expected standards.

A Brief History of VC* Investment in Brazil

The Brazilian PE market was in a dormant stage until mid-1994, which marked the beginning of Plano Real, the economic plan that stabilized inflation in the country through the introduction of a new currency, privatization of state-owned companies, and a series of structural reforms. Inflation was reduced to single-digit annual rates in 1996, from more than 10,000% annualized rate level in May 1994.

The government privatization effort resulted in the creation of the first true PE firms in Brazil, driven mainly by local investment banks and international institutions. The major targets in the first phase of the privatization program were the industrial companies, regional banks, and Telebrás, the national telecomunications monopoly. Telebrás was divided into several companies by geography and business segment, and sold to private investors in 1998.

One of the most famous and successful turnarounds involving Brazilian privatized companies was Embraer, at the time a quite problematic regional jet manufacturer, bought by a consortium led by Bozano Simonsen, a local investment bank, for US$ 192 million. Today, Embraer, the fourth biggest commercial aircraft manufacturer in the world, is worth more than US$ 4 billion.

Banco Nacional de Desenvolvimento Econômico e Social (BNDES), the chief federal agency for long-term funding (both equity and debt) which aims at promoting the country's development, has been a strong force in the privatization effort. BNDESPar, the BNDES private equity arm, is known for its rigorous standards, for being a pioneer in both the Brazilian PE and VC industries, and for realizing sound investment

---

* Throughout the present work, the term VC and PE are used to designate equity investments arranged in the form of negotiated agreements in private companies. The general partner of the VC/PE firm takes an active role monitoring the portfolio company, usually as a board member. Although not working with a rigid definition, VC is used to designate investments in fledging companies, while private equity is used for turnarounds and privatizations of big companies.

returns over the years. Through the CONTEC program, created in 1991 to capitalize small technology-based companies, BNDESPar invested over US$ 20 million in more than 20 companies, including two VC regional funds. Although some practitioners believe that BNDESPar[2] could play a much bigger role investing in VC funds than what is currently been done,[3] BNDESPar continues to invest in the Brazilian VC industry, as will be seen later in the chapter.

Venture capital firms were officially institutionalized in mid-1986, receiving a more favorable tax treatment than other investment vehicles.[4] The legislation approved was quite restrictive, limiting the investment scope of VC firms to companies with sales lower than $4 million and net asset lower than $8 million.[5]

Overall, the Brazilian VC industry is relatively young. The Internet wave attracted many experienced business people into VC from existing private equity funds, consulting companies, and the financial market. Many of them gathered in groups of two to four people to start their own VC firms. Nowadays, a reasonable share of the Brazilian VC funds, especially the local ones, are start-ups themselves.

There were a few VC players in the industry before the Internet wave, and we would like to spend a few lines talking about them. In the early 1980s, Brasilpar, a firm funded by the International Finance Corporation (IFC) along with French and Brazilian companies, was effectively operating as a VC firm. With US$ 14 million under management, the company made investments in IT, energy, and agribusiness. Results were disappointing and Brasilpar no longer operates as a VC.[6]

Another VC pioneer was Companhia Riograndense de Participações (CRP), founded in 1982. In 1990, operating out of the south of Brazil, the firm launched the CRP Caderi fund, relying on the IFC and a number of local private companies as investors. CRP Caderi is considered to be the first VC fund completely divested in the industry. Another early player was the Brazilian investment bank Bozano Simonsen, today part of Santander Central Hispano. Along with Advent International, a Boston-based global VC and PE firm Bozano Simonsen started a fund aiming to invest in companies with less than R$ 60 million in annual sales, in a mix of VC and PE investments.

At about the same time, GP Investimentos, one of the largest Brazilian PE firms, was catching the Internet wave in its early days. GP invested in Mandic, an Internet service provider, at the end of 1995 and successfully divested it in the beginning of 1998. It is also worth mentioning that, besides GP Investimentos, other PE funds (for instance Bank Boston Capital) were also making occasional VC investments in the mid- to late 1990s.

These early experiences were a source of encouragement for outside observers. But it was not until 1999, with the Internet frenzy, that venture capital in Brazil really exploded. A good way to access the explosion of the number of players in the VC arena is to look at the Brazilian Venture Capital Association (ABRC). Founded in mid-2000 by 26 members, 17 years after their European counterparts started the European Venture Capital Association (EVCA), ABCR currently has more than 60 members.[7]

An important mark regarding the general public interest on venture capital was the launch of Fundo IP.com by Investidor Profissional, a local investment firm. In early 2000, building on favorable market conditions, Investidor Profissional raised US$ 25 million from around 800 small investors[8] through a successful public offer of its first venture capital fund, Fundo IP.com, targeting Internet early-stage companies.

Nowadays, the Brazilian VC industry is made up of a number of well-known international players and a strong base of local firms. Some of the international players are Advent International, Merril Lynch, JP Morgan, Santander, GE Capital, Latinvest, Eccelera, and others. Local firms, like GP Investimentos, Votorantim Ventures, Stratus Investimentos, Dynamo, Investidor Profissional, e-Platform, Rio Bravo Investimentos and others, have been growing in relative importance in recent years.[9]

In the early twenty-first century, some initiatives were created to address the development of the Brazilian venture capital industry. One of them, and probably the most significant, is the Inovar Project, which attacks the development of VC in Brazil on different fronts, like the Venture Forum, training in VC, and the Fund Incubator. The Inovar's Fund Incubator[10] is an initiative of four investors to gather information and conduct joint VC funds analysis, due-diligence, investment, and monitoring. Inovar's Fund Incubator members are Finep, Sebrae, MIF, and Petros. Finep is the Brazilian government agency for innovation. Sebrae is a government-related nonprofit institution whose goal is to support small business creation and development in Brazil. MIF is the American Development Bank arm for VC. Petros is the second-largest Brazilian pension fund. These four institutions have an investment target close to US$ 40 million for the next 2 to 3 years. They recently invested US$ 10 million in the first fund approved by Inovar. The project is already in its third round of VC funds presentations. Up to now, three funds received Inovar's investments and three others are currently in the due-diligence process. Insiders expect to have new investors joining the four pioneers in the near future. Inovar's members like Finep, MIF, and Sebrae are also quite active on their own, providing funding to VC funds addressing their investment and development policies and working to support the industry in events like Finep's Venture Forum. Venture Forum is an event that brings together investors and entrepreneurs intending to raise capital and distributes awards in the form of more flexible debt financing agreements.

The first round of Inovar received 18 memorandum offerings of mostly local VC firms trying to raise their first fund. At that point in time, early 2001, most firms had made three to six investments in rapidly growing companies using their own resources but had divested few.

The VC Numbers in Brazil

According to Stratus Investimentos, a Brazilian VC/PE firm, at the end of 2001, the Brazilian VC/PE industry was composed of more than 80 players, whose combined capital under management ranged from US$ 6 billion to US$ 8 billion. The numbers seem consistent with those from the ABRC/FGV survey, conducted in the end of 2000, which accounted for a total of US$ 3.8 billion managed by the 31 VC institutions participating in the research.

Similar to the downward trend observed in other VC/PE markets in the year 2001, in Brazil VC/PE players invested US$ 678 million in 71 companies, down from more than US$ 800 million distributed in the 87 companies during year 2000 (see Figure 17.1).[11]

Another trend depicted in Figure 17.1 is the growing number of early-stage deals captured by the lower average deal size. The currency

Figure 17.1
VC/PE Deals and Investments in Brazil

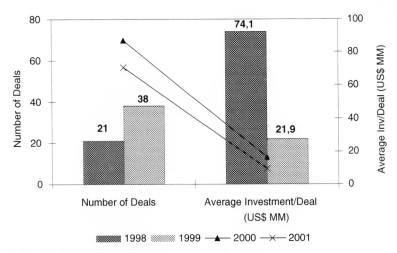

Source: Stratus Investimentos

devaluation is also a factor here, but the trend toward early-stage deals seems fairly strong.

In 2000 and 2001, total annual investment in VC in Brazil account for around 0.13% of GDP. This is far short of the U.S. figure, above 1%, but is somewhat in line with numbers from countries like Japan, Hungary, Poland, Denmark, Italy, Australia, Belgium, and Spain.[12] This evidence suggests that on a comparative basis there might not be a huge lack of formal VC investment in Brazil.[13]

As Figure 17.2 shows, at the end of 2001, from the 79 active VC/PE institutions investing in Brazil, 46% were international players, 33% were local players, 8% were family groups, 8% were corporate venture funds, and 5% were other types of organizations.[14]

The presence and importance of international players throughout Latin America is quite significant. According to the Latin American Private Equity Review and Outlook 2000/2001 edition, "most of the Latin American private equity investment has been raised from institutional investors abroad." Naturally, international players targeting local markets are, usually, better positioned to raise foreign money.

As of now, not a single venture-backed company made an initial public offer in Brazil. In this respect, the Brazilian VC industry is similar to the European one, where trade sales are the most important exit mechanism.

The role played by independent VC partnerships in Brazil is not as important as observed in the U.S. market (Botelho, Lange, and Harckbart 2003). Some of the international players operate through VC/PE divisions, not independent partnerships, and are investing money raised

Figure 17.2
Active Players in VC/PE in Brazil

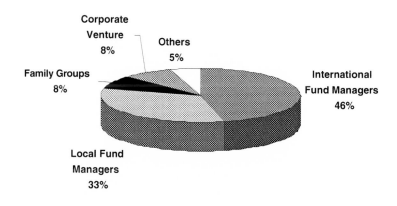

Source: Stratus Investimentos   Total: 79

from their private banking clients. Usually, the legal vehicle used for VC firms is the Emerging Companies' Fund structure, described by CVM's instruction 209 and the more recent ones modifying some of the original items, like instructions 209/94, 225/94, 236/95, and 363/02. CVM's instruction regulates the aspects involved in mutual funds investing in emerging companies. It states that these types of funds can only invest in companies whose total sales are less than R$ 100 million (US$ 40 million) at the moment of investment, and whose consolidated net asset is smaller than R$ 200 million (US$ 85 million). Funds shall have a 10-year time span, with a possibility of a 5-year extension. These funds can distribute shares with a minimum value of R$ 20,000 (US$ 9,000). Funds are allowed to have up to 35 investors without the burden of having to comply with CVM's full securities distribution requirements. Funds whose minimum investment shares are above R$ 400,000 (US$ 170,000) are also exempt from complying with CVM's full securities distribution requirements.

Similarly to European big players, international and big local players sometimes use more than one legal vehicle in order to have more investing flexibility. Some of the biggest international players choose to use offshore entities to make investments. Local players have usually been adopting CVM's Emerging Companies' Fund structure.

As happens in Europe, the definition of investments by companies' stage of development is blurred and investments are biased toward later-stage companies. According to the ABCR/FGV Survey (see Figure 17.3), almost 80% of the money invested during 2000 was targeted at later-stage deals; the number is very similar to the European one of 81% for late-stage investments during 2000.[15]

Figure 17.3
Investment by Stage of Development in 2000

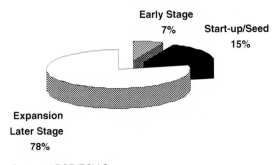

Source: ABCR/FGV Survey

But, there are significant differences regarding stages of development between Brazil and Europe. Certainly, the most significant of them is the relative importance of buyout transactions in both markets. Although in Europe buyouts are the single most important stage of investment, accounting for 41% of the transactions in the year 2000, they are smaller phenomena in Brazil.[16] One of the main reasons for this is likely to be the large difference in interest rates between the two regions. The explanation seems fairly straightforward: in Europe the annualized central bank target interest rate is in the 2 to 4% range, whereas in Brazil it is in the 18 to 19% range, making leveraged buyouts, an important buyout category in Europe, not nearly as attractive.

Also worth mentioning is a strong geographic cluster observed in the southeast region, concentrating more than 95% of the VC activity in Brazil.[17] The southeast region accounts for roughly 60% of the national GDP.

Qualitative Aspects of the VC Industry in Brazil*

Deal Flow

Business incubators are an important player in the Brazilian entrepreneurial environment. According to Anprotec, the Brazilian National Association of Incubators, at the end of 2001 there were 150 business incubators operating in Brazil, incubating an average of seven companies each. Figure 17.4 shows the exponential growth in the number of incubators in the last several years.

Usually, business incubators provide young companies with physical space at lower costs, office services, PR services, and business advice. Several of the incubators receive financial support from Sebrae, local government, foundations, and universities. Around 70% of the incubated entrepreneurs have at least a college degree, 36% of them in engineering. Regarding age, 60% are more than 35 years old. Software is the most sought after area, with 29% of the companies being software businesses. Usually, a company stays inside the incubator for around 2 to 4 years. The idea is to spur the development of local clusters, pursuing a similar pattern to the one observed in the United States, but with incubators being one of the driving forces, not just research institutions and private companies. The project is a long-term one and its impact is yet to be fully understood. However, its ability to attract young companies, more than one thousand of them in the end of 2001, cannot be ignored.

Endeavor, an international not-for-profit private entity aiming at helping entrepreneurs trying to develop their businesses, is playing a small

---

* This section, unless otherwise noted is based on Botelho and Pimenta-Bueno, 2002.

Figure 17.4
Exponential Growth in the Number of Incubators in the Last Several Years

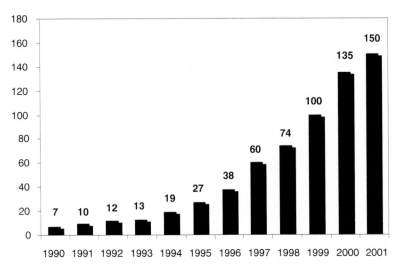

Source: Anprotec

but nonetheless important role in Brazil. Having heavyweight local and international business people on its board, Endeavor provides its entrepreneurs with access to its rich network of people and knowledge. Endeavor is also trying to broaden its scope by organizing open conferences and producing educational material.

Investment Size, Industry, Stage, and Geography Preferences

According to an article in *Exame* magazine in March 2002, most Brazilian VC players are targeting minority investments in the US$ 1 to 5 million range. Foreign investors seem biased toward bigger and later-stage investments, with a few eager to reach the US$ 50 to 100 million range. Local firms seem more willing to do early-stage deals. Regarding industry preferences, it was clear in our latest round of interviews that most VC firms are focusing on the IT, software, and telecom industries. The biotechnology sector is being exploited by a small number of firms, which usually have at least one of its partners with roots in the Brazilian biotech industry.

Considering the industry's age and size, we believe the Brazilian entrepreneur has a somewhat reasonable menu of options regarding stage of development, industry, and VC involvement in the venture. The Brazilian industry was perceived as having a diverse base of players. For each stage of development, a number of VC firms could be found with different preferences regarding the level of involvement in the venture and the general partners' background.

Our participation in the first round of the Inovar Project offered a rich source of insights about the VC industry in Brazil. Our perception is that the two major sources of fund managers were the financial markets and the private equity industry. When put together, fund managers coming from these two industries probably account for something close to 50% of the total number of fund managers at the first Inovar round. A logical derivation of this fact is that sophisticated term sheets, valuation methods, due diligence practices, and strong negotiation skills are likely to be found in the Brazilian VC industry.

One peculiar point is that the credit crunch experienced by young Brazilian companies is likely to modify the bargaining power of VCs and entrepreneurs, in comparison to other countries, when negotiating valuations and term sheets. On the other hand, for a number of reasons, the ability of young Brazilian companies to attract top-notch management and truly effective board members is likely to be inferior to their U.S. counterparts. In this scenario, having experienced and dedicated VCs on your side helping you attract and recruit top people might be a big edge.

Brazilian fund managers claim to provide entrepreneurs with the similar value-added services offered by their American counterparts. But, given the industry's early days, we believe there might be room for improvement regarding fund managers' understanding of technological issues and the particularities in the development of rapid/explosive growth companies. This is certainly a rich topic for research. Another interesting research avenue is local VCs' attitude towards deal syndication. Some of the VCs interviewed mentioned the lack of syndication in the local industry when compared to U.S. standards.

Entrepreneurial education is also an important driver for the future of venture capital in Brazil. As well-observed by Batlin and Bell (2001), "while engineering education is traditionally very sound and advanced, the relevant business education for entrepreneurship is still lacking." Although leading universities are teaching the basic entrepreneurial tools (business plans, marketing plans, valuation methods), courses are still guided solely by the teacher, with a strong theoretical approach and without intense student involvement. We foresee that a substantial amount of work will have to be done before Brazilians have top U.S.-level entrepreneurial education in the country.

General Partners Investment

One of the particularities of the Brazilian VC industry is the investment level undertaken by the general partners. Whereas in the United States the general partners are expected to contribute with 1 to 2% of the fund,[18] in Brazil higher levels have been observed. General managers and the firm's parent company are contributing in the range of 5 to 10% for the total capital under management, according to our experience at Inovar. The higher investment level is a strong sign that, in spite of the lack of a track record by most VC fund managers, parent companies and fund managers themselves are willing to make significant bets on their skills.

Targeted Rates of Return and Other Characteristics

Still regarding the Inovar experience, on an aggregated fashion, our perception is that Brazilian VC/PE firms are targeting annual portfolio returns in the 35 to 40% range. The 17 to 22% premium over the Brazilian Central Bank interest rate (SELIC) seems relatively larger than the ones found in the European and U.S. market, both in the 11 to 17% range, considering the aggregate returns for the industry in a 20-year time span. Taking into consideration the young age of the Brazilian VC industry, a spread between Brazil and more developed markets could be expected. The historical moment in which the first round of the Inovar Project took place might also have contributed to the distortion, considering that the effects of the technology stocks crash were not yet completely known by the beginning of 2001.

Other relevant information associated with Inovar's first round was the fact that VC funds were working with an expected lifespan of about 5 to 10 years, planning to invest in 15 to 30 companies during the fund's early years. Most VC firms were expecting to raise funds in the US$ 10 to 20 million range. The fee structures proposed were similar to U.S. standards except that most Brazilian VC funds intended to limit their carried interest to what would be earned above some inflation index (usually IGPM) plus 6% over year.

IPO and M&A Expectations

The perception of VCs regarding initial public offerings (IPOs) in Brazil is very cautious, with most investors not counting on an IPO window for the next 3 to 5 years. Many VCs argue that the lack of demand for small companies by local institutional investors is likely to play a significant role in the IPO issue. Interestingly, European VCs had similar points of view in 1996, as stated in the Better Exits document endorsed by the EVCA. One Brazilian investment banker interviewed pointed to the fact that his clients were not interested in IPOs with a floating smaller than US$ 50 million. Companies with negative earnings before interest, taxes, depreciation, and amortization (EBITDA) were also expected to have a hard time raising funds through public offers.

Some fund managers indicated that they might be using the SOMA market instead of BOVESPA, the biggest stock market in Brazil. SOMA is a smaller exchange targeting issuances of smaller companies and based on the market maker concept. It might be a more economically efficient alternative for smaller ventures.

Regarding mergers and acquisitions (M&A) exits, our talks indicate that local private equity funds have not started to actively buy VC funds out of later-stage companies. Some of them say they would consider the option, but they are more inclined to do primary issuances. Most VC funds in Brazil seem to be targeting strategic buyers as the primary exit target. A few fledging companies were bought by strategic investors in 1999 to 2000, but most of them were not venture-backed companies. So, much of the Brazilian market's capacity to absorb venture-backed companies through M&A deals is yet to be tested.

New Developments That Might Shape the Future of VC in Brazil

We believe that over the short-to-medium time span, the creation of BOVESPA's New Market, the new law of informatics, Resolution 2,829, the establishment of fund managers' track record, and the evolution of the country's macroeconomic conditions are likely to positively affect the Brazilian VC industry. With the approach of presidential elections, political uncertainty should not be underestimated. The New Market and the establishment of track record are directly related to VC's ability to exit and raise new funds. The law of informatics and the law of innovation might impact both funding and the deal flow side. The Resolution 2,829 increased pension funds' flexibility to make private investments in companies with good corporate governance practices, either directly or through funds. More on each item is commented on in the sections below.[19]

Corporate Governance, the New Market, and Public Interest in the Stock Market

The New Market, a project from BOVESPA, is an attempt to provide an environment of more transparency and shareholder protection to minority shareholders. Companies entering the New Market sign a contract with BOVESPA assuring that they will disclose certain additional information and concede certain shareholders' rights not enforced by the local law, depending on the level of corporate governance they are entering at.

As of the end of April, two companies had entered in the New Market, both old-economy style companies. Twenty companies have signed on for BOVESPA's first level of governance, which requires them to release additional information and to keep a minimum float of 25% of their equity value, but does not change minority shareholders' rights.

The current government has been trying to raise the public awareness of the stock market. BNDESPar made two successful secondary offerings, selling part of its shares of Petrobrás, the national petroleum company, and CVRD, the privatized iron ore producer. Part of both offerings was targeted at small investors, who used their FGTS[20] resources to acquire shares of both companies. A similar program aiming at raising VC funds with the general public might be a very interesting option. Although the current timing seems discouraging, Investidor Profissional's experience proved that there is demand for venture investing by the general public. The Canadian government's program of labor-sponsored venture capital funds, created in 1984, accounted for more than half of the country's venture capital pool by 1999. Labor-sponsored venture funds, composed primarily of average working people, managed over US$ 4 billion in the country by 1999.[21] The maximum annual individual investment, which qualifies for tax credits, is legislatively mandated and has ranged from $3,500 to $5,000. Tax incentives offered by the provincial and federal governments provide a total 40% tax credit to investors.[22] To say the least, given Brazil's previous experience with secondary offerings targeting small investors, this is certainly a promising road to be explored.

Resolution 2,829

Affecting the fundraising side of the venture industry, the recently approved Resolution 2,829 refers to the Brazilian pension fund investment restrictions and possibilities. Brazilian pension funds operating under the defined contribution plan[23] can invest up to 20% of their investments in the private equity asset class, venture capital included, both through funds and/or direct investments. The companies invested, either directly or through funds, are required to adopt good governance practices similar to the ones enforced by the New Market, and to formalize with the CVM, the Brazilian SEC, that if they are to issue shares in the national stock markets they will adopt good governance practices similar to the ones enforced by the New Market.

Besides the increase in allocation flexibility, the Resolution 2,829 is also likely to spur the adoption of good corporate governance practices by Brazilian emerging companies targeting venture capital. Given the importance of Brazilian pension funds as VC investors, it is likely that most VC funds will push for better corporate governance practices among their investees.

Although allocation flexibility is available, most pension fund managers do not have prior experience investing in VC funds. The lack of experience regarding VC and technology companies by pension fund managers is certainly a major constraint for the VC industry. More about the role of Brazilian pension funds in the VC industry is discussed in the Final Assessment section.

The New Version of the Law of Informatics and the Law of Innovation

The new Law of Informatics assures certain tax benefits to IT companies investing a minimum of 5% of their sales in R&D activities related to the IT sector in Brazil. Parts of the resources have to be invested in R&D activities taking place in Brazilian universities and research institutions. In 1999, the IT industry in Brazil had combined sales around US$ 12 billion, according to data from the Brazilian Ministry of Science and Technology. Some industry sources think the new law might contribute to the constitution of corporate VC funds and for the expansion of existing programs aimed at investing a share of the resources available.

The Law of Innovation, yet to be approved in Congress, intends to spur the creation and transfer of technology by researchers addressing four main factors. First, it would increase public universities' flexibility to hire/fire researchers involved in technological innovation projects. Second, it would allow public universities to partner with national technology companies and other entities for the development of new technologies. Third, it would allow the university and researcher to benefit from the economical gains of research licensing and technology transfer. Fourth, under certain circumstances and for a certain periods of time, researchers would be allowed to work for existing national technology companies or even start their own companies without losing their original job at the university. The project contemplates a number of other incentives for national technology companies, and experts believe that, given the quality of Brazilian public universities, the Law of Innovation has the potential to unleash a huge amount of technical knowledge to Brazilian small businesses.

The First IPO?

At the beginning of 2001, business newspapers started to talk about the possible first IPO of a venture-backed Brazilian company in the BOVESPA's New Market. Microsiga, a company developing and selling ERP software, was the top candidate, having big international investment banks as its underwriters. As the markets turned south, rumors disappeared. According to *Valor Econômico*, a Brazilian business newspaper, the IPO process was restarted in the beginning of 2002, after the Argentine contagion seemed less likely and the U.S. IPO conditions improved. Still according to *Valor Econômico*, the company was planning to sell 25 to 30% of its shares and raise a total of US$ 40 million for the company expansion plans. The IPO was expected for the second half of 2002, but was again postponed.

Establishment of Track Record and Successful Exits

The general partner's track record is widely known to be one of the most important investment criteria in the VC business for fund selection and investment decisions.[24] As previously pointed out, most of the Brazilian VC firms are start-ups themselves. Over the long run, as a track record is built up, fundraising is expected to improve. Successful exits might not only help fundraising but improve deal flow as well.

Political Uncertainty

The inauguration of the President-elect from the Workers' Party (PT), Luiz Inácio da Silva (popularly know as Lula), in March 2002, following Fernando Henrique Cardoso, who had governed the country since 1994, initially affected the financial market's mood. In fact, Lula adopted a very moderate posture and strong macroeconomioc stabilization policies that gradually reassured foreign investors.

Final Assessment

Gompers and Lerner (1998) highlighted three factors affecting VC fundraising in the United States on the aggregate level: the level of capital gains taxes, pension fund investment restrictions and R&D expenditures. The Brazilian government seems to be advancing in the last two fronts but retreating in the capital gain tax rate. From 2002 on, stocks' capital gain tax rate has increased to 20% from the previous 10% rate. Besides affecting financial returns, changes in capital gain taxes are know to be associated with changes in the level of entrepreneurial activity.

According to the Global Entrepreneurship Monitor (GEM) project report, Brazil is one of the most entrepreneurial countries in the world. Although with a high level of necessity-based entrepreneurs, Brazil's Total Entrepreneurial Opportunity Index, a better measure for opportunity-related entrepreneurial activity, ranks close to Ireland, and is higher than countries like the UK, Italy, Spain, France, Germany, Israel, Korea, India, and Singapore.[25]

Although Brazilian entrepreneurs hold positive perceptions of VC, there are some misconceived opinions and beliefs and correspondent negative feelings (Botelho and Jonathan 2004). The favorable view of VC held by high-tech entrepreneurs indicates a positive environment for the evolution of the VC model in Brazil. Nevertheless, efforts are in order to address negative feelings expressed in the opinions and beliefs of a few groups of Brazilian high-tech entrepreneurs, such as non-incubated, IT entrepreneurs, women entrepreneurs, and entrepreneurs from the state of São Paulo. High-tech entrepreneurs in Brazil mainly seek VC for establishing a partnership for strategic planning and express their confidence based on expected benefits: VC is perceived as mediating both developments in strategy and as accelerating growth.

Nowadays, Brazilian entrepreneurs face a severe credit crunch due to the high interest rate environment. Interest rates affect equity funding, debt funding, and even bootstrap alternatives. They severely affect the willingness of local investors to invest stocks and private equity. Brazilian pension funds, with around US$ 64 billion under management,[26] are likely to have a long way to go before hitting the 3.6% private equity allocation of their European counterparts. It is likely that deeper knowledge of VC on behalf of pension fund managers will be required before a major allocation increase to the VC asset class can be observed. Besides the private equity allocation itself, the willingness of local investors to invest in stocks, IPOs included, is likely to change significantly from a high interest rate environment to a low interest rate environment. Nowadays, Brazilian pension funds hold, on average, around 60% of their assets allocated in government certificates and fixed income, and 30% in stocks,[27] which gives considerable room for the expansion of the stock-related asset class.

It is in our belief that the Brazilian VC industry managed to attract talented general partners. BNDESPar's gradual move from direct investments in emerging companies to investments in VC fund is a strong sign of the maturity of the Brazilian industry.

Corporate venture capital investors, usually less liquidity-concerned due to their strategic motivations, might play a bigger role in Brazil than in more developed markets. In the United States, it took many years of venture capital activity before corporations started building corporate venture programs. In Brazil, a number of companies already have venture programs, ranging from heavyweight internationals Eastman, GE, and Intel, to locals CVRD, the largest iron ore exporter in the world; Promon, with IT-related interests; and Votorantim, a large family-owned industrial conglomerate centered on cement and paper and pulp industries.

Although venture capital is a business of exceptions, these exceptions can make a really big contribution to the economy. Companies like Cisco, Sun Microsystems, Oracle, Apple, Intel, Compaq, Staples, eBay, Genentech, and Neutrogena, are examples of the powerful exceptions venture capital was able to nurture. According to the NVCA, in the year 2000, venture-backed companies generated revenues totaling US$ 736 billion, an astonishing 7.4% of the U.S. GDP.

Significant numbers regarding both entrepreneurship and venture capital can already be seen in Brazil. Even though there are a good share of regulatory improvements to be made, like the so-awaited tax and pension reforms and other issues that have yet to be solved,[28] one can only imagine the transformation that will take place in the entrepreneurial activity and VC industry if and when Brazil's interest rates shift to more reasonable levels, as continuously forecasted by the government.[29]

References

Asset Alternatives. 2001. "Latin American Private Equity Review and Outlook 2000/2001 Edition." *Journal of Private Equity.*

Banco Nacional de Desenvolvimento Econômico e Social (BNDES). www.bndes.gov.br.

Batlin, M., and P. Bell. 2001. "Venture Capital in South America: Unlocking the Potential for Venture Creation in an Emerging Market." Working paper. Koblenz: WHU, Otto Beisheim Graduate School of Management, July.

Botelho, A. J. J., and E. Jonathan. 2004. "Brazilian High-Tech Entrepreneurs' Social Representation of Venture Capital." Paper presented at 24th Babson Kauffman Entrepreneurship Research Conference, Glasgow, Scotland, June3–5 and Laboratory for New Economy and Technology, Núcleo de Estudos e Pesquisas Gênesis, PUC Rio, Working Paper Series No. 01-2004.

Botelho, A. J. J., and J.A. Pimenta-Bueno. 2002. "Boosting Venture Capital in the Southern Cone–Innovation's Missing Thread?" Laboratory for New Economy and Technology, Núcleo de Estudos e Pesquisas Gênesis, PUC Rio, Working Paper Series No. 01-2002

Botelho, A. J. J., J. Lange, and G. Harckbart. 2003. "Do Brazilian Venture Capitalists Add Value to Their Portfolio Companies?" Paper presented at 23rd Babson College-Kauffman Foundation Entrepreneurship Research Conference at Babson College, June 5–June 7 and Laboratory for New

Economy and Technology, Núcleo de Estudos e Pesquisas Gênesis, PUC Rio, Working Paper Series No. 02-2003.

Botelho, A. J. J., T. Bruginski de Paula, M. C. Penido de Freitas, and M. C. Rossi. 2003. "Capital de Risco e Desenvolvimento Tecnológico no Brasil–Experiência recente e perspectiva–Relatório Final." Brasília, Centro de Gestão e Estudos Estratégicos, Junho.

BOVESPA. www.bovespa.com.br.

"Brasil Venture News 13." 2002. *Stratus Investimentos* newsletter. January.

"Brasil Venture News 14." 2002. *Stratus Investimentos* newsletter. February.

"Brasil Venture News 15." 2002. *Stratus Investimentos* newsletter. April.

Brazilian National Association of Incubators (Anprotec). 2001. "Panorama Anprotec 2001." http://www.anprotec.org.br/panorama.htm.

Brazilian Venture Capital Association (ABCR). www.abcr-venture.com.br.

Comissão de Valores Mobiliarios (CVM). www.cvm.gov.br.

Endeavor. www.endeavor.com.

European Venture Capital Association (EVCA). www.evca.com.

Finep. www.finep.gov.br.

Goldman Sachs and Co. and Frank Russell Company. 2001. "Report on Alternative Investing by Tax Exempt Institutions 2001." http://www.gs.com/insight/research/reports/2001_Goldman_Russell_Survey.pdf

Gompers, P.A., and J. Lerner. 1998. *What Drives Venture Capital Fundraising* NBER Working Paper No. w6906. Brookings Papers on Economic Activity: Macroeconomics: 149–192.

Gorgulho, F. 1996. *O capital de risco como alternativa de financiamento às pequenas e médias empresas de base tecnológica: o caso do Contec/BNDES.* Working paper. UFRJ–Universidade Federal do Rio de Janeiro.

Leite, C. R., and C.A. Souza. 2001. *Os fundos de private equity como uma alternativa de financiamento de capital de risco às empresas no Brasil, através da participação acionária e administrativa,* June.

National Venture Capital Association (NVCA). www.nvca.org

Revista Exame. March. "Onde está o dinheiro." Grupo Abril, 2002, 22.

Reynolds, P., W. Bygrave, E. Autio, L. Cox, and M. Hay. 2001. "Global Entrepreneurship Monitor, Executive Reports," London Business School and Babson College.

Sociedade Operadora do Mercado de Ativos (SOMA). "Como Abrir o Capital?" www.somativos.com.br

"Venture Capital Survey." 2000. Brazilian Venture Capital Association/Fundação Getúlio Vargas.

Notes

1. Estimated by BOVESPA as being more than four times higher than the costs of trading ADRs in the beginning of 2001.

2. The consolidated annual BNDES budget is around US$ 20 billion.

3. BNDESpar recently invested in a US$ 10 million regional fund managed by Rio Bravo Investimentos, targeting companies in the northeast part of Brazil. For more information, see http://www.bndes.gov.br/noticias/not497.asp.

4. Gorgulho (1996).

5. Ibid.

6. Ibid.

7. ABCR's Web site, www.abcr.org.br

8. Fund IP.com shares were sold at US$ 5,000 each.

9. Stratus Investimentos, a Brazilian VC firm.

10. From now on, for economy reasons, we use the terms Inovar Fund Incubator, Inovar Project, and Inovar interchangeably.

11. Source: Stratus Investimentos.

12. GEM 2001 Summary Report.

13. As previously said, VC definitions may vary from country to country. Direct comparisons should be viewed with caution.

14. Ibid.

15. EVCA.

16. Unfortunately, they were not computed in the ABCR/FGV survey.

17. Source: ABCR/FGV survey.

18. "Why and How to Invest in Private Equity," ECVA Investor Relations Committee.

19. Further information on these and other trends can be found in Botelho, Lange, and Harkbart 2003.

20. FGTS is a kind of pension fund managed by the government. Brazilian workers contribute monthly to the fund. The fund's resources can be assessed in case of the worker being fired without a fair reason, retirement, and so forth.

21. Wilson, Janet. "Canadian Labor Provides Stake for Tent Firms, Others." Los Angeles Times, September 26, 1999.

22. Kreiner, Sherman. "Fund Labour-Sponsored Investment Funds in Canada." http://www.uswa.org/heartland/7canlsif.htm.

23. The biggest Brazilian pension funds either adopted this model or are in transition to it.

24. See, for instance, the Alternative Investing by Tax Exempt Institutions 2001, by Goldman, Sachs and Co. and Frank Russell Company.

25. GEM 2001 summary report.

26. Brazilian government, December 2001.

27. Source: Brazilian government, December 2001. The data does not account for pension products open to any participant, like PGBL-related types.

28. Like the energy crises, for instance.

29. The Brazilian government is forecasting that interest rates will be lower than 13% by the end of 2003.

CHAPTER 18

Women in Business and Entrepreneurship in Chile

Judy "JJ" Jackson

Olga Pizarro

Entrepreneurship Defined

The terms *entrepreneur* and *entrepreneurship* have different connotations for different people, whether the people are business persons or other professionals, or whether they are practitioners. Moore and Buttner's (1997) research identified several different definitions of these terms: (1) "an independently owned and operated business with fewer than 100 employees and less than $100,000 gross receipts per year"; (2) "one who owns and starts a new and small business"; (3) "the creation of new organizations"; (4) "the process of creating something different with value by devoting the necessary time and effort; assuming the accompanying financial, psychic, and social risks; and receiving the resulting rewards of monetary and personal satisfaction" (p. 12). At the June 2000 Research Forum on Entrepreneurship in Latin America, held at Babson College in Massachusetts, the concept of *intrapreneurship* was mentioned in a discussion session. The term was used and understood as engagement in entrepreneurship within a larger business that is owned by someone else (e.g., a division or unit within a large company). Perhaps none of these should be considered in any way as the official definition of an entrepreneur or of entrepreneurship. The women in our study may in fact be categorized in one or all of the above, but we were loath to categorize them. We sought to illuminate the deeper meaning of the women's activities and the import of the choices they made.

Background for the Study

Along with highly touted mergers and acquisitions in big business, the economic vicissitudes of the past 10 to 15 years have spurred enormous growth in entrepreneurship. While the economic changes have been global and the percent of women entering the job market has increased worldwide (Moore and Buttner 1997), most of the literature on entrepreneurship has focused on activity in the United States and parts of Europe. The body of literature on women in entrepreneurship continues the growth that took hold in the 1990s. However, similar to the majority of research on entrepreneurship in general, the focus has been largely on women in the United States and parts of Europe. Researchers seem particularly drawn to the study of women who have been successful in big corporations. Studies by Ericksen (1999) demonstrate researchers' abiding interest in women who have made it big, or who have climbed to the top of an otherwise masculine ladder.

Few studies have focused on women in South America, specifically women in Chile. Research by De Rubinstein, Valdés, and Pardo (1991) looked at determinants of women's participation in general in the labor force, using national census data and long-term labor trends in Santiago. While their study focused on employment in general, their findings helped to frame some of the dimensions of our own research. They found, for example, that generally trends in education influenced women's participation in the work force—the more education women had, the higher their level of participation. Chilean women, however, seemed to buck that trend, because their employment participation rates were lower than that of women in other parts of Latin America, although their education levels were at least as high, if not higher than the education and training levels of most other women in the third world. Barrientos, Bee, Matear, and Vogel (1999) looked closely at Chilean agribusiness. Their focus, however, was narrowly on the participation of women in the fruit export sector, looking at circumstances in the women's temporary and permanent employment status. The inclusion of entrepreneurship as a discussion point was endorsed at the 1997 meeting of the International Labour Organization. Certainly, discourse on entrepreneurship in the international arena may help to increase future focus on this research area in regions additional to the United States and parts of Europe. Hopefully, the discourse will also help to spur more research and change the fact that the literature retains scant mention of women entrepreneurs in Chile.

Objectives of the Study

The first objective of this study was to compile fundamental and useful information to contribute to the limited research on Chilean women in entrepreneurship. To the extent possible, we wanted to determine the level of participation–how many women entrepreneurs are there in Chile? We wanted to discern their motives–why did they choose to become entrepreneurs? What did they hope to accomplish? We wanted also to identify the areas of their impact–what effect might their work have on the Chilean economy and on their families? Finally, we wanted to determine whether their impact could be measured–how many people did they employ, and what financial contribution did they make to the growth of the city or region? The second objective was to raise questions that might promote further research in this area. Given the considerably high percent of Chilean women with a post-secondary education, what might this foretell about the future increase of their participation in entrepreneurship? What impact have these women had on the family structure and other social institutions? How might their experiences resemble those of women entrepreneurs in, say, the United States or parts of Europe?

Context of the Study

The market-oriented Chilean economy boasts special strength in its financial institutions, offering considerable investment reliability. Services represent some 54% of Chile's GDP, with industry representing about 38% and agriculture representing the remaining 8%. In the year 2000, women represented approximately 40% of the labor market. The unemployment rate among women was only one percentage point higher than that of men. This data point is noteworthy because women make up approximately 50.5% of the country's population (Fact Book on Chile 2002). The May 2002 report of the Union Association of Pension Funds Administrators showed that, in February 2002, the average wage of women grew 1.6% over the February 2001 level. In the same time period, the average wage of men grew only 0.01%. According to the report, the wage differential between men and women's average income diminished dramatically. Specifically, over the last 3 years, men's average income went from 31.5% to only 12.8% higher than that of women.

We focused our investigation on women entrepreneurs, as well as intrapreneurs (women engaged in entrepreneurial activity within an established business). We sought to determine the level of participation, motivation, and success of Chilean women in these areas, including especially those who owned and operated their business. Our research design involved both quantitative and qualitative data gathering and analyses. The findings may be useful in the design of a blueprint to foster greater involvement and success of women entrepreneurs.

Research Design and Methodology

Sample of Participants

Had we a choice, we would have utilized a purely random sample method of identifying women for the study. However, we found no existence of a directory or other database of executives organized by gender in Chile. Nor did we find evidence of any comprehensive database on women in business or entrepreneurship. Thus, we were compelled to use the method of convenience (or opportunity) sampling to identify a potential population from which we could draw our sample of participants. We did so with the help of different organizations in Santiago and Concepción. The organizations included private associations of businesswomen, a national finance organization providing funding for women-owned start-up businesses (FINAM), and word of mouth through informal professional networks. Through these organizations, we identified nearly 1,000 women. We invited all of them to participate in the study.

Mail Survey

Guided in part by previous studies on women in business that were done in the United States (Bell and Nkomo 2001; Langowitz 2001) and in Poland (International Forum for Women 2000), we developed a 63-item questionnaire. This survey instrument solicited detailed information on the participants and their activities, and organized the information in the following sections.

- Company profile data provided such information as the type of industry' size of company, number of employees, dollar estimate of annual sales, ownership structure, managerial levels of the company, and the demographics of the management structure.

- Participants' position in the company provided information on the number of employees that the participants supervised, if any; participants' assessment of their own stature or respect in the company; participants' sense of their company's competitiveness; and their salary levels and movement or promotion through company ranks.

- Participants' self perception as a manager gave us insight into what motivated the participants; how they see themselves and how they perceive that others see them; and their hopes or goals for the company and its employees.

- Educational and personal background information yielded a profile of the participants, their support structures during their educational and career development, how they attributed their success, their family circumstances, and what pressures they faced that were related to home and family.

We distributed the questionnaire to the nearly 1,000 women professionals and executives in Santiago and Concepción, with the assistance of the aforementioned organizations that helped us to identify the participants. The 10% return rate that we got represented a first step in an area of research that holds much promise for future investigation.

Interview Protocol

Using a loosely structured protocol, we conducted interviews with 20 of the 100 respondents. Interview questions solicited information about the participants' youth; the nature of their relationship with their parents or guardians when they were growing up; their educational experience and mentors they have had; and their relationship with their husbands/ partners and children, if any. The interviews yielded contextual information about the women's educational and professional experiences, as well as insights into their motivations for the work that they chose to do. Most interviews were conducted at the participants' place of business, giving us a professional context and a sense of their level of pride of association. Some interviews took place (by invitation) in the participants' homes. This gave us a rare glimpse into the private structures that undergird the participants' success, and a chance to see some depth of relationships that helped to explain the choices made and successes enjoyed.

Findings

Company Profiles

As summarized in Table 18.1, the company profiles largely reflected the composition of the country's economic structure. Over half of the companies were service providers, with nearly one-third in industrial enterprises. Most were small-to-medium private companies (96%), and most (54%) had fewer than 50 employees. At least 50% of the companies were in development or dynamic development, which means they were poised (or preparing for) expansion or increased volume of activity. Most of the companies, even the smallest ones, were using up-to-date technology, from the latest in computer office equipment (including software), to state-of-the-art printing presses, to modern automated machinery for mass production. Annual sales of the companies spanned a wide range. Much like the situation in the United States, most of the managerial ranks were generally dominated by men, including the companies in which the workforce was at least 50% women.

Table 18.1
Summary Profile of the Companies Represented in the Study

	Type of Industry
56%	Service (utilities, textiles, public administration, hotel, transportation, education)
32%	Industry (construction, mining, forestry, mineral extraction, production, printing)
12%	Finance (banking and other lending/investment industries)
	Company Ownership
26%	Joint stock
28%	Private domestic
28%	Other structure
10%	Company owned
8%	State owned
	Annual Sales
31%	$400,000
34%	$2,800,000
35%	Wide variation
	Workforce
30%	10 employees
24%	11–50 employees
18%	51–100 employees
11%	101–500 employees
8%	501–1000 employees
9%	1001–6000 employees
63%	50% women in the workforce
47%	Women at or near managerial levels in businesses that they do not own
	State of the Company
25%	Dynamic development
25%	Development
30%	Planned stability
12%	Stability forces by external conditions
2%	Temporary problems
1%	Serious problems
5%	Other

Respondent Profiles

The participants in the study were by and large well-educated women—88% earned at least one college degree, with most obtaining their degree within the last 20 years. This may explain the observation that the age spread of 63% of the women is between 40 and 59 years old. Most of the respondents earned educational degrees in the areas of business or engineering. About 71% of them were owners or general managers in their businesses. They reported participating actively and frequently in the personnel decisions of their companies, as well as in the control and evaluation of work plans and the company's general direction. Despite this level of involvement and control, many reported that they do not assert that they are always right. Thus, decision-making seemed to be a shared exercise. They reported that they are aware when employees are having problems, often including personal or family issues. This kind of managerial magnanimity allows them to easily win the support of others in the company. Fostering collaboration and delegating responsibility to subordinates is thus made easier, and they frequently participate in the planning and timing of activities, in addition to recruitment and hiring.

The women almost all reported heavy demands from both professional and personal areas of their lives. More than half of the respondents are married, and 82% of them have children. With more than 50% indicating 41- to 50-hour workweeks, many reported that this level of involvement frequently leaves them overworked and with little or no time for themselves. Table 18.2 summarizes respondents' personal and professional profiles.

Table 18.2
Summary Profile of the Participants in the Study

23%	Earned a postgraduate (e.g., MBA) or doctoral degree
65%	Earned an undergraduate degree
5%	Earned a technical or vocational degree
9%	Earned a high school diploma or equivalent
1%	Less than a high school diploma
54%	Earned their terminal degree since 1980
45%	Earned degree(s) in business/economics or engineering
63%	Age range 40–59
26%	Age range 20–39
58%	Married
82%	Have 1–3 children
56%	Primary wage earner

Approximately 37% of respondents reported an annual income over $34,300, with 54% of them indicating that their compensation fulfills their expectations. The majority of the respondents reported that they were the highest or primary wage earner in their home. Table 18.3 shows the salary ranges of the participants.

Success Characteristics and Personal Values

Most of the respondents attributed their success first to their own personal motivation, then to their professional reputation, with the least deference paid to their academic training. Respondents who were interviewed also attributed their success to a years-long commitment to development of interpersonal and communication skills, as well as their ability to balance family life and professional careers. We do note here that, characteristic of the lifestyle in Chile, all of the women we interviewed employed domestic helpers who kept the house, cooked, and assisted or were charged with caring for the respondents' children. Table 18.4 shows the percent rank of the factors to which the participants attributed their success.

Table 18.3
Salary Ranges of Study Participants

Percent of Participants	Salary Range
7%	Below $8,600
25%	$ 8,600–$17,100
13%	$17,100–$25,700
18%	$25,700–$34,300
9%	$34,300–$42,800
17%	$42,800–$60,000
11%	Over $60,000

Table 18.4
Rank of Factors to Which Respondents Attributed Their Success

82%	Own motivation
65%	Professional reputation
63%	Interpersonal skills
60%	Prior professional experience
59%	Communication skills
52%	Ability to balance home and career
46%	Academic training

With such a high percentage of participants relying on their own motivation to achieve success, it was understandable that the attribute these women most valued with regard to the company was their leadership skills or style. Similarly, it is not surprising to note that what the women strive toward most in the company was client or customer satisfaction. Second to customer satisfaction was the satisfaction of employees. Table 18.5 shows what percent of the respondents valued which specific attributes.

Motivations for Having Started the Business

Typically, our interview subjects showed a deeply held sense of altruism in the reason for having either started or sustained their business. Isabella Jaras was a superb illustration of the care that the women business owners gave to their employees. Mrs. Jaras founded Nutra Bien in partnership with her brother, Patricio. As the wife of a graduate student in the United States, Mrs. Jaras baked and sold cookies to the university cafeteria and local mom-and-pop stores to supplement her husband's meager stipend. Other women family members have assumed positions in the company in various capacities, particularly management. The company has provided for employees to have tutoring or to take courses at the local vocational school, and to receive special consultation on health issues and education planning. Typical of many of the women in the study, company profit in the traditional sense was not the most sought after goal for the Jaras family. The promotion or protection of the family's well-being was a significantly motivating factor in most of the women's entrepreneurial activity. Table 18.6 shows respondent priorities with respect to goals for the company.

Table 18.5
Specific Values and the Percent of Participants Who Held Them as Keys to Their Success

85%	Leadership skills or style
75%	Knowledge and broad views
54%	Responsibility for subordinates
50%	Interpersonal skills

Table 18.6
Company Goals Most Sought After by Respondents

96%	Client/customer satisfaction
72%	Employee satisfaction
61%	Growth of the company
59%	Maximization of company profit

Conclusions and Implications for Future Research

Although the sample of respondents in our study was small, this was a good first step toward providing impetus for further research on women in entrepreneurship in Chile. The country's economy shows much promise for entrepreneurial endeavors. The educational level in the country is high among both men and women, indicating relatively little gender bias regarding college and university participation. The labor atmosphere suggests no major difference in regard between men and women, an indication that is corroborated by the women we interviewed. Present are all the elements needed for increasing the participation of Chilean women in entrepreneurship.

References

Barrientos, S., A. Bee, A. Matear, and I. Vogel. 1999. *Women and Agribusiness.* New York: St. Martin's Press.

Bell, Ella L., J. Edmondson, and Stella M. Nkomo. 2001. *Our Separate Ways: Black and White Women and the Struggle for Professional Identity.* Boston: Harvard Business School Press.

De Rubinstein, E., I. Vial de Valdés, and L. Pardo. 1991. "Determinants of Women's Employment in Chile: A Life History Approach." In *Women, Households, and Change,* edited by. E. Masini and S. Stratigos. Tokyo: United Nations University Press.

Ericksen, G. K. 1999. *Women Entrepreneurs Only: 12 Women Entrepreneurs Tell the Stories of Their Success.* New York: John Wiley and Sons.

Langowitz, N. S. 2001. *The Top Woman-Led Businesses in Massachusetts.* Babson Park, MA: Babson College.

Moore, D. P., and E. Holly Buttner. 1997. *Women Entrepreneurs: Moving Beyond the Glass Ceiling.* Thousand Oaks: Sage Publications.

"Polish Women Managers 2000 Survey." 2000. International Forum for Women. Babson Park, MA: Babson College.

Ulshoefer, P. "Globalization and Regionalization of the Economy and Their Effect on Employment." International Labor Organization, http://www.ilo.org/public/english/dialogue/actrav/publ/109/109e4.htm.

Union Association of Pension Funds Administrators. 2002. Annual report.

CHAPTER 19

Women Entrepreneurs in High-Tech Firms in Brazil

Eva G. Jonathan

Changing Times for Women

Recent fast and deep-seated changes in the economy and the productive processes have brought about a major restructuring of work organization. Many new jobs have been created as a consequence of the increase in micro, small and medium ventures. Worldwide, the great economic, social, and political relevance of these enterprises has been acknowledged.

In Brazil, 56.32% of all enterprises created in 1999 were micro enterprises (SEBRAE 2000). Besides being an important means of generating employment, these ventures promote innovation and wealth, paving the way for a sustained economic development.

Female Entrepreneurship

Since 1970, the number of females working has increased significantly, accounting for changes in the size and composition of the Brazilian labor market (Bruschini 1994). The female employment rate in small and medium enterprises reached 44.53% in the metropolitan areas (Melo 2001).

Female leadership has also flourished. In 1994 to 1995, 17.08% of high-level management positions were occupied by women; in 1999 to 2000, women occupation reached 26.17% (Numeros 2002). On the other hand, business ownership has meant for many women a growing pass-key to their inclusion or maintenance in the labor market. Recent research indicates that 25% of the working-women segment were leading their own businesses (Vilella 2002). When both formal and informal sectors are considered, women-owned businesses compose nearly half of the universe of micro and small ventures (OECD 1998), attesting to the importance of female entrepreneurship in Brazil.

Women and High Technology

Women's relationship with technology is socially constructed (Silva 1998) and has been undergoing many transformations. Although science and technology have been historically defined as masculine activities (Monteiro 1998), present flexibility of gender roles has enabled a greater transit of women in these areas (Posthuma 1998).

Brazilian women have increased their working activities in the technology sector, especially in the information technology (IT) environment where old gender stereotypes and prejudices are being demolished (Rapkiewicz 1998; Leal 2001). In 2002, 54% of all professional workers in IT were women; the increase of their empowerment and technical competence was also observed in telecommunications (Jornal Telecompare 2002). Taken together these data suggest a change in relation to gender discrimination in the whole technological sector.

Following the trend, Brazilian women have increasingly reached high-level management positions in technological firms (Tuszel 2000; Vieira 2001). However, female ownership of high-tech firms seems still to be modest, since it was observed that only 6.67% of the Internet projects submitted for financial support belonged to women (NEXXY Capital Research 2001). The interpretation of these data demands caution, for it cannot be ruled out that Brazilian high-tech women entrepreneurs were not interested in that kind of business financing.

Women Entrepreneurs and Business Financing

It has been argued that the growth of high-tech firms contributes to the expansion and internationalization of the Brazilian economy, and that venture capital (VC) funds play an important role in promoting such growth process.

Women entrepreneurs' difficult relationship with VC has been frequently reported. For example, in 1999 the amount of American VC investments given to women entrepreneurs was not proportionate to the number of women-owned businesses at that time (Brush et al. 2000). Female businesses are perceived as risky, leading to higher loan rates, which, in turn, inhibit women's acceptance (Coleman 1998). This author understands, however, that such risk perception is not a gender issue and can be best explained by the small size and young age of female enterprises, an aspect also pointed out by Mahot (1998).

Women's problems with VC money have also been attributed to three other sets of reasons. The first one refers to structural barriers concerning traditional socialization of women, its stereotypes, and prejudices (Brush et al. 2000; Greene et al. 1999). The second set refers to culturally constructed abilities, experiences, and professional interests leading women to act in areas (retail, services, and manufacturing) that are distant from VC interests (Mahot 1998; Greene et al. 1999; Brush et al. 2000). These interests concentrate on entrepreneurs who are in the fast-growing, hot areas, who like risk, and who want to accelerate growth in order to obtain success (Zider 1998). The third set of reasons concerns women entrepreneurs' typical strategic choices. These strategies involve being sensitive and attributing great value to the maintenance of good interpersonal relationships (possibly modified by the entry of VC), as well as acting in a careful, cautious, and conservative way (Mahot 1998; Greene et al 1999; Brush et al. 2000).

Although, as previously discussed, more women have been joining the high-tech sector, women's partnership with VC still remains to be better understood. For if it is true that VC's search for female enterprises has not been significant, it is also true that women entrepreneurs do not tend to search for these investments (Carter and Kolvereid 1998). When external money is needed, they appeal to relatives (Mahot 1998) or to the traditional financial market (Allen and Carter 1996). In Brazil, 29% of women business owners report using business earnings as a form of financing (National Foundation of Women Business Owners 1999). Caution toward risk (Sawyer and McGee 1999) may influence the observed behaviors. On the other hand, women entrepreneurs' perception of success and business growth may help explain their poor relationship with VC.

Business Growth and Success

Women entrepreneurs perceive that business growth demands a purpose; growth for its own sake does not interest women entrepreneurs (Kamau, McLean, and Ardishvili 1999). According to these authors, growth is frequently a consequence of women entrepreneurs' intensive social networking with employees, clients, bankers, other entrepreneurs, and suppliers, among others.

It can be argued, then, that women choose a business growth strategy other than partnership with VC. But, fundamentally, high-tech business growth has to be desired and actively pursued, and is related to the entrepreneur's psychological characteristics and value system, to his or her desire and ability to search for market opportunities (Sexton 1993). Do high-tech women entrepreneurs desire business growth?

Studies of nonspecific women entrepreneurs indicate that they do not tend to measure success by business growth. The five most important success-defining criteria are self-fulfillment, effectiveness, profits, goal achievement, and employee satisfaction (Moore and Buttner 1997). Similarly, in Brazil, women business owners in the nontechnological sector place very little emphasis on business growth. Self-fulfillment, effectiveness, and profits are the three most important success measures, and success rests on both subjective and objective parameters (Jonathan 2001). One infers that success is a social and psychological construct influenced by values and world vision (Morel d'Arleux 1999) and it mediates entrepreneurs' attitude toward business growth.

Moreover, Brazilian women executives are significantly less motivated by money than those from developed countries. Like Brazilian women entrepreneurs, Brazilian women executives mainly define success as self-fulfillment and satisfaction. These feelings derive from work's challenges, a good work environment, and relationship opportunities, rather than from wages (Lobos 2002). Likewise, IT women executives tend to define success as self-fulfillment associated with loving their work and entrepreneurial activities (Entrevista 2002).

Additionally, success is related to reaching a balance between women entrepreneurs' personal, family, and professional lives (Entrevista 2002). Such balance implies perceiving work and family benefiting and helping each other; it also concerns experiencing both demands positively, as a double challenge rather than as a double working journey issue that constrains women (Jonathan 2001).

The empirical study described in the next section aims to increase the understanding of gender dimension in the realm of high-tech firms and thus contribute to building knowledge about Brazilian entrepreneurship.

Studying High-Tech Women Entrepreneurs

Although female entrepreneurs are a fast-growing segment of the small-business population, gathering big samples of high-tech Brazilian women entrepreneurs is a far-removed possibility. Thus, a small size study was set up in order to deepen the understanding of Brazilian female entrepreneurship. The general aim was to describe women's symbolic world rather than to compare high-tech women and men's entrepreneurial characteristics.

Literature on female entrepreneurship suggests controversial issues that deserve further examination. How do Brazilian women in charge of high-tech businesses–a segment considered to be of rapid growth–perceive business growth? How do they experience and signify success? How do high-tech women entrepreneurs see their partnership with VC? These were some of the specific questions discussed in the study.

Methodological Notes

The study was carried out with 16 women entrepreneurs of the state of Rio de Janeiro, divided into two intentional samples: Ten women-owned businesses in the IT area, and six women-owned businesses in the area of biotechnology.

High-tech women entrepreneurs were contacted by phone. At an arranged meeting, participants first filled out a questionnaire concerning general personal and business descriptive data. Afterwards, in-depth semi-structured interviews were carried out. Seven topics were addressed in the interview: (1) entrepreneurial history and motivation, (2) encountered facilities and difficulties, (3) success definition and measures, (4) business growth perception, (5) perception of business financing and of VC, (6) social networks, and (7) significance of entrepreneurial role.

Interviews lasted for about one hour and were tape recorded. After transcribing the tapes, a content analysis of participants' discourse was performed.

Describing the Sample

Except for ownership share and marital status, no major differences concerning the descriptive data were observed between the two research groups. Results from the collapsed samples indicated that women had a high educational level: 81.2% had a graduate degree. Women averaged 40.4 years old (ages ranged from 29 to 61 years), 43.7% were married, 37.5% were single, and 18.7% were separated. However, it was observed that the proportion of singles in the IT group (50%) was larger than in the biotechnology group (16%). Around half of the entrepreneurs in each group had children.

In general, women entrepreneurs reported being actively involved in running their businesses, working around 10 hours a day. Businesses were in operation for 5 years average (ranging from 7 months to 24 years) and employed an average of 27 people (ranging from zero to 120 employees). Considering the whole sample, women owned 52.6% of their firms, but ownership shares were higher among biotechnology entrepreneurs (65.2%) than among IT women (40.1%).

Analyzing and Discussing Results

Data were organized along the main interview topics. Between as well as within subjects, analysis was performed on the transcribed material. Categories that emerged from the content analysis are italic in the text to facilitate their apprehension. Entrepreneurs' discourse illustrating the results was freely translated into English and is presented with some editing.

On being a high-tech woman entrepreneur. Women described their entrepreneurial experience from several angles. Much attention was given to motivation to create ventures and difficulties encountered in running a business. Both these issues are indirectly related to success.

Results indicated that the need for achievement, the need to innovate implementing one's own ideas and values, as well as opportunism and the perception of competence were the main motives leading women entrepreneurs to create high-tech ventures.

> [T]o do something new . . . with our own ideas, our own values and get credit for it.
>
> IT entrepreneur, 31 years old

> I saw a possibility; it didn't exist in Rio . . . we were pioneers. I had the knowledge and there was a market need for it.
>
> biotechnology entrepreneur, 49 years old

It can be argued that need satisfaction and the use of one's intellectual and technical potential are sources of self-fulfillment, a feeling strongly linked to the women's perception of success (Moore and Buttner 1997; Jonathan 2001; Lobos 2002). This issue will be further discussed in the next section.

Women entrepreneurs faced a great variety of difficulties with a proactive attitude. Women often perceived them as natural, as passageways.

> Difficulties are considered natural; they stop existing and become just stages to move through.
>
> IT entrepreneur, 36 years old

At a business level, both groups of women entrepreneurs reported problems with *business financing*; this issue will be discussed in another section. On the other hand, while IT entrepreneurs stressed strong *competition* as a major difficulty, biotechnology entrepreneurs emphasized their search for *autonomy*.

You have problems conquering your own space . . . having a well-known name.

IT entrepreneur, 31 years old

[I]t takes courage to conquer autonomy, to part from the protection of the university and be out in the market.

biotechnology entrepreneur, 39 years old

Data suggest that women entrepreneurs had different perspectives on market difficulties and business survival. This may be explained by the fact that business creation in biotechnology is a relatively recent endeavor, rendering less competition. University research and laboratories originate this kind of business, while entrepreneurs maintain their strong scientific links with the university.

At a personal level, data revealed that prejudice against women in technology is a controversial issue. While some high-tech women entrepreneurs had not experienced any kind of discrimination, others reported gender and/or age discrimination.

I have suffered all kinds of discrimination for being a woman and for being young.

IT entrepreneur, 45 years old

I have never felt any discrimination for being a woman; but rather because of my age.

biotechnology entrepreneur, 49 years old

However, no battles seemed to have been lost; high-tech women entrepreneurs were quite assertive in dealing with their feminine (and age) issues.

[I said] don't look at me as if you saw a woman; you are looking at a professional that is a woman. . . . One can deal with it easily, provided you put yourself . . . at a more professional and stronger position.

IT entrepreneur, 37 years old

I have already suffered (gender) discrimination, but I've used it much more in my favor than the other way around.

biotechnology entrepreneur, 47 years old

The fact that these women owned high-tech businesses may be seen as a proof of gender roles' flexibility (Posthuma 1998), confirming women's greater presence in high-level management positions in the technological sector (Tuszel 2000; Vieira 2001). Data suggest, however, that the breakup of stereotypes and prejudices against Brazilian women in technology (Rapkiewicz 1998; Leal 2001) is still an ongoing process.

What does it mean to be a high-tech woman entrepreneur? Results indicated that participants perceived that their businesses played a central role in their lives. This was confirmed by the great amount of daily hours dedicated to the ventures. As entrepreneurs, women were conscious of this and acknowledged the difficulties involved in facing triple demands. They stressed their need to balance their personal, professional, and family lives. Ways of reaching such balance varied within as well as between women entrepreneurs. However, results indicated that women entrepreneurs tended to meet challenges with an affirmative rather than a regretful attitude.

> I manage quite well to harmonize [business, family, and personal lives]. . . . There are moments . . . I have to give something up, but with creativity one can do it [reconcile demands].

> > biotechnology entrepreneur, 49 years,
> > divorced, about to remarry, one child

> It is a triple challenge; if one of these [challenges] is not met, it's not the same thing. . . . The three [demands] have to be together. . . . They have to be coordinated.

> > IT entrepreneur, 35 years old, married, six children

The assertive way in which these high-tech women entrepreneurs faced the triple demands is similar to the behavior of women business owners from the Brazilian nontechnological sector (Jonathan 2001). The fact that business ownership is a chosen life strategy and not a forced or irrelevant occupation motivates women to be assertive and search for balance. Challenges and victories, rather than constraints and burdens of the "double working journey," define high-tech women entrepreneurs' confrontations with difficulties.

Success. An analysis of how high-tech women entrepreneurs defined success revealed that, although women placed great emphasis on internal and subjective measures of success, they also used external and objective business performance measures. Participants often made this dual positioning explicit.

There are two kinds of rewards: the financial and the emotional one. . . . When you are well emotionally, you are happy with what you are doing . . . even if money gets sometimes short, there is this other side that gives you stability.

> IT entrepreneur, 37 years old

However, the internal definition of success tended to be crucial for women entrepreneurs.

Success is something very personal . . . success comes from your inside.

> IT entrepreneur, 61 years old

Self-fulfillment, directly or indirectly mentioned, was the measure of success most often used. Business existence, its survival, was seen as a symbol of personal conquest.

[Business success brings] personal satisfaction because it [the firm] exists; it's real.

> biotechnology entrepreneur, 52 years old

Success meant great satisfaction and pleasure derived from love for working activities.

I consider myself successful because I work in something that gives me enormous pleasure.

> IT entrepreneur, 46 years old

[I feel successful] for adoring what I do . . . an enormous pleasure.

> biotechnology entrepreneur, 49 years old

Goal achievement and professional recognition/trust defined success as well. Some women stressed the first kind of measures.

Yes, I consider myself successful because I attain everything I fight for.

> biotechnology entrepreneur, 52 years old

I link [success] with some goals I have established.

> IT entrepreneur, 31 years old

Others emphasized the second kind.

The criterion I'm using to measure success is technical recognition; for me that's what preferably feeds my ego.

> biotechnology entrepreneur, 47 years old

When you know that what you do is a good-quality service, people trust you professionally.

> IT entrepreneur, 37 years old

Additionally, high-tech women entrepreneurs, especially biotechnology professionals, linked success to social benefits/contribution.

[Success] is mediated by the self-fulfillment of doing something good to someone . . . of being useful, of improving things [the environment].
[Success means] to be able to offer quality of life to other people . . . creating jobs. . . . It gives me pleasure to enable another person to earn a better salary.

> biotechnology entrepreneur, 39 years old
> biotechnology entrepreneur, 30 years old

At a business level, the financial criterion was the most often used measure of success. In this context, profits tended to be emphasized by IT professionals more than by biotechnology entrepreneurs.

The success of a business implies [making] money . . . it's an obligation.

> IT entrepreneur, 45 years old

However, profits were often seen as a consequence. As one IT entrepreneur, 31 years old, said, "Money is a result . . . it's not our main goal." On the other hand, financial health also played an important role in defining business success.

[I consider myself successful] for never having asked for a loan.
. . . I think that's indeed a measure of success.

biotechnology entrepreneur, 49 years old

Finally, high-tech women entrepreneurs also related success to the good quality of their products and services, as well as to the long-term internal and external partnerships they managed to establish. These data suggest that women were using effectiveness and social networking as measures of their success.

In summary, high-tech women entrepreneurs used both subjective and objective criteria to define success. Success was defined mainly in terms of self-fulfillment. Together with goal-achievement, professional recognition/trust, and social benefits/contribution, it relates to a self-actualization cluster. On the other hand, profits, financial health, effectiveness, and social networking were the main measures of success at a business level. In spite of being in the hot, fast-growing segment of the economy, business growth was not used by high-tech women entrepreneurs to define success.

Overall, high-tech Brazilian women entrepreneurs use similar success measures as American women entrepreneurs (Moore and Buttner 1997) and as Brazilian nontechnological women entrepreneurs (Jonathan 2001; Lobos 2002). Data confirm that success is much more a question of self-fulfillment than a money issue (Lobos 2002). The fact that IT entrepreneurs attributed a relatively greater emphasis to profits, while biotechnology entrepreneurs tended to emphasize social benefits/contribution suggests that these women do not share the same set of values and world visions (Morel d'Arleux 1999). This is an issue that deserves further investigation.

Business Growth. Market expansion; increase of sales, incomes and profits; bigger headquarters; and more employees were all used to define business growth. However, the need for quantitative business growth was rarely seen as a priority. Participants' views of business growth tended to stress two points: quality improvement and gradual growth. High-tech women entrepreneurs, especially IT entrepreneurs, perceived quality (of products, services, and processes) as a goal for business growth.

[The aim is] quality. Growth but with quality . . . quality of the process . . . of all aspects.

IT entrepreneur, 36 years old

[N]ow we are working on this [quality] certificate like ISO 9000.

IT entrepreneur, 45 years old

Although some entrepreneurs expressed the desire for business-size stability, the majority emphasized slow development. Gradual growth was seen as a strategy to guarantee quality and the venture's identity.

> [W]e don't want to give a step bigger than our legs. . . . We are going to do it gradually . . . without loosing autonomy and the firm's identity.
>
> biotechnology entrepreneur, 39 years old

> I expect not to grow so much, for the idea is to improve processes rather than to swell.
>
> IT entrepreneur, 36 years old

Data suggest that quality improvement is a major purpose orienting high-tech business growth; business growth is not a goal in itself (Kamau, McLean, and Ardishvili 1999). Brazilian high-tech women entrepreneurs desire business growth (Sexton 1993) but, at emphasizing gradual growth as a strategy to maintain quality, they contradict general expectations of fast high-tech business growth (Zider 1998). Their attitude does not favor a relationship with VC.

Business Financing and Venture Capital. IT and biotechnology entrepreneurs had similar general attitudes toward business financing. They tended to perceive business financing as a major problem.

> [It's difficult] to have money to pay for a competent team.
>
> biotechnology entrepreneur, 52 years old

> [T]he worst phases . . . were related to obtaining funds for making investments.
>
> IT entrepreneur, 34 years old

Overall, women entrepreneurs tended to show a conservative attitude toward business financing. They preferred using business earnings and their own, their partners', or their families' resources as forms of business financing. Traditional bank loans and credit cards were occasionally used. Sometimes governmental agencies financed their research, infrastructure, or training programs.

Results indicated that VC financed 12.5% of all high-tech women entrepreneurs. However, no biotechnology entrepreneur had an established partnership with VC. Among biotechnology entrepreneurs, VC funds were either an unknown (50%) or an unfavorable/incompatible form of business financing. Their desire to keep ownership and control over their ventures grounded their disagreement with VC's goals and procedures.

> VC is investing . . . with the intent of selling the business. . . . None of us was interested in selling the business.
>
> biotechnology entrepreneur, 30 years old

> I have already been searched [by VC] . . . they wanted a new plant as well as my soul . . . at the first capital replacement, they take you out of the business.
>
> biotechnology entrepreneur, 49 years old

However, among IT women entrepreneurs, 50% held a favorable attitude toward VC, 40% held an unfavorable attitude, and 10% were unfamiliar with VC. Among those with a favorable perception, 60% of them had an established partnership with VC. Mere acceptance of VC funds, as "a necessary evil to be used by those who needed them" contrasted with attributing to VC an important role in business growth and in improving the quality of products, personnel, and strategic decision-making.

> [I]t's fundamental . . . without it [VC] you don't get the expansion of businesses.
>
> IT entrepreneur, 29 years old, no established partnership with VC

> I wanted them [VC group] . . . I chose them . . . to give us credibility and not just money . . . to expand our commercial activity . . . to train people . . . to get more qualified employees and . . . a more consistent product. . . . Investors have helped us with decision-making.
>
> IT entrepreneur, 36 years old, established partnership with VC

Among IT women entrepreneurs, aside from thinking that "they squeeze you out," different motives grounded their unfavorable positioning toward VC. Fears of loosing quality or the firm's focus, as well as feelings of insecurity and of being unprepared were often-quoted motives.

[T]hey [VC] want to make money in a short time . . . you loose quality.

IT entrepreneur, 31 years old, no established partnership with VC

[W]e are going very carefully with . . . VC. . . . They didn't want to hear. . . . We didn't know it. . . . We were totally unprepared.

IT entrepreneur, 45 years old, established partnership with VC

Worldwide, women entrepreneurs perceive business financing as a major problem (Moore and Buttner 1997). Brazilian high-tech women entrepreneurs share this perception. In general, they tend to act in a cautious and conservative way (Mahot 1998; Greene et al. 1999; Brush et al. 2000). They prefer to finance businesses with business earnings (National Foundation of Women Business Owners 1999), with their own or relatives' resources (Mahot 1998), or with resources from the traditional financial market (Allen and Carter 1996). None of these strategies draws high-tech women entrepreneurs close to VC funds. Additionally, as argued previously, their preference for gradual growth does not favor partnership with VC.

Apart from unfamiliarity, Brazilian high-tech women entrepreneurs have mixed feelings and attitudes toward VC. They fear losing quality and, more importantly, their ventures' control and ownership. On the other hand, IT–but not biotechnology–entrepreneurs have favorable beliefs and feelings. VC funds are considered important for bringing about business growth as well as improvements in decision-making strategies, in market credibility, and in the quality of products, employees, and processes.

In the high-tech environment, VC and entrepreneurs form a couple that has to stay together (Botelho and Jonathan 2002). In view of the results reported here, there seems to be a call for designing business-financing policies that will better address the needs, feelings, and perceptions of Brazilian high-tech women entrepreneurs.

Summary

Brazilian women have increasingly been joining the high-tech sector of the labor market. Some of these women choose to create their own businesses and, as IT and biotechnology business owners, they reveal a rich entrepreneurial culture.

Brazilian high-tech women entrepreneurs seek to run their ventures because they want to achieve, innovate, and implement their own ideas and values. They are confident of their technical and professional abilities and perceive the market as offering an opportunity to come forward with their qualifications.

Things are not easy for them. Yet they persevere and are assertive as they cope with competition, search for autonomy, and deal with gender and age discrimination. Triple demands challenge high-tech women entrepreneurs, and, although business is central in these women's lives, they search to balance personal, family, and work demands. Their strategies to thrive vary but, apparently, they are successful.

They define success with both subjective and objective criteria. Overall, success means self-fulfillment. Goal achievement, professional recognition, and the promotion of social benefits also contribute to self-actualization and define success. At the business level, money and profits are acknowledged as measures of success but they are not extremely emphasized. Financial health, effectiveness, as well as social networking also define success. The fact that biotechnology entrepreneurs place a relatively greater emphasis on promoting social benefits as a success criterion, while IT emphasize profits, is an issue that demands further examination.

Business growth is neither a success measure nor a goal in itself. As they pursue gradual business growth in order to maintain quality, women entrepreneurs are going against the prevalent fast-growth expectations of the high-tech environment. Thus, their partnership with VC is not favored. Unfamiliarity, fears, disagreements, and ill feelings, as well as positive attitudes, compose high-tech women entrepreneurs' social representation of VC. It constitutes a challenge to keep women entrepreneurs properly informed and to design business-financing policies that adequately meet needs, feelings, values, and belief of Brazilian high-tech women entrepreneurs. Yet, these challenges have to be met because these women's entrepreneurial contribution to the expansion of the Brazilian economy is important.

References

Allen, K. R., and N. M. Carter. 1996. "Women Entrepreneurs: Profile Differences Across High and Low Performing Adolescent Firms." *Frontiers of Entrepreneurship Research,* Wellesley, MA: Center for Entrepreneurial Studies, Babson College. Accessed September 4, 2001, from http://www.babson.edu/entrep/fer/papers96/sum96/allen.html.

Botelho, A. J. J., and E. G. Jonathan. 2002. "A representação social do capital de risco entre empreendedores de alta tecnologia." Unpublished research report, Rio de Janeiro, Instituto Genesis, PUC-Rio.

Bruschini, C. 1994. "O trabalho da mulher no Brasil: tendências recentes." In H. I. B. Saffioti and M. Munõz-Vargas (eds.), *Mulher Brasileira é Assim.* Rio de Janeiro: Rosa dos Ventos, 63–93.

Brush, C. G., N. M. Carter, P. G. Greene, M. M. Hart, and E. J. Gatewood. 2000. "Women and Equity Capital: An Exploration of Factors Affecting Capital Access." Accessed October 1, 2001, from: http://www.babson.edu/entrep/fer//XI/XIA/html/xi-a.htm.

Carter, N. M., and L. Kolvereid. 1998. "Women Starting New Businesses: The Experience in Norway and the United States." *Women Entrepreneurs in Small and Medium Enterprises,* Organization for Economic Cooperation and Development (OECD), Proceedings/IBM, 185–202.

Coleman, S. 1998. "Access to Capital: A Comparison of Men and Women-Owned Small Business." *Frontiers of Entrepreneurship Research,* Wellesley, MA: Center for Entrepreneurial Studies, Babson College. Accessed September 4, 2001, from http://www.babson.edu/entrep/fer/papers98/V/V_B/V_B_text.htm.

"Cresce a presença feminina nas áreas de TI e telecomunicações." 2002. *Jornal telecompare, Catho online,* 86 ed. Accessed April 27, 2002, from http://www.telecompare.com.br/inputer_view.phtml?id=4127.

"Entrevista." 2002. *Jornal carreira e sucesso, Catho online,* 74 ed. Accessed March 6, 2002, from http://www.catho.com.br/jcs/inputer_view.phtml?id=1831&print=1.

Greene, P .G., C. G. Brush, M. M. Hart, and P. Saparito. 1999. "Exploration of the Venture Capital Industry: Is Gender an Issue?" *Frontiers of Entrepreneurship Research,* Wellesley, MA: Center for Entrepreneurial Studies, Babson College. Accessed September 6, 2001, from http://www.babson.edu/entrep/fer/papers99/IV/IV_A/IVA%20Text.htm.

Jonathan, E. G. 2001. "Mulheres empreendedoras: quebrando alguns tabus." *Anais CD-ROM,* (No. 69), *III Encontro nacional de empreendedorismo (ENEMPRE),* UFSC, Florianópolis, Santa Catarina, December 5–6.

Kamau, D.G., G. N. McLean, and A. Ardishvili. 1999. "Perceptions of Business Growth by Women Entrepreneurs." *Frontiers of Entrepreneurship Research,* Wellesley, MA: Center for Entrepreneurial Studies, Babson College. Retrieved September 17, 2001, from http://www.babson.edu/entrep/fer/papers99/IV/IV_C/IVC%20Text.htm.

Leal, R. P. 2001. "A informática à espera das mulheres." *Jornal do Brasil, Caderno Internet,* July 12.

Lobos, J. 2002. *Mulheres que abrem passagem–e o que os homens têm a ver com isso.* São Paulo: Fundação Getúlio Vargas.

Mahot, P. 1998. "Funding for Women Entrepreneurs: A Real–Though Disputed–Problem." Women Entrepreneurs in Small and Medium Enterprises, Organization for Economic Cooperation and Development (OECD), Proceedings/IBM, 217–226.

Melo, H. P. 2001. "O feminino nas manufaturas Brasileiras." In R. M. Muraro and A. B. Puppin, (eds.), *Mulher, gênero e sociedade.* Rio de Janeiro: Relume Dumará: FAPERJ, 124–136.

Monteiro, R. H. 1998. "Inventing Women Science, Technology and Gender." *Cadernos Pagu,* Campinas, no. 10: 445–448.

Moore, D. P., and E. H. Buttner. 1997. *Women Entrepreneurs: Moving Beyond the Glass Ceiling.* Thousand Oaks, CA: Sage Publications.

Morel d'Arleux, C. 1999. "Success as a Psychological and Social Construct: The Influence of the Entrepeneur's Nature on His/Her Conception of Success." Accessed September 11, 2001, from http://file:///A/puc3_arquivos/IV_H_text.html

National Foundation for Women Business Owners (NFWBO). 1999. "International Surveys 1997 and 1998 National Foundation for Women Business Owners and IBM." March.

NEXXY Capital Research. 2001. "Perfil dos projetos e empreendedores voltados à Internet." Unpublished research report.

"Números." 2002. *Jornal carreira e sucesso, Catho online,* 88 ed.. Accessed March 6, 2002, from http://www.catho.com.br/jcs/inputer_view.phtml?id=2551&print=1.

Organization for Economic Cooperation and Development (OECD). 1998. "Women Entrepreneurs in SMEs: A Major Force in Innovation and Job Creation, Synthesis."

Posthuma, A. C. 1998. "Women Encounter Technology: Changing Patterns of Employment in the Third World." *Cadernos pagu,* Campinas, no. 10: 449–451.

Rapkiewicz, C. E. 1998. "Informática: domínio masculino?" *Cadernos Pagu,* Campinas, no. 10: 169–200.

Sawyer, O. O., and J. E. McGee. 1999. "The Impact of Personal Network Characteristics on Perceived Environmental Uncertainty: An Examination of Owners/Managers of New High Technology Firms." *Frontiers of Entrepreneurship Research,* Wellesley, MA: Center for Entrepreneurial Studies, Babson College. Accessed March 8, 2001, from http://www.babson.edu/entrep/fer/papers99/V/V_A/V_A%20Text.htm.

Serviço Brasileiro de Apoio à Pequena e Média Empresa (SEBRAE). 2000. "II Sondagem SEBRAE 2000–A mulher empresária." *SEBRAE estudos e pesquisas,* 9, no. 2, (November). Accessed May 17, 2002, from http://www.sebrae.com.br (link: "microempresa").

Sexton, D. 1993. "Psychological Traits and Their Applicability in Predicting Growth Propensities in High-Tech Founders." In *Advances in Global High-Technology Management,* vol. 3, edited by M. W. Lawless and L. R. Gomez-Mejan. Greenwich, CT: Jai Press.

Silva, E. B. 1998. "Des-construindo gênero em ciência e tecnologia." *Cadernos Pagu,* no. 10: 7–20.

Tuszel, L. 2000. "Mulheres avançam na área tecnológica." *Gazeta mercantil Latino-Americana, seção negócios,* (December 4–10).

Vieira, E. 2001. "Fim do clube do Bolinha?" *Revista info,* Agosto, 48–57.

Vilella, J. 2002. "Mulheres avançam em microempresas." *Jornal do Brasil, economia e negócios,* (September).

Zider, B. 1998. "How Venture Capital Works." *Harvard Business Review,* (Nov.–Dec.): 131–139.

Index

About the Contributors

PABLO JAVIER ANGELELLI is currently an enterprise development specialist in the Micro, Small, and Medium Enterprise Division at the Inter-American Development Bank (IADB), where he conducts research in different areas related to competitiveness and small business development, such as business development services, industrial clusters, and entrepreneurship. He started his professional career in 1994 as a local consultant in a World Bank Program to promote small and medium enterprise exports between 1994 and 1997. After that he worked for public and private organizations related to private sector development until he joined the IADB in 2000. He received his Bachelor's degree in Economics from the National University of Córdoba and a Master's degree in Economics and Industrial Development from the National University of Mar del Plata and National University of General Sarmiento.

IMANOL BELAUSTEGUIGOITIA is director of the Family Business Center at Instituto Tecnológico Autónomo de México (ITAM). He got his PhD in management from the Universidad Nacional Autónoma de México (UNAM), while receiving the National Award for an outstanding thesis on the influence of organizational climate on commitment and effort in family firms. He spent one year as Visiting Scholar at the Blank Center for Entrepreneurship at Babson College, where he taught and researched organizational behavior, entrepreneurship, and family business. At the same time, he collaborated with the Institute for Latin American Business.

As a consultant, educator, researcher, and speaker, he has been on the radio since 1998 with the program known as *Reflections on Family Firms*. Dr. Belausteguigoitia is a member of the Family Firm Institute and Endeavor, an international organization created to support entrepreneurs.

ANTONIO JOSÉ J. BOTELHO holds a PhD in political science from MIT, and graduate degrees from Cornell University and Université Paris IV. He held a National Science Foundation Postdoctoral Minority

Fellow at the Johns Hopkins University. He is a member of the editorial board of the journals *Perspectives on Global Development and Technology, Journal of Information Technologies and International Development,* and *Science, Technology and Society.* Botelho's research deals with venture capital, entrepreneurship and small and medium enterprise growth factors of technology-based firms and technology transfer. He is currently a principal researcher on the project Diffusion and Effective Use of Information Technology: A Latin-Asian Dialogue on Initial Conditions and Policy Challenges, funded by the Social Science Research Council and Ford Foundation; and scientific coordinator of the Brazil case of a comparative project on the software industry in Brazil, China, and India.

JOHN R. BOURNE is professor of electrical and computer engineering at the Franklin W. Olin College of Engineering and professor of technology entrepreneurship at Babson College. He was previously professor of electrical and computer engineering and professor of biomedical engineering at Vanderbilt University, where he was on the faculty since 1969. He also held the position of professor of management of technology between 1991 and 1998.

Dr. Bourne received his PhD in electrical engineering in 1969 from the University of Florida. In 1982 he served as a Visiting Professor at Chalmers University in Goteborg, Sweden, and in 1990 he was a Visiting Researcher at Northern Telecom. Dr. Bourne has been the Editor-in-Chief of the Begell House Critical Reviews in Biomedical Engineering since 1979. He founded the *Journal of Asynchronous Learning Networks* and remains as editor.

EDWARD G. CALE, JR., who has been a professor of information systems at Babson College since 1988, holds a BS in electrical engineering from Stanford University, as well as an MBA and a DBA from Harvard University. In 1997, Dr. Cale founded the Institute for Latin American Business (ILAB) at Babson, where he currently serves as the Faculty Director. The institute's primary mission is the build relationships between Babson College and sister universities in Latin America. Before entering the academy, Dr. Cale was an operations manager in Fairchild Semiconductor, one of the founding businesses in Silicon Valley. Additionally, he has consulted with several Fortune 100 companies and federal and state agencies. Dr. Cale's areas of expertise include strategic use of information technology, planning for and managing the information technology organization, and Latin American business issues. His research interests include end-user computing systems, systems implementation, and the diffusion of management pedagogy.

RICARDO AGUILAR DIAZ holds a Bachelor of Management from the Instituto Tecnológico de Costa Rica (ITCR) and has prior education in industrial engineering. Mr. Aguilar Diaz has taken courses in natural resources management and agricultural economics at the University of Manitoba, Canada. He has worked as a professor in the ITCR Business School, as well as in the Industrial Production Engineering School, where he founded the entrepreneurial program and the industrial liaison office, and was involved in the development of the incubator center. From 1995 until 2002 he worked as Vice Rector for Research and Development. Currently he is working as a coordinator for the Environmental Management Systems for Central America Program (PROARCA/ SIGMA), in its private sector branch. This project is sponsored by the USAID. Mr. Aguilar Diaz is a member of the Asociación Latino-Iberoamericana de Gestión Tecnológica (ALTEC), and has published many articles related to company-university linkage, research and development politics, technological innovation, and entrepreneurship.

JOSÉ DORNELAS has a PhD in entrepreneurship from University of São Paulo (USP), Brazil. He has been teaching at a number of universities in Brazil, including USP, Ibmec, and Faculdade Trevisan. He was the first Brazilian professor (2001–2002) to do postdoctoral study at Babson College in the United States, where he worked with the entrepreneurship center to apply concepts from Babson's innovative curriculum to Brazil. He is also the author of *Empreendedorismo* and a book on business incubators in Brazil. As an entrepreneur, Dr. Dornelas has founded two companies in Brazil and has helped thousands of entrepreneurs write their business plans through a Web site (www.planodenegocios.com.br) that provides tools for those who want to start a new business. Nowadays, Dr. Dornelas has been focusing his work on corporate entrepreneurship, as a consultant to large corporations interested in this area. He is also working on his third book, *Empreendedorismo Corporativo,* to be published in August 2003.

GERMÁN ECHECOPAR has a PhD and MA in economics, University of Notre Dame, United States, and a Bachelor of Science, Industrial Engineering, from Pontificia Universidad Católica del Perú. Dr. Echecopar specializes in the economics of innovation, focusing on industrial innovation systems and innovative entrepreneurship. At the university's Adolfo Ibáñez Business School, he teaches managerial economics and entrepreneurship and innovation in the undergraduate and MBA programs. He is director of the university's Centre for Entrepreneurship.

Professionally, he has been partner and general manager of Agrícola y Ganadera Galeano (Lima, Peru) during 1984–1989, partner and director for Agrícola y Ganadera el Chilco (1987–1992), and senior consultant for Business Consulting and Technology Services (Lima, Peru) during 1996–1997. Since 1998, he has been partner and director for Zona 5 (Talca, Chile), an Internet provider. He has consulted for the International Development Research Center and the Canadian Advanced Technology Association. At the Universidad de Talca, Professor Echecopar has been director of the Economics Department (1998–2000) and director of the MBA Program (1999–2002).

JEANNINE HOROWITZ GASSOL is associate professor in the Department of Administrative and Economic Sciences at the University Simón Bolívar in Caracas, Venezuela. She received a BS from the University of California, Berkeley; a PhD. from the University of East Anglia, Norwich, England; and an MBA from the Instituto de Estudios Superiores de Administracion (IESA) in Caracas, Venezuela. Dr. Horowitz is director of the Entrepreneurship Program of the Department of Administrative and Economics Sciences at the University Simón Bolívar. Dr. Horowitz has worked as a scientist and teacher in the area of biotechnology in Europe, the United States, and Latin America, both in university and in industry. Her research has resulted in several publications, presentations at international conferences, and a patent. Her present interest at the university focuses on economic development with emphasis in management of technology, entrepreneurship, and innovation. She has designed several courses in these areas and directs both undergraduate projects and graduate theses. She worked as consultant and U.S. office director for the Programa Bolívar, an international program financed by the Inter-American Development Bank in the field of small business development, and has also worked as business and development consultant for numerous businesses and government organizations.

GUSTAVO HARCKBART is a partner at Fides Asset Management, a Brazilian hedge fund, responsible for stock picking and quantitative research for the company's funds. Prior to that, Mr. Harckbart was a Visiting Scholar at Babson College, where he focused his research on venture capital in Brazil and in the United States. His work on how Brazilian venture capitalists add value to portfolio companies will be presented at the next Babson Kauffmann Conference on Entrepreneurial Research. Mr. Harckbart also worked for Petros, the second-biggest Brazilian pension fund, where he was a stock analyst in a number of industries and was also responsible for the analysis of investment opportunities in the venture capital arena. Mr. Harckbart has a master of science degree in finance and investment analysis from PUC-Rio University and concluded his undergraduate degree in Mechanical Engineering at the Federal University of Espírito Santo.

ALICIA CASTILLO HOLLEY holds an MBA from Babson College, and a Master of Science and an engineering degree from Universidad Central de Venezuela. Prior to her engagement in entrepreneurship, she worked in Venezuela, Switzerland, and the United States on new product development and commercialization.

For 6 years she worked in Chile to promote entrepreneurship, teach courses on entrepreneurship at the Universidad Adolfo Ibáñez, launch a consultancy firm to help entrepreneurs create and grow businesses, carry out research to understand the entrepreneurial and angel investors' mind-set, and establish a venture capital fund for the seed stage. She has helped over 500 people create business models and trained over 4000 people on business creation, funding for emerging businesses, intrapreneurship, and change management. She has secured investments for over $1 million, participated as board member for several emerging companies, and has been a member of several committees to foster venture capital and commercializing of innovations.

Currently she lives in Houston, Texas, where she continues to foster entrepreneurship by consulting for individuals, firms, and institutions in the field of wealth creation throughout Latin America.

JUDY "JJ" JACKSON is Associate Provost for Institutional Engagement at New York University in Manhattan. Her responsibilities include spearheading the design and implementation of a university-wide diversity plan and engagement strategy. Dr. Jackson was formerly a member of the senior administration at Babson College, MIT, and Cornell University. Dr. Jackson has designed and implemented academic retention programs that have been acclaimed and supported by education, industry, and government organizations. She holds a Bachelor of Arts degree from the University of North Carolina at Greensboro, an interdisciplinary Master of Arts from Bucknell University, and a doctorate in administration, planning, and social policy from the Harvard University Graduate School of Education.

GONZALO JIMÉNEZ is Albert von Appen Professor at Universidad Adolfo Ibáñez, teaching corporate strategy and family business at the Escuela de Negocios de Valparaíso, Universidad Adolfo Ibáñez since 1993. He has won seven Best Professor awards and is now director of the Albert von Appen Family Business Center. He is also Founding Partner and Managing Director of PROTEUS, a professional strategy firm consultancy, advising companies operating in South America, since 1995. He holds a degree in economics and a Master of Science in Finance (1987) from Universidad de Chile where he was a Universidad de Chile Scholar, followed by an MBA at the École Nationale des Ponts et Chaussées in Paris (1990–91). He has carried out corporate strategy studies at Harvard Business School, attended a Colloquium on Participant-Center Learning (CPCL) HBS (June 2000), and acted as Rockefeller Scholar, Harvard University (2001) on a Luksic Scholarship. Mr. Jiménez has 10 years of experience previous to PROTEUS as consultant, director, and board member for a variety of firms in Chile and Europe. He is the co-author of *Corporate Headquarters: An International Analysis* and *Ethos y Estrategias Corporativas de los Grupos Latinoamericanos.*

EVA G. JONATHAN is a psychologist, with an MA in social psychology (PUC-Rio, Brazil, 1974). She is a lecturer at the Psychology Department of PUC-Rio, Brazil, and a researcher for the Instituto Genesis para Inovação e Ação Empreendedora, PUC-Rio, Brazil, with main interests in entrepreneurship and innovation, especially in female entrepreneurship.

JULIAN E. LANGE is an associate professor of entrepreneurship and the Benson Distinguished Entrepreneurship Fellow at Babson College. Dr. Lange is known internationally for his teaching and research in entrepreneurship, and for the practical application of the principles of entrepreneurship to business and government.

JUAN CARLOS LEIVA is coordinator of the Entrepreneurship Program at the Technology Institute of Costa Rica (ITCR) and was also manager of the Incubator Center in the same ITCR. He has extensive experience in the formation and training of entrepreneurs, support services to the enterprise creation, entrepreneurship promotion, and investigation. In addition he teaches entrepreneurship, management, and marketing at the ITCR. Previous to joining ITCR, Mr. Leiva spent 4 years in the finance sector, where he served as chief of a bank agency and an educational credit institution.

He holds a Master's degree in Economy and Industrial Development with a focus on small and medium enterprises from the National University of General Sarmiento, Buenos Aires, Argentina. He also has a postgraduate diploma from University of Valencia in Training for Trainers in Enterprise Creation. In addition, he obtained his degree in business administration in the Technology Institute of Costa Rica.

Mr. Leiva was Costa Rica's contributor to the IADB research "Entrepreneurship in Emerging Economies: The Creation and Development of

New Firms in Latin America and East Asia." He also writes about entrepreneurship and small and medium enterprises in different magazines and journals.

JUAN JOSÉ LLISTERRI is currently Principal Enterprise Development Advisor of the Micro, Small and Medium Enterprise Division at the Inter-American Development Bank. He leads policy discussions and provides advisory services and operational support on enterprise development-related matters, including legal and institutional framework, financing, technology, market access, and nonfinancial services, with an emphasis on small and medium enterprises. Before joining the bank in 1992, he served as the general director of the Institute for Small and Medium Enterprise in Spain, and represented his country in front of the European Union and OECD on enterprise development matters. He was also general manager of the Regional Development Agency of Madrid. He holds both law and economics degrees from the University of Deusto, Spain, and was awarded a Visiting Fellowship to the Institute of Urban and Regional Development at the University of California at Berkeley.

PEDRO MÁRQUEZ is a graduate of the University of Calgary (PhD and MA) and is professor of corporate strategy and public administration at ITESM, Mexico City. He is author of several articles on business ethics, family business, and Mexican business environment, and at present is head of management and international business at ITESM's business school.

ANGÉLICA MORA is general manager of the Entrepreneur Virtual Incubator Center and Chief Officer at the Export Program in Monterrey Technological Institute, Campus Mexico City. She is also consultant and recognized expert in e-business. Her current work is on the project Entrepreneur Transformation, an initiative aiming to foster the e-business culture and the evolution of companies in the new economy, collaborating with engineer Alfredo Capote, former vice-president for IBM's Latin America division.

VERONICA PARDO holds a Bachelor's degree in Business Administration from the Universidad del Pacífico, Lima, Perú, and a Licentiate title in this same field. Ms. Pardo is a professor of entrepreneurship in the Business Administration and Accounting School of the Universidad del Pacífico and a manager of the Office of Entrepreneurial Spirit of this university. Ms. Pardo has had experience in starting up and managing businesses.

ADRIANA PAREDES holds a Bachelor's degree in Business Administration from the Universidad del Pacífico, Lima, Perú, and a Licentiate title in this same field. Ms. Paredes has carried out specialized studies in marketing at the University of Uppsala, Sweden, and participated in an internship program in Brazil. Currently, Ms. Paredes works as assistant of the Office of Entrepreneurial Spirit of the Universidad del Pacífico and is a researcher at the Business Administration and Accounting School.

JOSÉ ANTONIO PIMENTA BUENO, MSc, is general coordinator, general coordination, and co-coordinator for the Brazil Pole, New Venture Financing Project at the PUC-Rio.

OLGA PIZARRO is director of the MBA program at Universidad Del Desarrollo in Concepción. She holds a MBA from Universidad Adolfo Ibáñez, a Bachelor of Commerce and Economies degree and a Bachelor of Mathematics degree from Universidad Concepción. Ms. Pizarro has worked as a professor at Universidad del Desarrollo and at Universidad de Concepción. She taught short courses in professional programs to firms and foreign students. She has worked as Senior Consultant at Anguita and Asociados, representing them for the eighth region.

SOLEDAD PORTILLA has a business degree at Universidad del Desarrollo. She also has an economics degree with a public politics mention from the Pontificia Universidad Católica de Chile. Ms. Portilla is sub-director of the Business Research Center at Universidad del Desarrollo. Her research is on competitiveness and entrepreneurship in Chilean regions, gender differences in entrepreneurship, and entrepreneurship inside of the firm. She teaches several courses on economics, and she is coordinator of the Economy Area at the Business and Economics Faculty of the Universidad Del Desarrollo.

JORGE ENRIQUE JIMÉNEZ PRIETO has a Master's degree in SME Management from the Université du Quebéc at Trois Rivières. He was a professor at Universidad ICESI and Director of Research of the Center for Entrepreneurship Development. He is co-author of the book *Crear empresa: Misión de todos*, and was director of the project "Red PyMe" that Universidad ICESI did under an IDB grant. He is author of several articles.

DENNIS M. RAY is the 3M Endowed Chair of Global Strategy and Management at the University of St. Thomas, where he teaches courses on global and technology entrepreneurship and international business strategy. His doctorate in international relations and economics was received from the Graduate School of International Studies at the University of Denver, and he was a postdoctoral fellow in Chinese studies at UC Berkeley. He has held teaching positions at California State University at Los Angeles, the University of Calgary, Brock University, and the University of Auckland.

Dr. Ray co-edited a special issue of the *Journal of Development Studies* (1988), a United Nations publication that focused on entrepreneurship and economic development. In 2001, he was a consultant to Industrial Research Ltd., leading to the creation of a private investor–entrepreneur network that has placed over $2 million in seed capital in promising New Zealand start-ups. He was the founding director of a global business accelerator, a spin-off of the Austin Technology Incubator, at the IC2 Institute at the University of Texas at Austin.

ALEXANDRA SOLANO holds a Bachelor of Industrial and Systems Engineering at Monterrey Tech (Mexico City) and is finishing the Global MBA for Latin American Managers at Thunderbird. She is in charge of the Entrepreneurship Program Coordination for the Academic and Projects Division at Monterrey Tech Campus Ciudad de Mexico. She transferred project oriented learning methodology for business creation training in campus, and she participated in the design, development, and implementation of the new strategy for the entrepreneurship program imparted across the Monterrey Tech System. Traveling extensively in America and Europe, she negotiates joint-venture agreements with major investors and sponsors in order to receive financial support for the business plans developed by students and alumni.

PEDRO ARRIAGADA STUVEN has a PhD in economics from Boston University. He is professor of business economics at Universidad del Desarrollo, Chile and Visiting Professor at Pepperdine University, Malibu, California. Dr Arriagada Stuven is a member of the board of several private companies, and President of the Fundación Miguel Kast and of PAS Centro America.

SERGEY UDOLKIN DAKOVA is Dean of the School of Business Administration and Accounting, president of the Executive Committee of the Management Consulting Center, and director for the Project of Technology for Education of Universidad del Pacífico.

He has been professor for the Departments of Accountancy and Administration since 1980 and for the Graduate School of Administration since 1992. In addition to holding various administrative positions and teaching at Universidad del Pacífico, Mr. Udolkin also has taught at special courses designed for executives from many companies and leaders from different organizations and has given conferences in managerial events. He has also worked as principal consultant of the Management Consulting Center since 1980. Mr. Udolkin's research is focused on the areas of technology, strategic management, and cost and managerial accounting.

He received his Bachelor's degree and license in accounting from Universidad del Pacífico in 1980. He earned a master's of business administration from the University of Texas at Austin in 1991.

RODRIGO VARELA received a PhD in chemical and petroleum refining engineering from Colorado School of Mines. He is the founder and director of the Center for Entrepreneurship Development at Universidad Icesi and the founder and director of the Latin American Congress on Entrepreneurship. He is the author of *Innovación Empresarial–Arte y Ciencia en la Creación de Empresas* and many other books and articles. He was a member of the ICSB board of directors and is a member of the academic committee of several international journals.

About the Editor

SCOTT TIFFIN has been active in entrepreneurship and innovation research and promotion in Latin America for many years. While living in Uruguay and working for the International Development Research Centre as a program specialist in innovation systems, he started the first research projects on venture capital in Latin America and worked in biotechnology network promotion and electronic commerce research. As director for the Institute for Latin American Business at Babson College, United States, he launched research and teaching projects relating to entrepreneurship in several countries in the Latin America region. This work ended in his directing the first research conference on entrepreneurship in Latin America. He is currently Director, Research and International Relations for the School of Business at the Universidad Adólfo Ibañez. He also writes a column on entrepreneurship for *AmericaEconomia*. Dr. Tiffin has been a consultant for many international organizations in the field of local innovation systems. He has also set up his own company innovating decision-support software and has been a professor at several other business and engineering schools. Scott's PhD is in technology management from the Université de Montréal in Canada, and he has prior education in environmental science, ocean engineering, and mechanical engineering.